The Taste of Hidden Things

I had dinner with Sara Sviri at the home of Guy and Sarah Stroumsa in Jerusalem. October 1997

Sara Sviri

The Taste of Hidden Things

Images on the Sufi Path

Sara Sviri

THE GOLDEN SUFI CENTER

First published in the United States in 1997 by
The Golden Sufi Center
P.O. Box 428, Inverness, California 94937

Cover Photo of Bahā' ad-Dīn Naqshband's tomb in Bukara, Uzbekistan.
Printed and bound by Thomson-Shore, Inc.
using recycled paper.

Library of Congress Cataloging in Publication Data,
Sara Sviri
The Taste of Hidden Things: Images of the Sufi Path
1. Spiritual life
2. Psychology
3. Sufism

Library of Congress Catalog Card Number: 96-078735
ISBN 0-9634574-8-9

for all my teachers

Contents

Throughout this book, in an effort to maintain continuity and simplicity of text, God, the Great Beloved, is referred to as He. Of course, the Absolute Truth is neither masculine nor feminine. As much as It has a divine masculine side, so It has an awe-inspiring feminine aspect.

Preface

This book is an attempt to describe a mystical system. It is not an historical account, nor is it a comparative study. I would like to think of it as a portrait of a system, a *living* system, as I have come to know it over many years. Like human beings, mystical systems, too, have many aspects, many faces, and appear to the beholder through his or her own eyes. From this angle the book presents a personal view, an intimate account of the Sufi path. And yet in writing it my wish has been to let the path speak for itself—in poetic images, in dreams, in dicta, in anecdotes—highlighting its past as well as its present. It has been my wish to share with the reader the conviction that now as centuries ago, the mystical path carves its hidden routes within the hearts of men and women who, at certain moments in their lives, awake to an insatiable hunger, to an irreconcilable nostalgia for something which they cannot clearly define, and which is nevertheless powerful enough, *when this awakening becomes an inner commitment*, to shape their destiny.

Sara Sviri

London, September 1996

1

The Niche of Light

My image dwells in the heart of the King.
Rūmī[1]

There is a special pleasure for a person to look and see himself in the mirror.
Ismail Hakki Bursevi[2]

The central image of the Sufi path is the human heart. Sufi teaching, in all its variegation, revolves around the heart as that organ in which the Divine mysteries are hidden, and where the mystical journey takes place. The heart lies at the very center of the mystical quest.

A spiritual journey often starts when a person dimly senses that there are areas in his, or her, psyche which are unreachable through the ordinary vehicles of perception. A person becomes dimly aware that he seldom fully lives, that his life is made up of split-off, unconnected moments which seem to have no center. The quest is a quest for a center from which everything emerges and to which everything returns.

Sufis believe that there is a substance in the heart which does not belong to the world of forms and appearances, but to the Formless, to the Oneness of Being. Yet this substance resides within the complexity of the human organism, with its physical, emotional, and mental components. Life is governed by an ever-increasing multiplicity and complexity. It is shaped by an ever-expanding process of aggregation and fragmentation, adding up and sorting out. We find our place in the world through the fact that we are distinct and separate beings. So how can Oneness be experienced?

To designate the antithetic states of fragmentation and centeredness, Sufis have coined terms. By the term *tafriqa,* which means dispersion and segmentation, they have designated the fractured, fragmented, and uncentered parts of existence; by the term *jam'*—aggregating, bringing together—they have designated the states of centeredness and oneness; and by the term *sirr*—secret—they have designated the hidden point at the core of the human heart where all dispersed things come together. Al-Qushayrī, an 11th-century master from the town of Nishapur, explains that *tafriqa* pertains even to intimate, one-to-one acts of worship, when the center of worship is man rather than God. He says:

> When man speaks to God in the language of intimate discourse *(najwā)* asking, or calling, or praising, or giving thanks—he is in the place of *tafriqa*; and when he listens with his innermost *(sirr)* to what his Lord discloses to him, or to what He shows him in his heart, he is witnessing [in the state of] *jam'*.[3]

Oneness is not a theological concept, and despite countless attempts it cannot be defined by creeds or philosophic formulae. But it can be experienced; it can sometimes be glimpsed and tasted as a genuine state of being. These glimpses show that the sought-for center is not out there, but within the depth of the seeker himself.

What is the heart? It is an enigmatic and mysterious organ. In one sense, Sufis say, the heart is nothing but a hollow piece of flesh within the cavity of the chest. But at the same time it is also the treasure-house of divine mysteries. It is in the heart of hearts, in the innermost chamber of this spherical organ, whose center is an ineffable point that cannot be pinned down, that the human and the Divine commune and embrace. To this enclosed and guarded shrine no creature is allowed access, not even an angel. It is guarded zealously by the Divine Beloved, because this place belongs to Him alone.

One of the earliest mystics in the Sufi tradition who pondered and taught the mystical function of the heart is the 9th-century mystic Abū ʻAbdallāh Muḥammad ibn ʻAlī al-Ḥakīm at-Tirmidhī, from Tirmidh, on the shores of the Oxus river in Central Asia. Unlike most contemporary Sufis, Abū ʻAbdallāh did not belong to a group or a circle. He did not have a flesh-and-blood teacher. Nevertheless, he was held in great esteem by fellow mystics. In his autobiographical sketches (from which I quote in the third chapter), he relates how people in his town would dream about him and would seek him out as a spiritual guide. In his voluminous corpus of writing there are letters to seekers, letters which reflect his spiritual authority and contain valuable information about the early history of Sufism. Masters of later generations—for example, Ibn al-ʻArabī and Bahā' ad-Dīn Naqshband—paid homage to him and acknowledged the inspiration that his teaching and spiritual energy gave to them. Abū ʻAbdallāh is no doubt one of the main contributers to Sufi psychology, to that mystical science which points not to the ego or the psyche *(nafs)* as the focus of the inner work, but to the heart. Here are some passages from his vast opus in which he explains the phenomenon of the human heart and its mystical relationship with God:

> The heart is the king and the limbs are its servants; each limb functions according to the will and the command of the heart, yet the will of the heart comes from the will of God. God nominates none over the heart but Himself; none can see what the heart contains. God alone places in the heart and removes from the heart whatever He wills....
>
> The heart is the source and the abode of God's Unity and the object of God's observation.... God watches over the heart for it is the container of His most precious jewels and the treasure trove of the true Knowledge of Him.[4]

> Satan (Iblīs) flows within the human body through the blood-stream.... When God wills a person to be His beloved, or friend, or prophet, He plucks out the arteries from the inner recesses of the heart, so that Satan will have no access there.[5]

> God made this hollow piece of flesh into His treasure trove. He has given it eyes to see the invisible and ears to hear His words, and He has fixed in it a window to the chest, for the heart is a lamp whose rays of light shine in the chest. Thus God has made this hollow piece of flesh into the source of true knowledge, which is supreme wisdom and mystical understanding. God placed within the heart the knowledge of Him, and the heart became lit by God's Light. Then God spoke in a parable and said: *"Compared to a niche wherein is a lamp"* (Qur'ān 24:35). The lamp of the Divine Light is in the hearts of those who believe in the Oneness of God.[6]

> Apart from the remembrance of God, anything that takes place in the chest creates a shadow which falls in front of the heart's eyes.... When things take place in the chest, namely, if one is distracted by and occupied with thoughts and desires, the shadows which they produce create a smoke screen in front of the heart's eyes. The light then becomes concealed in the depth of the heart, and the chest becomes like a house whose lamp is covered. Such a man is veiled from God.[7]

> By means of the Divine Lights the heart becomes polished so that it shines like a polished mirror. When it becomes a mirror one can see in it the reflection of all existing things and the reflection of the Kingdom of God as they *really are*. When one sees the Glory and Majesty of God in His Realm, then all the lights become one light and the chest is filled with this shining light. This is like a man who observes his reflection in a mirror and sees in it at the same time the reflection of everything in front and behind him. Now when a ray of sun hits the mirror, the whole house becomes flooded with light from the meeting of these two lights: the light of the sun-ray and the light of the mirror. Similarly, when the heart is polished and shining, it beholds the Realm of Divine Glory and the Divine Glory becomes revealed to it.[8]

In a treatise entitled *The Difference Between the Chest, the Heart, the Inner Heart, and the Kernel of the Heart*, a treatise attributed—perhaps erroneously—to al-Ḥakīm at-Tirmidhī, the author explains the concentric structure of the heart. The heart is conceived of as a multi-layered spherical organ, each layer finer than the outer one that envelops it. Each layer has a function which is meant to serve the heart as a whole. The well-being of any layer depends on the well-being of all other layers. Ultimately, all layers are seen as protective sheaths for that which lies at the center. That which lies at the center is the source of light, wisdom, and mystical knowledge. As the eye can't see without the light which resides in its center, neither can the heart's eye. But for the eye to see, light is not enough. It should also be clear from infection and illness. All its parts should be kept clean and intact. So it is with the heart's eye. To illustrate the multiple structure of the heart, the protective function of each layer, and the need to keep all of them intact, the author suggests several analogies. Here are a few abridged passages culled from this treatise:

> The name "heart" is a general name which refers to its inner stations. There are spaces within and without that [which is commonly known as] heart. [In this respect] the name "heart" resembles the name "eye," since "eye" refers to all that is included within the rim of the eyelids: the white of the eye, the black [of the eye], the pupil, and the light in the pupil. What is external is the container for the inner which lies within it.
>
> The name "house" too is general, since it refers to all that is included within its walls: the rooms, the hall, the courtyard surrounding the rooms, the bedchamber, the store-house. Each of these spaces has a specific function which sets it apart from the rest.
>
> The name "almond" too is general. It includes the outer shell which covers the husk, the kernel, and the oil within the kernel.

The author then comments on the esoteric aspect of this layered physiology:

Know that the higher the knowledge, the more concealed, the more guarded, the more hidden it is. Laymen, however, use the name "heart" to refer to all its inner spaces.

Then the analogies between the heart, the eye, the house, the holy city of Mecca, the lamp, and the almond are drawn in more detail. Here are some of the statements the author makes:

The chest in relation to the heart is like the white of the eye in relation to the eye, or like the courtyard in relation to the house, or like the container of water in relation to the lamp, or like the outer shell in relation to the almond.

The chest *(ṣadr)* is the space into which desires and inclinations enter. This is the domain of the lower self *(nafs)*.

The heart *(qalb)* lies within the chest, and is like the black of the eye within the white of the eye. This is the abode of the light of faith, humility, piety, love, fear, hope, and content.

The inner heart *(fu'ād)* is the third station. It is like the pupil of the eye within the black of the eye, or like the kernel within the almond. The *fu'ād* is the place of Divine knowledge and visions. The inner heart is in the center of the heart, just as the heart is in the center of the chest, like a pearl within the shell.

The kernel of the heart *(lubb)* is like the light of seeing within the eye, like the light of the lamp within the wick, like the oil concealed within the kernel of the almond.

The external parts protect and cover that which lies within them.

Beyond these there are ever-finer stations, loftier spaces, and more exquisite subtleties. The root of all of them is the light of Unity.[9]

The concentric view of the heart, as will become highlighted in chapter six, is all-important in Sufi mystical psychology. Terms, however, may vary from one author to another. The inner kernel of the heart in the above description is named *lubb*, which strongly implies a concealed inner part, or the marrow, the essence of an object. Sometimes this innermost point in the center of the heart is named *ḥabb*, which literally means "seed."[10] More often it's known as *sirr*, secret.

This aspect of mystery and *secret* which lies at the center of man's relationship with God is poetically illustrated in *The Conference of the Birds*. The 13th-century poet 'Aṭṭār uses a parable to allude to the closeness which binds man's heart and God, a closeness so intimate that it cannot be interfered with or shared by anyone except these two. He has the hoopoe, the birds' guide, explain to the birds their special kinship with the Symorgh, their hidden king, in search of whom they are setting off, by telling them of the formidable king Maḥmūd's love for his slave Ayāz. When the slave is sick and ailing, even the fastest, most motivated messenger can't surpass the speed with which the king arrives at his bedside. The messenger, who had been ordered to hurry to Ayāz, galloped "like wind" only to find the king already there, by the bedside. "You could not know / The hidden ways by which we lovers go," the king tells him:

> … "You could not know
> The hidden ways by which we lovers go;
> I cannot bear my life without his face,
> And every minute I am in this place.
> The passing world outside is unaware
> Of mysteries Ayaz and Mahmoud share;

> In public I ask after him, although
> Behind the veil of secrecy I know
> Whatever news my messengers could give;
> I hide my secret and in secret live."[11]

The hidden kinship between God and man, and the way in which it's played out in the depth of the heart, are taken further by al-Ḥakīm at-Tirmidhī. He writes:

> God placed the heart within the cavity of the human chest, and it belongs to God alone. No one can have any claim on it. *God holds the heart between two of His fingers,* and no one is allowed access to it: not an angel, nor a prophet, nor any created being in the whole of creation. *God alone turns it as He wishes.* Within the heart God placed the Knowledge of Him and He lit it with the Divine Light.... By this light He gave the heart eyes to see.[12]

In the Arabic language "heart," *qalb*, and "turning," *taqallub*, derive from the same linguistic root. Thus the image of God holding the human heart between two of His fingers, and turning it whichever way He wishes, illustrates the most intrinsic property of the heart: its submissiveness to God's will. The very nature of the heart is to be held in God's grasp and be turned around without resistance.

This image also alludes to the Sufi way of understanding the conjunction of surrender and freedom *(ḥurriyya)*: when the heart surrenders willingly to the Divine hold, it becomes free of the manipulation of the lower self, the *nafs*. Paradoxically, such freedom is reflected by a letting go of choices, a state which Sufis have termed just so: "to relinquish making choices"—*tark al-ikhtlyār.*[13] Abū 'Abd ar-Raḥmān as-Sulamī, an influential 11th-century master from Nishapur, writes, "Man does not become a true servant *('abd)* until he becomes free *(ḥurr)* from all save God."[14]

When the will of the heart becomes one with the will of God, then whatever God chooses for the seeker the heart accepts with no resistance, for "Whichever way you turn, there is the face of God" (Qur'ān, 2:115).

For theologians, philosophers, and politicians, the issue of free will and free choice is all important; they endlessly debate the multifaceted, especially the moral, ramifications of the acquisition or the loss of free choice. For mystics, on the other hand, the intrinsic issue which the journey confronts them with is how to be relieved of the willful, choice-making *nafs*, how to relinquish the right to own a free will in the face of the transcendent will of God. They come to realize that for the heart, which is the place of mystical surrender, there is only one wish: to be utterly receptive to the Divine will, to simply turn in whichever way it's made to turn.

The image of a heart being turned between two fingers of God reflects the vicissitudes of the heart in its quest for Oneness: when turned this way or that, it is made to undergo many different states *(aḥwāl)* and stages *(maqāmāt)*; it is tossed and turned relentlessly; it is swung between feelings, moods, impasses in constant crests and troughs: "And our hearts are ever restless until they find their rest in Thee."

Ibn al-'Arabī, an Andalusian mystic who died in Damascus in 1240, boldly and unconventionally sees this fluctuation, the *taqallub* of the *qalb*, as a reflection or incarnation of the Divine attribute of love, which is defined by a never-resting, creative dynamism. He says:

> The goblet of love is the lover's heart, not his reason or his sense perception. For the heart fluctuates from state to state, just as God—who is the Beloved—is "Each day upon some task" (55:29). So the lover undergoes constant variation in the object of his love in keeping with the constant variation of the Beloved in His acts....
>
> Love has many diverse and mutually opposed properties. Hence nothing receives these properties except that which has the capacity ... to fluctuate along with love.... This belongs only to the heart.[15]

Behind the fluctuation and variegation which the heart undergoes—known in Sufi terminology as *talwīn* or *tafriqa*—Sufi teaching points to the heart of hearts, the *sirr*, as the immutable point where the still state of oneness—*jam'*, or *tamkīn*—is unveiled. The state of *jam'* lies beyond the oscillating states and stations of the heart. In the state of *jam'* the polar states are not simply reconciled, they are *transcended*. Thus, the restless circumambulation around the *sirr*, this mysterious kernel of being, brings about, if persevered in, the sought-for state of Oneness.[16]

From this vantage point the heart is both the pilgrim and the very goal of the journey. The final stage of "The Inner Pilgrimage to the Essence of the Heart" is described by 'Abd al-Qādir al-Jīlānī, an 11th-century mystic from Jīlān on the shores of the Caspian Sea,[17] in *The Secret of*

Secrets, a fine treatise which describes the mystical travel through the inner planes. He writes:

> Then the pilgrim returns home, to the home of his origin.... That is the world of Allāh's proximity, that is where the home of the inner pilgrim is, and that is where he returns.
>
> This is all that can be explained, as much as the tongue can say and the mind grasp. Beyond this no news can be given, for beyond is the unperceivable, inconceivable, indescribable.[18]

A symbolic description of God's light which resides in the depth of the heart is contained in one of the best-known verses of the Qur'ān—the verse of Light (24:35):

> God is the Light of the heavens and the earth;
> the likeness of His Light is as a niche
> wherein is a lamp
> (the lamp in a glass,
> the glass as it were a glittering star)
> kindled from a Blessed Tree,
> an olive that is neither of the East nor of the West
> whose oil wellnigh would shine, even if no fire
>   touched it
> Light upon Light
> (God guides to His Light whom He will.)
> (And God strikes similitudes for men,
> and God has knowledge of everything.)[19]

This poetically haunting passage is the focus of many commentaries. Much ink has been spilled by Muslim scholars in the attempt to make sense of its enigmatic images: the niche, the lamp, the tree which is neither of the East nor of the West, the olive oil which kindles the lamp with an invisible fire. For most commentators the identification of God with anything, even with "light," presented an insurmountable theological problem which they felt obliged to explain away. Sufis, however, have understood the entirety of this verse as a metaphor for the human heart in which God's light resides and by which man is guided on his mystical journey. Most Sufi commentators didn't hesitate to take the verse at face value: God is Light, and this Light resides in the heart; God *is* in the heart.

The center of this prophetic image is a niche *(mishkāt)*—a recess, an unexposed space, a *temenos*, an inner shrine. In this recess a lamp is placed to throw light over the enclosed area. The lamp is lit and then placed within a glass. The glass protects the lamp but does not reduce its light; on the contrary, it increases it, for the glass is translucent, spotless, shining like a glittering star.

But what is the fuel that kindles the lamp? What sets it alight? The oil comes from a sacred tree, an olive tree, which is neither of the East nor of the West, a cosmic tree beyond the boundaries of space—*the tree of life* whose oil shines forth though no fire touches it; and there is "Light upon Light."

Behind the details which make up this numinous image lies the perception of a universal Oneness. The tree, the niche, the light in the lamp are seamlessly interconnected. That inner sanctuary within the heart of men is linked to the Source of Life, the cosmic tree which nourishes it with the loftiest and rarest of energies: the Divine Light. There, in the secret of secrets, is the guarded vessel which holds and protects God's light.

'Abd al-Qādir al-Jīlanī, in the opening of his *The Secret of Secrets,* addresses the reader with a sermon which contains a running commentary on the mystical meaning of the Light verse. He says:

> Dear friend, Your heart is a polished mirror. You must wipe it clean of the veil of dust which has gathered upon it, because it is destined to reflect the light of divine secrets.
>
> When the light from *Allah* (Who) *is the light of the heavens and the earth* ... begins to shine upon the regions of your heart, the lamp of the heart will be lit. The lamp of the heart *is in a glass, the glass is as it were a brightly shining star....* Then within that heart, the lightning-shaft of divine discoveries strikes. This lightning-shaft will emanate from the thunderclouds of meaning *neither of the East nor of the West, lit from a blessed olive tree* ... and throw light upon the tree of discovery, so pure, so transparent that it *sheds light though fire does not touch it.* Then the lamp of wisdom is lit by itself. How can it remain unlit when the light of Allah's secrets shines over it?[20]

He continues his homily in a benevolently didactic style, describing the awakening of mystical consciousness within the heart and the illumination which follows:

> If only the lamp of divine secrets be kindled in your inner self the rest will come, either all at once, or little by little....
>
> The dark skies of unconsciousness will be lit by divine presence and the peace and beauty of the full moon, which will rise from the horizon shedding *light upon light,* ever rising in the sky, passing through its appointed stages ... until it shines in glory in the centre of the sky, dispersing the darkness of heedlessness.[21]

Meditation on the verse of Light, and the experience of the mystical power contained within the heart, produced an even more poignant commentary from the pen of Najm ad-Dīn Kubrā, a 13th-century mystic from Central Asia. In his autobiographical book *The Whiffs of Beauty and the Revelations of Majesty*, Kubrā focuses on the enigmatic expression *light upon light*. For him, it describes the *kinship*, the *correspondence*, and the *mutual attraction* of the celestial Divine lights and the lights which reside in the human heart. He writes:

> There are lights which ascend and lights which descend. The ascending lights are the lights of the heart; the descending lights are those of the Throne. Creatural being is the veil between the Throne and the heart. When this veil is rent and a door to the Throne opens in the heart, like springs toward like. Light rises toward light and light comes down upon light, "*and it is light upon light*" (Qur'ān 24:35)....
>
> Each time the heart sighs for the Throne, the Throne sighs for the heart, so that they come to meet....
>
> Each time *a light rises up from you, a light comes down toward you,* and each time a flame rises from you, a corresponding flame comes down toward you.[22]

Then, in an astonishing comment which highlights the function of the heart as *a magnetic center* which draws the divine lights *down*, Kubrā adds:

> If their energies are equal, they meet half-way.... *But when the substance of light has grown in you,* then this becomes a Whole in relation to what is of the same nature in Heaven: *then it is the substance of light in Heaven which yearns for you and is at-*

> *tracted by your light,* and it descends toward you. This is the secret of the mystical approach.[23]

Polishing the mirror of the heart, tearing the veils which surround the self, increasing the strength of the inner lights—all these bring the Divine lights *down* to the human arena, because that is where the mystical life is lived.

For Sufis the arena where the mystical states are tasted and where the inner layers unfold is *here*; the time in which it takes place is *now*. "The Sufi is the child of the moment *(aṣ-ṣūfī ibnu waqtihi),*" writes al-Qushayrī, the 11th-century compiler from Nishapur, citing a statement often pronounced by the Sufi masters. "What they mean," he explains, "is that the Sufi is occupied with what is right for that moment." Then he adds:

> The poor [of heart, *al-faqīr*] is not concerned with his past or with his future; he is concerned with the moment in which he is.[24]

The mystical life is *now*, where one *is*, not in an eschatological future. This existential outlook is reiterated time and again by the masters. Al-Ḥakīm at-Tirmidhī, in the 9th century, writes in a letter to Muḥammad ibn al-Faḍl, a mystic companion from Balkh:

> My brother, in your letter you pray that God should comfort us of all our miseries in paradise: He

> who is veiled from God in this life will be comforted neither in this life nor in the next.[25]

And Bhai Sahib, the 20th-century master from Kanpur, says emphatically:

> My disciples, if they live as I expect them to live, and they follow me in everything, they realize God IN THIS LIFE. Absolutely.... God MUST be realized in one life, in this life.[26]

To live and to exist means to experience. In Sufi terminology an experience, in particular a mystical experience, is named "taste"—*dhawq*. Figuratively, Sufis imagine themselves as guests invited to a banquet. If they don't procrastinate, and arrive at the banquet on time, they'll be served the most delicious food. It's like nothing they have ever tasted; it cannot be described. It is served in the most exquisite tableware; the guests are seated on the softest silky cushions; enchanting music and the sound of trickling water tinkle in their ears; sweet, unfamiliar scents pervade their senses. They are beside themselves with astonishment and joy. Other guests are slower to arrive. They are held up by other business, by other attractions which they hesitate to leave behind. They arrive late. The banquet is almost over; they are served only leftovers. Of the true delicacies they get, second-handedly, only a description. Returning home, the guests who enjoyed the full banquet are at a loss to describe their mouthwatering experience to those who have stayed behind. It's to no avail; the listeners can't really share the experience. The flavors, the sounds, the scents, the textures, the colors—all this richness can be known only directly, through the experience of the real banquet, through *being* there.

Being, existing, tasting, and experiencing are thus interrelated. This relatedness is borne out by Sufi terminology. The term for existence, or being—*wujūd*—is etymologically and semantically linked with the term for a strong emotion or ecstasy—*wajd; wajd* is used synonymously with *dhawq*—tasting a mystical experience; and both *wajd* and *dhawq* are synonymous with *ḥāl*—a brief and powerful mystical experience. *Ḥāl* itself is often used synonymously with *waqt*—time, moment, the present moment. Thus this existential terminology, which was devised early in the history of the Sufi tradition, reflects the concept of time not as a linear sequence of units of a measured duration, but as an existential, vertical moment which is characterized by a strong emotional response to an inner experience.[27]

An anonymous 10th-century Sufi author, probably one of the Baghdadi disciples of al-Junayd, gives a short and intriguing definition of ecstasy *(wajd)*. He writes:

> The ecstasy of the Sufis is the [sudden] encounter of the invisible *(al-ghayb)* with the invisible *(bil-ghayb)*.[28]

The unnamed author then goes on to say:

> These are realities which they find *(yajidūna)* within their innermost secret *(sirr)*, [realities which emanate] from the divine Truth *(al-ḥaqq)* without "how."

According to this definition, the Divine Truth—*al-*

Ḥaqq, one of God's names—in its Hiddenness *(ghayb)* is encountered *suddenly* within the hiddenness of the human heart, and from this sudden encounter—*muṣādafa*—of the Divine *mysterium* with the human *mysterium*, an ecstatic moment is born. In the subtle semantics of Sufi terminology this ecstatic moment is connected with finding: "ecstatic moments" *(wajd)* are realities which Sufis *find (yajidūn)* within their innermost. In Arabic the infinitive form *wujūd* means both "to find" and "to be." "To find," which ordinarily refers to a successful outcome of a search, is linguistically identical with "to be," "to exist." Thus the Divine Realities which seekers *find* in their heart of hearts are also, according to this semantic allusion, the Divine realities which *exist* within their innermost, realities which have been there all along. When a genuine encounter occurs between the human being and that which is found in his innermost—in other words, when the human being becomes in some way, "without how" *(bilā kayfā)*, aware of what lies within his own hiddenness—he experiences a special mystical state which is called *wajd*, ecstasy. The mystical sense of this important statement can be paraphrased as follows: "The mystic *finds*, therefore the mystic *is* "; or: "To *be* is to *find* and *live* the Divine Hiddenness within." And in Rūmī's words: "Make this heart drunk, so that it can find today the things it lost yesterday."[29]

'Aṭṭār, using the evocative imagery of "mirroring," describes the realization of Truth within the heart as the outcome of *reflection*. Truth, ultimate Reality, cannot be seen directly; but it can be revealed in its reflection upon the translucent, empty heart which contemplates it. He says:

If you would glimpse the beauty we revere
Look in your heart—its image will appear.
Make of your heart a looking-glass and see
Reflected there the Friend's nobility;
Your sovereign's glory will illuminate
The palace where he reigns in proper state.
Search for this king within your heart; His soul
Reveals itself in atoms of the Whole.[30]

The vision that springs from the overwhelming experience in which the mystery of Being is discovered within the heart led Sufis in ecstasy to pronounce statements, or utterances *(shaṭaḥāt)*, for which they were persecuted and even executed.[31] Abū Yazīd al-Bisṭāmī, one of the earliest ecstatics, whose utterances baffled sober Sufis as well as pious legalists, cried from the level of the convergence *(jam')* of the human and Divine *mysteria* in himself: "Glory be to me! How lofty am I!" *(subḥānī! mā a'ẓama sha'nī!)*. And, describing the inner transformation which this shattering experience has brought about, he exclaimed:

I shed my self *(nafs)* as a snake sheds its skin,
then I looked at myself, and behold! *I am He.*[32]

And al-Ḥallāj, the 10th-century martyr of love, from the state he names "*the essence of union*" *('ayn al-jam')*, cried out in ecstasy, "I am the Truth" *(anā al-ḥaqq)*. These famous words, as well as other so-called "heretical" utterances, sent him to the gallows in the center of Baghdad.[33]

The merging of the human being with a transcendent Being to the point of losing the separate identity of the "I" is poignantly described by Michaela Özelsel, a modern seeker, in her *Forty Days* diary, an account of a "traditional solitary Sufi retreat" *(khalwa).* On the 39th day of her retreat she records the following subtle and hard-to-describe experience:

> "I" see "myself" from behind, with arms and legs spread wide, tiny by comparison, flying toward this immense cloud bank. Drawn as if by a powerful magnet, falling in as if into the sea.
>
> Then "I" stop seeing "myself." Now there is only one perceiving. Inside this cloud bank I spread out farther and farther.... Then I come apart and dissolve completely in this fog that is purest love and mercy. As if a glass of tea were tossed into a great sea. The tea gets thinner and thinner till finally its "tea-being" is lost in the "water-being," leaving only one sea water.
>
> Having now become one, "we" spread out immeasurably, endlessly, farther and farther. "We-I-he" are so dissolved, so spread out, that we embrace the whole universe. But again, there can be no talk of "embracing," because that would imply boundaries, whereas love has no boundaries. The whole cosmos, in fact, consists of purest love. It is one single Being of immeasurable love and mercy....
>
> But it won't be possible to make that understandable to anyone; I already don't understand it myself anymore as I am writing down my (whose??) experience. It seems monstrous to me to even think such a thing, let alone speak it. Still, I know with every fiber of my being that it is so.[34]

So the experience of Oneness is the coming together of the *mysterium* in man with the *Divine Mysterium.* In this sense the seeker, the pilgrim on the path, is none other than that *hiddenness* which resides in the heart of hearts. "The seven heavens and the seven earths contain me not," says a Sufi tradition, "but the heart of my servant contains me."[35] Mystics who live in keeping with this vision are not inclined to be drawn into spectacular acts of power or to outline complex theosophical systems. They live, either soberly or intoxicated, in the light and presence of the *mysterium*—that *ghayb* which is the source and goal of all being, yet is beyond all being—knowing that they will find it nowhere out there, but within themselves, "closer" to them "than their jugular vein" (Qur'ān 50:16). "The inner pilgrim," writes 'Abd al-Qādir al-Jīlānī, "wraps himself in the light of the holy spirit, transforming his material shape into the inner essence":

> The inner pilgrim wraps himself in the light of the holy spirit, transforming his material shape into the inner essence, and circumambulates the Ka'ba of the heart, inwardly reciting the ... name of God. He moves in circles because the path of the essence is not straight but circular. Its end is its beginning.[36]

These wise, direct, and compassionate words of 'Abd al-Qādir al-Jīlānī promise further secrets, further mysteries, along the circular road of the never-ending mystical path.

2

The Path of Effort and the Effortless Path

All of existence is ease, and ease is mercy....
Though there may be weariness along the way,
it is a weariness in ease.
Ibn al-'Arabī [1]

I wish not to wish, I want not to want.
Abū Yazīd al-Bisṭāmī [2]

A few years ago I taught a course on Sufism in an adult-education program run by the University of London. The people who enrolled in this course came from different backgrounds: some were graduates who wished to fulfill an academic requirement; some were intrigued by the title; some knew little about Sufism and wanted to know more; some were aspirants. Within a short time, however, this group of strangers coalesced into a lively and engaging class. The emphasis that the Sufi tradition places on direct "taste" *(dhawq)*, on concrete experiencing, was echoed by the group's openness and attentiveness, not only to the literary material but also to one another, and to their own responses—in thoughts, images, and dreams—to the texts discussed. A few weeks after the course had ended I received a letter from N., an Anglican pastor who had been a rather reticent participant in the class. The thick, brown envelope contained about twenty poems. They were—so I understood from the covering letter—the fruit of N.'s reflections on the themes which were brought up during the course. The poems moved me deeply. They presented a fresh, sensitive, and modern understanding of the way Sufism relates to the "self" and the quest. One of these poems is called *muḍṭarr*.

Muḍṭarr is Arabic for "constrained," for someone who is in a state in which he can make no choices, who is forced into a situation without any freedom of choice on his part. Sufi authors have used this word in a particular context: when the seeker sees that all his efforts to attain God are futile, he reaches a point of despair, a point of total helplessness. He comes to realize that his very effort, necessary though it is, is the root of his failure; his very attainments are the cause of his failing. He discovers that all effort springs out of will, and will is a manifestation of the self, the "I," the *nafs*,[3] that which is believed to be "man's worst of all enemies."[4] Out of despair the seeker lets go of all claim to know how to proceed or what to do. He is stuck, he is a *muḍṭarr*. Here is how N.'s poem captures this point:

> It is always like two people trying to pass
> through a door at the same time.
> We collide with that eager, bothersome wayfarer
> who wants to go everywhere with us,
> but is the main reason why we lag behind.
> Do we humor this ubiquitous companion? Berate or
> ignore?
>
> The path of spiritual enlightenment
> stretches away in front, and we don't
> get past the first hurdle because we
> are occupied with this little self,
> this little pleasure-seeker, who

applauds every successful step forward,
and pulls us back to admire it.
We find ourselves in the desert,
the valley of confusion, stationary.
Longing to be detached from the shadow
which clings, and not yet grasping
the fringes of God's robe.

The Absolute cannot free us from
this paralysis, lift us straight to the place
of clear seeing, until
we are *constrained*—yoked without knowing it
to the end we desire,
receptive as a cup waiting to be filled,
looking at nothing and
consequently no longer distracted
by the cavorting exhibitionist;

alone
and therefore, to our astonishment,
joined.[5]

What connects us with bygone generations of Sufis is the fact that now as then the mystical quest is a journey through a psychological obstacle, a paradox: while the quest is from the *mysterium* within to the Divine *Mysterium (ghayb)*, "from the alone to the Alone,"[6] we soon find that there are two in us who walk on the path: *"It is always like two people trying to pass through a door at the same time."* Who is this in us that wants to partake in everything we go through? Sufi psychology draws our attention to an entity more ostentatious than the unconscious "shadow," an entity that we think we know only too well: our own self, our *nafs*, our sense of I-ness, our *ubiquitous* ego. The *nafs,* by definition, is that part of the psyche which ascribes everything to itself. It is the seat of I-consciousness. It is the psychic component from which we perceive ourselves as separate from one another: "I" opposite "thou." The *nafs* views everything from the angle of its bottomless neediness, its appetites *(shahawāt)*: it needs love, security, success, recognition, excitement. It also needs to own and possess all of our experiences. Through the *nafs*, therefore, we feel gratified or frustrated, successful or failing.

"He who knows himself (or: his self) knows his Lord" is a prophetic *ḥadīth* often quoted in Sufi literature.[7] Thus, like the adepts of old who were faced with the injunction "Know thyself!" on the gateway to the temple of Apollo in Delphi, the Sufi seeker too, before entering the sacred space within, has to "know" what the self is, who *he* is, who in truth is the one in him who walks the mystical path. He needs to understand what makes the self the main obstacle on this journey. In the pursuit of this knowledge, past joins present: ancient Sufis, modern Sufis, Muslim Sufis, Jewish Sufis, and Christian Sufis are all in the same boat. The seeker discovers that it is not only difficult, it is in fact *impossible* to get rid of *"this little self, this little pleasure-seeker, who applauds every successful step forward."* The self is always with us. To counsel "Get rid of the ego" is to ask the impossible; one simply cannot do it. Sufi teachers and the experiences that their energy creates for their disciples show that the *nafs* will not be chased away by will power and persuasion. The experience of an ego-less state can only be *granted*. It can be *given*, and it is given only when the seeker becomes truly *constrained*.

In the 11th century al-Hujwīrī, a wandering Sufi from Afghanistan and the author of *Kashf al-Maḥjūb*, a well-known compilation, summed up this teaching succinctly:

> Man is clay, and clay involves impurity, and man cannot escape from impurity. Therefore purity bears no likeness to acts *(af'āl)*, nor can the human nature be destroyed by means of efforts.[8]

One of the bewildering findings that come from examining our human nature is this: the arena in which the *nafs* thrives most is the arena of *effort (mujāhada, jihād)*. Effort cannot be divorced from the self which executes it. The very contribution the seeker offers—the efforts he makes and the actions he takes in order to change his nature—is thwarted by this very nature. How can he ever transcend his nature? Nevertheless, according to Sufi teaching, effort is indispensable and has been assigned an important place in the mapping of the journey. Effort is part and parcel of the endeavor to pass through and actualize the different "stages" and "stations" *(maqāmāt)* which make up the journey and which are mapped in Sufi manuals. These stations are reached through the intentional and disciplined work that the wayfarer puts into the process of transformation required by the mystical quest. For a long time the seeker is involved in nothing else but the "training" of his self *(riyāḍat an-nafs)*. Al-Qushayrī reports that his master, Abū 'Alī ad-Daqqāq, used to say: "He who embellishes his exterior with effort *(mujāhada)*, God graces his interior with vision *(mushāhada)*."[9]

A *maqām*, a station on the path, is defined by al-Hujwīrī in the following way:

> Station *(maqām)* denotes anyone's "standing" in the way of God, and his fulfillment of the obligations appertaining to that "station" and his keeping it until he comprehends its perfection *so far as lies in man's power.*[10]

The stations on the journey reflect the arduous process by which human strength and perseverance are put to the test and are stretched to their limit. From this angle the journey is effortful and demands tremendous will power. The self participates in this process; the self, in fact, carries this process through and is its agent. But here lies the paradox: when the self makes an effort, it cannot avoid a certain bargaining, an awareness, a self-appraisal(!). Something inside us tirelessly takes notes and whispers: "I" have made an effort; "I" expect to see progress; indeed, "I" can notice in myself a significant change; or simply, "I" can see it now! Or the self can become defensive and self-righteous: I have been wronged, it's not *my* fault, someone else is at fault, I meant well, and so on.

These ego-centered calculations and observations are unavoidable. They are part of the inner dynamic of integrating the experiences and making them conscious. In Sufi manuals, and especially in the teaching of the Nishapuri "Path of Blame" *(al-malāmatiyya)*, this introspective self-appraisal of the *nafs* is called *riyā'*.[11] It is, indeed, *like two people trying to pass through a door at the same time.* Hence, sooner or later, effort becomes the doorway through which not surrender sneaks in but inflation and conceit *('ujb)*. This is a law which has to be reckoned with on the path of psychological transformation. For the sincere seeker this subtle law creates a vicious circle: Without effort he can't progress; the outcome of his effort indicates the progress he has made. But when he takes stock of his effort and his progress, he is caught in the web of the ever-present, manipulative, and plotting self. He cannot detach himself from his self.

When we set ourselves a goal and the goal is won, our *nafs* is gratified. Even when the goal is altruistic and virtuous, in fact especially then, we can't prevent the ego from claiming its share in our noble achievement: "*We collide with that eager, bothersome wayfarer / who wants to go everywhere with us, / ... this little pleasure-seeker, who / applauds every successful step forward, / and pulls us back to admire it.*" No matter how selfless our aspirations, it is almost impossible to remain selfless in the process of actualizing them. Most interesting is to observe how the ego identifies with mystical experiences. No experience, regardless of its loftiness, is immune from being "owned" or "claimed" by the ego, which will always ascribe it to itself: *my* visions, *my* dreams, *my* experiences, *my* intuition, *my* perseverance, *my* surrender. The *nafs* is therefore recognized in Sufi psychology as that sly trickster, the power-driven part within our human makeup which undermines the process of the quest in endless cunning ways, because the object of the quest always *transcends* the ego, while the ego, by definition, is *self-centered.*

The point at which the sincere seeker encounters the full consequence of this vicious circle becomes a turning point. When he comes face to face with the impossibility of extracting himself from the ego, he becomes *constrained.* This is a point of no return. Here the wayfarer sees, with clarity and disillusionment, that it is impossible to attain the object of his quest, sincere though it is, through his own will and effort. Disillusionment, bewilderment, and true humility replace the conceited inflation. When he sees the futility of his efforts, he recognizes his human limitation. He has come to know himself. This knowledge can never be attained through dogma, creed, or moralistic preaching, only through a real experience. Sufi teaching is unequivocal: only at this point can man come to know his true position in the scheme of things. He is a "slave" *('abd)*; his human nature is "slavehood" *('ubūdiyya)*. With the same breath man realizes God's Sovereignty *(rubūbiyya)*: "He who knows himself knows his Lord." The only choice that remains for him now is whose slave he chooses to be: God's or his ego's.

At this point the tables are turned. The ego-centered impulses shut down. The *nafs* lets go of all claims to know or understand what to do, where to go. This is the dark night of the soul: *"The Absolute cannot free us from / this paralysis, lift us straight to the place / of clear seeing, until / we are* constrained*—yoked without knowing it / to the end we desire, / ... looking at nothing and / consequently no longer distracted / by the cavorting exhibitionist; / alone / and therefore, to our astonishment, / joined."*

The term "constrained" derives from a Qur'ānic verse:

> He who answers the constrained *(al-muḍṭarr)* when
> he calls unto Him,
> and removes the evil
> and appoints you to be successors in the earth,
> Is there a god with God? (27: 62)

In the state of "constraint" one loses the freedom of choice. This is one of the most difficult things for modern

Western man and woman to accept. To lose the right to choose—*tark al-ikhtlyār*—to lose the notion of "free will," is an affront to our cherished fought-for human rights: does it mean that we shall have to give up the liberty and equality which our culture boasts of, which make it so advanced, so liberal, so politically correct? It is also an offense to our psychological struggle for self-esteem, self-realization, and individuation. Do we have to give these up too? But strange though it may appear, the state of constraint *(iḍṭirār)* and slavehood *('ubūdiyya)* reflects, according to Sufi psychology, *true* freedom *(ḥurriyya)*. The point of emptiness and despair brings about a liberating detachment from ego-centered impulses. Alongside the despair one savors for the first time the taste of freedom from the bond with the *nafs*. Despair over the loss of power to control his destiny allows the seeker to become free of inner as well as outer blame or praise. From here he can fall no further: if he fails, he fails; if he is accused, he is accused; if he is misunderstood, so be it. Things are no longer seen solely from the angle of the self. In spite of the depression, a new horizon appears in the seeker's consciousness.

Michaela Özelsel, who exerted herself to experience a traditional Sufi "forty-day solitude" *(khalwa, chilla)*, gives a poignant description of this state in her diary:

> Day 19. I feel only emptiness, burned-out, endless emptiness. No traces of this indescribable inner peace, the "poorhouse of not wanting," that had come in the night for a few seconds like a beam of light through the cloud-cover of pain: I still keep wanting to decide for myself which way to go. I still have a lot to learn before I become the Sunken One who is moved along by the currents of the ocean....

> Day 20. I give up, declare myself helpless, admit to myself my complete helplessness. I have to face the fact that even my greatest voluntary offering of renunciation the night before last has brought me nothing. I realize that in this matter I was also making my own plans, was "figuring my own figuring." ... I feel completely trapped in utter helplessness. I have nothing more to give, nothing more to do. My scheming reason, always trying to take control for itself, has finally and conclusively cornered itself in a hopeless blind alley. I can't go on....
>
> Day 21. I'm fairly calm, I don't understand anything anymore. There's nothing more for me to do but do what was assigned to me: *zhikrs*, prayer, some reading.... Pain is healed by pain, love only by a still greater love.... No more defenses! Only one goal, one prayer, makes any sense: true *Islām,* peace in absolute surrender.[12]

Years ago, while I was working on my doctoral thesis on al-Ḥakīm at-Tirmidhī, the 9th-century Muslim mystic from Transoxania, I was going through something similar to the state of constraint. I encountered an impasse in myself and in my work. This impasse lasted for a long time. One day I came across some passages in the writings of at-Tirmidhī which responded perfectly to my inner experience. The impact of the teaching contained in these passages has remained with me ever since. Of all the mystics of the Sufi tradition, it was al-Ḥakīm at-Tirmidhī who, at a very early stage in the development of Sufi psychology, analyzed minutely this turning point on the path. Here is a perceptive description, based on his own experiences and insights, of the state of constraint on the effortful path, cited from his *The Way of the Friends of God (Sīrat al-awliyā')*:

And when the seeker has exhausted all his sincere efforts, and has found that his *nafs* and its lowly features are alive, he becomes bewildered, and his sincerity breaks. He says: "How can I extract from my *nafs* the sweetness of these things?" He realizes that he can do it no more than white hair can turn black.

He says: "I have harnessed my *nafs* with my sincerity towards God, but how can I hold it harnessed? It has broken off and gone loose. When shall I capture it?" And so he falls into the wilderness of bewilderment. There, in the emptiness of wilderness, he strays alone and desolate. He is no longer close to himself, nor has he reached God's closeness.

He becomes constrained *(muḍṭarr)* and bewildered; he does not know whether to go forward or backward. Despairing of his sincerity, he cries out to God, empty-handed, his heart empty of any effort, and thus he says in his heart's communication: "You who know all hidden things, You know that there is not even one step in the arena of true effort left for me.... You rescue me!"

Then Compassion *(raḥma)* reaches him and he is spared. From the place where his sincere effort stopped, his heart is lifted up in a flash to the platform of proximity at the Divine Throne, and in the spaces of Unity he expands. This is the meaning of God's words: *"He who answers the constrained when he calls unto Him...."*

This verse informs you that the passion of your heart for sincere self-exertion will not remove the evil from you and will not answer what you call for, until your call and the passion of your heart be purely directed towards God alone, who made the hearts passionately constrained and in need of Him....

> The constrained who is left without provision, and who strays bewildered in the wilderness not knowing which way to go, is spared by Divine Compassion and is delivered by Divine Help.... He who wanders constrained in the wastelands of the road to Him is the one who truly merits Divine Compassion and Relief.... He is spared by Compassion because his call is truly sincere. *It cannot be truly sincere until he becomes constrained, with nothing to hold on to and with no one to turn to.* He who looks with one eye to God and with the other eye to his effort is not truly constrained, and his call is not truly sincere. When the call of this constrained one is answered, his heart is lifted in a flash to the abode of the free and noble.[13]

The seeker's psyche, modern or old, male or female, Western or Eastern, in its struggle to shake off the shackles of ego-identification comes up against the same experiences and pronounces them in almost identical terms. The point of constraint occurs at different stages of the journey. It may take the seeker in a storm or may come as a still, small voice when he is least ready to give up making plans and efforts. Stubbornly the seeker holds on to his perceptions of right and wrong, fair and unfair, shoulds and shouldn'ts. He thinks with a well-meaning self-righteousness that he knows what is required of him. But eventually he is taken right to the edge of knowledge and understanding. There he melts. "In a flash" he knows surrender.

To be driven to the edge is to be driven beyond fear and despair. Despair in itself is a state beyond fear. When the seeker gives up all hope of being in control, and yet "knows"—consciously or in his heart of hearts—that he is vertically aligned with a higher source of power, he knows surrender: "*until / we are* constrained—*yoked without knowing it, / to the end we desire, / receptive as a cup waiting to be filled, / looking at nothing....* "

God is one, but He reveals Himself in many faces. Constraint is experienced through being exposed to Divine Majesty and Might *(jalāl)*, a measure which is complemented by Divine Compassion *(raḥma)* and Beauty *(jamāl)*. It is said in the Qur'ān that one of the measures of God is craftiness, deviousness, and ruse *(makr)*: "Do they feel secure against God's devising? None feels secure against God's devising but the people of the lost" (7:99).[14]

Many will view with abhorrence such a perception of God, will resist and fight the idea that there exists an aspect of Divine Power for whose vagaries and arbitrariness human beings are mere pawns. Why would God deceive us? Why would He play tricks with us, torment us, destroy us, take everything away from us? And if this indeed be the way He is, what kind of a God is He? Most participants in the London class on Sufism voiced such resistance. Once again I found in N.'s poems an understanding of the subtleties underlying this bewildering topic. In the following poem he ponders the objective which hides behind this hard-to-accept, devious guise of God:

Showing the unattractive face may be
a gambit, turning you from the worn,
time-hallowed image which has become
repugnant, to seek new appearances

in another place. But God has many disguises,
and the closely-guarded secret
is a deviousness that will not balk
at loading you with shit to draw you
into grace.

The experience of God's Majesty and Power can be encountered through life's tribulations or through the unpredictable behavior of a spiritual guide. For the seeker this experience is presented, usually as a bitter test, either by the teacher's apparent ruthlessness, unfairness, fickleness, and arbitrariness, or by a grim situation in life. Whichever it is, there comes a point at which the seeker is left confused, bewildered, and alone, *"with nothing to hold on to and with no one to turn to."*

In *Daughter of Fire,* a modern record of a Sufi training written by a European woman, Mrs. Tweedie documented many bewildering experiences to which her master Bhai Sahib's behavior exposed her. He would be tender, compassionate, and radiant, and then, without warning, he would become strict, demanding, tyrannical. The more stubborn, self-opinionated, and righteous she was, the more ruthless he had to become, in a manner that appeared to her mind incomprehensible and unjust. In her desperation—she recorded in her diary—she exclaimed one day:

> "Oh, please, help me! I am so confused!"
>
> "Why should I?" He looked straight at me. "If I begin to help you, you will ask again and again for help: how will you cross the stream? You must do it yourself; I will not help. We all had to cross the stream alone."
>
> "Don't you realize that this is the way? I am telling you, showing you the way. THE ONLY WAY.

> Why don't you realize that you are nothing? Complete surrender it means! It takes time. It is not done in one day.... It takes time to surrender.... "
>
> "How long?"
>
> "The whole life, twenty, thirty years. If you live 1000 years, 1000 years won't be enough. Sometimes you are near, sometimes very far away. I am helping you, as a matter of fact, but you cannot be aware of it, and I will never say so. My harsh words help you; my sweetness never will.... You have renounced the world; all the material things.... But ... have you renounced ... your character, your will, everything? The character one gets inherited from the parents, and together with the will it molds the life of a person. If you have not renounced your will, your character, in your case the surrender has not yet begun."[15]

A modern disciple, a very ancient teaching. How can one renounce the will, by will? Through effort? Will and effort cannot do it: *"Man is clay, and clay involves impurity.... Therefore purity bears no likeness to acts, nor can human nature be destroyed by means of efforts."* But it can *be done.*

The mystery of suffering and pain lies right there. Why "suffering"? Because when one goes through the valley of pain, especially when one suffers an unjustifiable injury, a deep frustration, a failure, a rejection by a loved one, and especially when one realizes that he has no remedy for his situation, then he may truly give away the illusion that he is in control. Then he may truly discover the incapacity, the impotence of his ubiquitous partner, the ego. This is a subtle piece of teaching. But the outer teaching cannot become a true realization unless the seeker is given a direct experience of it. Pain and suffering are not glorified in their own right. Suffering in itself does not redeem anyone; only suffering which culminates in a state of constraint *(iḍṭirār)*, a state in which the seeker wakes up to the reality of his smallness and powerlessness, can redeem. This sobering-up may herald a true transition, a real transformation. And where the mystery of pain becomes unraveled there is redemption. Here are a few Sufi sayings which bring this idea home:

> Tests are the lamp of the mystics, the true awakening of those who keep wakeful at night, and the destruction of those who are heedless.

> Poverty is an ocean of suffering, but the whole of suffering is Divine Glory.

> Suffering is the seed of repentance and the threshold of love.

> The Divine can be revealed only there where created beings are weak.

> Suffering introduces God utterly alone to the heart.

It is through the very failings of certain people's freedom of choice that Divine Mercy comes nakedly to give itself to all of its fullness.

God's Mercy comes to us through what outwardly appears as contradicting His Law (namely, through suffering, deviousness, injustice, pain ...), and is then given wholly, directly, inwardly. This is what suffering is about. It is through the application of misfortunes and heartbreak as remedies that Divine Mercy comes into the heart and transforms the personality where efforts failed. This is known as "testing," *balāʾ*, and according to a well-known *ḥadīth* no one suffered more *balāʾ* than God's elect, the prophets and the Friends of God.

He who reveals the secret of God to other human beings and wishes to make this moment of Union last in himself, experiences a suffering that exceeds the power of created nature. If he experiences nothing, it is a sign that the moment of Union is withdrawn from him.[16]

You are bewildered at my severity ... though I am mightily severe, a thousand gentlenesses are hidden in my severity.[17]

According to the System, the *Shishya* (disciple) is constantly kept between the opposites, ups and downs; it creates the friction necessary to cause suffering which will defeat the Mind. The greatest obstacle on the Spiritual Path is to make people understand that they have to give up everything.[18]

And Rūmī, this master of love, surrender, and ecstasy, describes the paradoxical relationship between the human lover and the Divine Beloved in these wild images:

> That beauty handed me a broom saying, "Stir up the dust from the sea!"
>
> He then burned the broom in the fire saying,"Bring up the broom out of the fire!"
>
> In bewilderment I made prostration before him; he said, "Without a prostrator, offer a graceful prostration!"
>
> "Ah! How prostrate without a prostrator?" He said,"Unconditionally, without personal impulse."
>
> I lowered my neck and said,"Cut off the head of a prostrator with Dhu'l-Faqār."[19]
>
> The more he struck with the sword, the more my head grew, till heads a myriad sprouted from my neck;
>
> I was a lamp, and every head of mine was a wick; sparks flew on every side.
>
> Candles sprang up out of my heads, east to west was filled with the train.
>
> What are east and west in the placeless? A dark bath-stove, and a bath at work.
>
> You whose temperament is cold, where is the anxiety of your heart? How long this dwelling at rest in these baths?[20]

These pieces of poetic beauty and mystical paradox can make sense only from the vantage point of a real experience. We know through experiencing. Sufis call this way of knowing *dhawq,* "tasting." When we read the biographies and sayings of the friends of God, the *awliyā'*, we are put in touch with our own confusion and broken hearts. "It's the same with everything," says Rūmī; "you don't understand until you *are* what you are trying to understand." On the mystical path "knowing" and "being" are identical. We understand through our state of being, and the scope of our knowledge expands with the expansion of our being, with the unveiling of the veils which have covered our being. The non-ceremonial "widening of the horizons" through *dhawq* is the true and only initiation on the path.[21]

The Sufi tradition has distilled the teaching that at the beginning of the mystical path effort is indispensable. At the beginning almost everything the seeker goes through on the path is effort. In fact, not right at the very beginning—then there might be a short space of grace, a glimpse into the future, an outlook into the spaces of possibilities. It is in a way like having an auspicious initial dream at the beginning of analysis or at the beginning of a journey. The process seduces the aspirant. This space, however, does not last long. The paradoxical dynamic of effort and self soon takes over. At this stage of the journey the wayfarer is called *murīd*. *Murīd* means an aspirant, someone who wants, who has a wish, an intention, a goal, who aspires to attain a lofty object. It has become conventional to render it, somewhat inappropriately, "novice."

Al-Ḥallāj, the 9th- and 10th-century mystic from Baghdad who was executed because of his ecstatic and ostentatiously "heretical" utterances, describes three phases on the path to God.[22] In the first phase, the phase of "novicehood" *(irāda)*, the *murīd* progresses from station to station through the path of effort *(mujāhada)*. This is the ascetic phase of the journey, and in this phase, whose length can never be known in advance, one is put to constant tests of perseverance and loneliness. Here the *murīd* encounters the danger of identifying with effort, with practices, with the willful aspect of the path. But this is only the beginning.

The second phase according to al-Ḥallāj is the phase of constraint *(iḍṭirār)*, of passive purification. In this phase, since the *murīd* has lost his self-will, he becomes *murād,* the one who is aspired after. The one who seeks becomes the sought, the one whose aim is God becomes God's aim, the one who desires God becomes God's desire, the path of effort becomes the effortless path. At this phase one has glimpses of Oneness in flashes of intuitive insights, in dreams, or in deep states of meditation. Here one loses all desires, all wishes, all sense of will: one has given up "willing," one has given up making intentional efforts. This state of being cannot be attained by design; it is purely *given,* it's pure Grace *(faḍl, luṭf)*.

The third phase is named by al-Ḥallāj *'ayn al-jam'*, the core of union, the quintessence of Oneness. Oneness is experienced as an immutable state of being, as a centered point of stillness where fluctuation ceases, where the "impulsive self" *(an-nafs al-ammāra bi-s-sū')* becomes the "serene self" *(an-nafs al-muṭma'inna)*.[23]

In this phase the mystic goes back to life and lives an ordinary life in an extraordinary way. His resistances have fallen away; he does not identify with the self anymore. It's not that the self, or ego, has died; as long as he is alive, in body, psyche, and mind, the self is there. But there is no *identification* with it. It has lost its manipulative power; it has become subservient, in full consciousness and humility, to an energy which is many times mightier than itself. This state does not necessarily manifest itself, although sometimes it may, in outward states of ecstasy and drunkenness. The mystical experiences of intimacy and love become more and more introverted, more and more contained: "And thou shalt see the mountains, that thou supposest fixed, passing by like clouds" (Qur'ān 27:88).[24]

At this stage of inner peace and surrender, one lives in a state of complete receptivity, complete fluidity, complete transparency, in complete attentiveness to the Divine hint. Such a one may also develop the capacity to put all appearances against himself or herself, to change personas and colors according to the needs of the moment. It is very demanding and at the same time very inspiring to be around such people. They become transmitters of Divine energy. There is a particular stillness around them and a constant sense of meaningfulness. This is the stage of *wilāya*, the stage in which the mystic becomes the friend of God, a *walī*. Through men and women who have reached this stage, grace and blessing flow. It is said that when the friends of God are seen, God is seen; when they are remembered, God is remembered.[25] Some of those who have reached this stage become teachers, guides, beacons of light; some remain hidden, unknown to the world, working from the mystery of the inner secret of being.

A famous *hadīth qudsī*, probably the most frequently quoted piece of tradition in Sufi literature, describes this state of being thus:

> My servant does not draw near to me by performing the obligatory commandments; he draws near to me by acts of devotion, and then I love him. And when I love him, I become his ears, his eyes, his tongue, his hands, his legs and his heart: he hears by Me, he speaks by Me, he handles by Me, he walks by Me and he comprehends by Me.[26]

One of the most penetrating and mysterious pieces of Sufi poetry was written from this state of being. It is a poem by al-Ḥallāj. The state of nearness and merging conveyed in it was too shocking for al-Ḥallāj's contemporaries. Even al-Junayd, al-Ḥallāj's teacher and a mystic who knew deep states of ecstasy, could not approve of the outspoken way in which his former disciple had divulged the secret of Oneness. But al-Ḥallāj's poetry survived. Many Sufis, albeit not without a great deal of apologetics, were nourished on it, and it didn't fall into oblivion. We too may have a taste of it, and through it glimpse that state of intimacy and merging in which there is no duality between the seeker and the object of his search. Here is al-Ḥallāj's poetic description of the state which he names *'ayn al-jam'*, the essence of Oneness:[27]

> Your spirit is mixing with my spirit
> Just as wine is mixing with pure water.
> And when something touches You, it touches me.
> Now "You" are "me" in everything!
>
> You are there, between the linings of the heart and the heart, You escape from it
> (By slipping) like tears from eyelids.
> And You infuse the (personal) consciousness inside my heart
> As spirits are infused into bodies.

Ah! nothing immobile moves without
You, You move it by a hidden spring
O, Crescent (of the moon), which appears (as much) on the fourteenth (of the month)
As on the eighth, the fourth and the second!

I have become the One I love, and the One I love has become me!
We are two spirits infused in a (single) body.
And to see me is to see Him,
And to see Him is to see us.

Here am I, here am I, O my secret, O my trust!
Here am I, here am I, O my hope, O my meaning!
I call to You ... no, it is You Who calls me to Yourself.
How could I say "it is You!"—if You had not said to me "it is I"?
O essence of the essence of my existence,—O aim of my intent,
O You Who make me speak, O You, my utterances,—You, my winks!
O All of my all,—O my hearing and my sight,
O my assembling, my composition and my parts!
O All of my all,—the all of all things, equivocal enigma,
It is the all of Your all that I obscure in wanting to express You!
O You, by Whom my spirit was hanged, already dying of ecstasy,
Ah! keep its token in my anguish! ...
O Highest thing I ask and hope for, O my Host,
O food of my spirit, O my life in this world and the next!
Let my heart be your ransom! O my hearing, O my sight!
Why do you keep me so long at such a distance?
Ah, though You hide in what is invisible to my eyes,
My heart already beholds You in my distance, yes, in my exile![28]

3

Dreams and Destiny

The primary imagination I hold to be the living power and prime agent of all human perception, and as a repetition in the finite mind of the eternal act of creation in the infinite I AM.

Samuel Taylor Coleridge[1]

A God who cannot be imagined does manifest Himself in visible symbols, and the visible symbols are real manifestations of God, and to grasp them one must have imagination.

Thomas Merton[2]

Part One: Light in the Darkness

Dreams, Sufis say, speaking of "true dreams" *(ar-ru'yā aṣ-ṣāliḥa)*, are symbolic messages which arise from the knowledge hidden in the center of being. In the wilderness of unknowing through which the seeker travels, these encoded messages give a forecast and a foretaste of things to come. They are often the *only* indication which points in the direction the seeker needs to proceed. Not all dreams are "true dreams"; most dreams are spun, Sufis say, by the needs of the lower self, or by the mind churning the events of the day. Such dreams are usually confused and fragmented, and are characteristically called "dreams in confusion" *(aḍghāth al-aḥlām)*. But occasionally there appears a dream, or a series of dreams, which bears the hallmark of a true knowledge, a knowledge which, though concealed from mind and sense perception, responds directly and instructively to the true needs of the dreamer's soul. Such dreams often have an aura of numinosity which doesn't require interpretation. Their meaning looms clear on the inner horizon. They have a feeling quality which touches the dreamer and awakens in him dormant emotions, perceptions, a new insight into the direction his life is taking. The dreamer, if he is sincere in his quest for truth and meaning, will listen, understand, and respond to the inner taskmaster who reveals himself in the dream, and who knows him better than he knows himself.

Ibn al-'Arabī, the 13th-century Andalusian mystic, whose formulations of mystical knowledge have left a lasting impression on the Sufi tradition, describes the paradoxical nature of that hidden knowledge to which, "until it is unveiled instant by instant," consciousness has no access. He writes:

> God deposited within man knowledge of all things, then prevented him from perceiving what He had deposited within him.... This is one of the divine mysteries which reason denies and considers totally impossible. The nearness of this mystery to those ignorant of it is like God's nearness to His servant, as mentioned in His words, "We are nearer to him than you, but you do not see" (56:85) and His words, "We are nearer to him than the jugular vein" (50:16). In spite of this nearness, the person does not perceive and does not know.... *No one knows what is within himself until it is unveiled to him instant by instant.*[3]

Modern depth psychology too is based on the premise that an aspect of the human psyche is buried so deep that it cannot be considered part of consciousness, yet does surface in various guises, most predominantly in dreams. Jung, a modern explorer of the knowledge hidden in the *unconscious*, describes it as having, paradoxically, its own "consciousness." "Certain dreams, visions, and mystical experiences," he writes, "... suggest the existence of a consciousness in the unconscious."[4] The knowledge compressed in the unconscious exceeds by far the knowledge available to consciousness. "Today we know for certain," Jung writes, "that the unconscious has contents which would bring an immeasurable increase of knowledge if they could only be made conscious."[5] One of the characteristics of analytical psychology is the understanding that the unconscious has both a continuous and a purposive existence: "The unconscious perceives, has purposes and intuitions, feels and thinks as does the conscious mind."[6] Jung describes the unconscious as "a multiple consciousness" with its own luminosity.[7] The ego-consciousness, according to Jung, is surrounded by a multitude of "luminosities" *(scintillae,* luminous particles) which sometimes emerge as images, dreams, and "visual phantasies." The alchemists of past times, he says, called these luminosities "seeds of light broadcast in the chaos" or "the seed plot of a world to come."[8] And Gerhard Adler, in one of the finest elaborations on Jung's ideas, explains:

> The totality of these *scintillae* (sparks, luminous particles) produce a 'light' which becomes visible to the observing conscious mind as a consciousness in the unconscious.... Thus, when one analyzes dreams... one finds frequently a process of 'realization' taking place in the unconscious which is full of inner consistency, coherence, and intelligence.... This I have called ... "the logos of the unconscious."[9]

This "inner consistency, coherence, and intelligence" is that which *knows* in spite of outer unknowing, is that which, in spite of outer chaos, is a master architect of meaning. When it unmasks itself in a dream, it often becomes the seeker's only confirmation and support, especially in periods of anguish, loss of direction, and despair. Yet in order to become realized in life, it demands of the dreamer attentiveness and trust. To trust the message inherent in the dream means to be prepared to go through the inner and outer changes which it heralds.

In the *Mathnawī* Rūmī tells a story about "childhood friends." In this story, Joseph, who is now a formidable and mighty prince in Egypt, second only to King Pharaoh, reunites with a childhood friend, a friend from his remote days in the land of Canaan. It was there, in his youth, that dreams of an august destiny were revealed to him. Naïve and immature, yet already skilled in the arcane art of dream interpreting, Joseph disclosed his dreams to his siblings and thus incurred their envy and hate. In their plot to kill him they threw him into a pit, but he was rescued, sold to a caravan of Arab merchants on their way to Egypt, and bought there by a minister to King Pharaoh. There, after many tribulations, events turned in his favor. He was the only man in Egypt who could interpret some perturbing dreams the King had had. His understanding of the King's dreams saved Egypt and its neighboring lands from a long and devastating famine.

Now, Rūmī tells us, when Joseph is the *de facto* ruler of Egypt, a childhood friend comes to visit him. This friend used to be "a pillow friend," a friend with whom one shares the most intimate secrets, as adolescents do, whispering softly to each other into the night (which is Rūmī's way of alluding to the intimacy with *the Friend).* In their intimate, *tête-à-tête* reunion, the friend asks Joseph:

> ..."What was it like when you realized
> your brothers were jealous and what they planned to do?"
>
> "I felt like a lion with a chain around its neck.
> Not degraded by the chain, and not complaining,
> but just waiting for my power to be recognized."
>
> "How about down in the well, and in prison?
> How was it then?"
> "Like the moon when it's getting
> smaller, yet knowing the fullness to come.
> Like a seed pearl ground in the mortar for medicine,
> that knows it will now be the light in a human eye.
>
> Like a wheat grain that breaks open in the ground,
> then grows, then gets harvested, then crushed in the mill
> for flour, then baked, then crushed again between teeth
> to become a person's deepest understanding.
> Lost in Love, like the songs the planters sing
> the night after they sow the seed." [10]

In these endearing, down-to-earth images Rūmī describes the inner certitude and strength which sustained Joseph even in the bottom of the pit, because of his unfailing trust in the dream-visions which predicted his destiny. Because of his trust and certitude he could endure patiently the vicissitudes of his life until that turn of events in which his destiny unfolded. Thus dreams of destiny, when understood with Joseph's attitude and intuition, become a hint from a veiled master-plan yet to unfold, the *"seed plot of a world to come"*; and secretly they are celebrated—*"like the songs the planters sing the night after they sow the seed."* To him who knows the language of dreams, destiny—which is encapsuled as seeds in the dark luminosity of the depths—shines bright as the full moon in the darkness of night.

A modern woman, a flute player, dreamed:

> I am sitting at the back of an orchestra, observing, not taking part in the playing, but still in it. I am watching Celia playing the most difficult flute solo brilliantly. She is illuminated by the dazzling music she is playing. I and everyone else, the musicians and presumably the audience too, are absolutely stunned at the brilliance of Celia's performance.
>
> Then I am in a small dormitory of about four beds on an upper floor. I am there with a few other young flute-playing females: we are all there waiting for Celia to join us after the concert, so that we can congratulate her on her playing. But Celia does not come. So I go by myself downstairs to a room in an old manor-style house, looking for Celia. It is an old-fashioned, grand room with an institutional feel about it, but there is no one there. All the same, I know that Celia has been there, in front of two elderly gentlemen who had offered her great rewards if she produced her very best at the concert. She had done this, and came to claim her just reward, but they now said that although it had been excellent it wasn't worth anything really. So she had gone away.

The dreamer is an unfulfilled flute player. In her youth she had embarked on a promising career, then married, gave birth to two children, and gave up her career as a performer. Years later, through inner work, she gradually realized that her attitude toward professional performing had been ambivalent from the start. She had viewed the heroes of her youth—her teachers and the excellent musicians with whom she played—with a mixture of admiration and disapproval. She admired their brilliancy and had often described it in the same "dazzling" terms with which she described Celia's recital in the dream. But at the same time she also accused them of "a huge ego trip." She also discovered how she had identified with social and family norms, according to which motherhood and wifehood did not go hand-in-hand with pursuing a career as a musician. But above all she discovered the pain of abandoning her potential and love for flute-playing. This pain became associated for her with her longing for a lost paradise.

Now in her dream, Celia, a colleague from the past who is a professional flute player as well as wife and mother, is giving—in the dreamer's language—a *dazzling* performance of *a most difficult solo, illuminated* by the music she produces. Everyone is *stunned* at the *brilliance* of it.

No doubt, this is the dreamer's own brilliancy and excellence which she sees in Celia. There is something angelic, divine, in the way Celia's performance is perceived in the dream. This transcendent quality, projected onto Celia, comes from that luminous center within the dreamer herself. Celia is not a mere shadow figure, and this isn't simply a compensatory dream. It comes from the soul, from the "seeds" of beauty planted there, still waiting in the darkness, yearning to see the light, to grow, and be harvested. They are revealed to the dreamer now, in the throes of her inner process, as shining images which strive to be freed from the repressing, inhibiting stamp of moralistic conceptions such as "all this is nothing but an ego trip."

The femininity and freshness of the dream are emphasized by the group of women, the young flute players, who are waiting with the dreamer for Celia, their alter ego, in order to share with her the exuberance of her performance. Yet Celia does not materialize. Perhaps the time to realize the promise of the dream is not yet right. The dreamer is given to understand that there is more, perhaps deeper, inner work to do. She separates herself from the group of women; she has to walk alone now in order to find Celia. She climbs down the staircase into the old, formal hall which has *an institutional feel about it.* There, in the realm of impersonal, authoritative male figures who censor and clip down her own exuberance and buoyancy, she finds out what is holding Celia back: Celia has been slighted by the judges. They are not willing to grant her the promised award in spite of her outstanding performance. The dreamer understands the message: she will have to follow her destiny *in spite* of these judges in her, *alone*. She will have to rely now on nothing but her genuine aspirations, her faith in the dream, because she must not ignore any more the beauty of her own inner music and her soul-messages.

Through the images of a dream she has made contact with seeds of fresh possibilities. Her task now is to believe strongly enough in her dream, and to follow its hints in faith and sincerity. If she does, these seeds will flower and will mature fruitfully, and will fulfill what her soul has destined for her.

Part Two: Imagination

The art of dreaming and dream interpreting has always been part of the Sufi tradition. According to medieval theories, dreams, as well as visions, which appear during mystical states, are explained as symbolic representations of transcendental, spiritual realities. These realities, or *meanings (ma'ānī*—close to the Platonic *ideas)*, are archetypal; they belong to a realm of incorporeal entities, a realm which lies beyond the grasp of ordinary, corporeal sense perception. This realm is named "the World of the Imaginal" *('ālam al-mithāl)*. When one is dreaming, the formless archetypes appear in front of the mind's eye in recognizable forms and images. This process in which *meanings* become *images* is facilitated through the activity of a special faculty, the imaginative faculty *(al-khayāl)*.[11]

Mystics and philosophers have maintained that imagination, as one of the functions of the psyche, operates in the twilight zone between the world dominated by the senses and the world dominated by transcendent reality. By clothing the transcendent and the formless in *images*, imagination bridges these two worlds. Its ability to function in this way increases in states in which sense perception is withdrawn and the psychic energy is directed inward rather than outward, that is to say, in sleep, in voluntary "active imagining," in meditation, and in mystical states. By producing such images, imagination acts for the dreamer as a revealer of things to come; it points to, or prophesies, future events which lie dormant in the realm of the spirit.

A Sufi master who has understood the essence and function of imagination in an all-encompassing epistemological way is Ibn al-'Arabī. Ibn al-'Arabī combines a philosophical understanding of the function of the imaginative faculty with insights inspired by his mystical tradition and experiences. He sees in the imagination *the main tool of perception* on any level on which perception takes place, not only in dreams and mystical visions. Pondering the quintessence of imagination, Ibn al-'Arabī finds that it is a *barzakh*, an isthmus. *Barzakh* is a term of Persian origin (?) which appears in the Qur'ān (55:19),[12] and which Ibn al-'Arabī describes as "something that separates two other things while never going to one side."[13] This means that while imagination lies at the ephemeral line which separates the world of sense-perception and the world of formless *meanings*, or spiritual realities, it belongs neither to the one nor to the other. It's a realm in its own right, which acts as a bridge between the *sensible*—that which is grasped by the senses—and the *intelligible*—that which is wholly spiritual. Thus imagination becomes the means whereby messages from the world of spiritual realities can be perceived. In the words of Ibn al-'Arabī:

> Imaginal things... are the meanings that assume shape *(tashukkul)* in sensory forms; they are given form by the form-giving faculty *(al-quwwat al-muṣawwira)*, which serves the rational faculty.[14]

The very essence of a *barzakh* is doubleness. Hence, as a *barzakh*, imagination has a double, paradoxical nature. "Imagination," says Ibn al-'Arabī, "is neither existent nor nonexistent, neither known nor unknown, neither negated nor affirmed."[15] Anything which is perceived, he implies, has a double aspect: it exists and does not exist at one and the same time.

This doubleness is best exemplified in two related phenomena: in the reflection of images upon a mirror and in dreams. When a person looks in a mirror, explains Ibn al-'Arabī, what he sees is both there and not there. If he says, "I am there, in the mirror," he is making a statement which is both true and untrue. This is also the case of dreams. When, through the activity of imagination, the spiritual realities are clothed in images, the dreamer sees entities and objects which are both there and not there, which both exist and do not exist. But dreams and reflections, Ibn al-'Arabī maintains, do not exhaust the full extent of the double nature of the reality which we perceive. Doubleness is the very nature of any kind of perception, on any level of existence.

By virtue of its bringing together the realm of sense perception and the realm of spiritual realities, Ibn al-'Arabī assigns to imagination highly exalted functions. For him imagination is that which brings opposites together *(al-jam' bayna al-aḍdād)*.[16] It is a *coincidentia oppositorum*, an idiom which for many philosophers and mystics describes God as that which reconciles all opposites.[17] This explains why in dreams even Divine attributes can be perceived in a corporeal form. The friends of God, says Ibn al-'Arabī, see images of highly spiritual beings such as angels, prophets, the Heavenly Throne *(al-'arsh)*, and even God Himself. He writes:

> The Prophet said, "I saw my Lord in the form of a youth." This is like the meanings (i.e., spiritual

> entities) that a sleeper sees in his dreams within sensory forms. The reason for this is that the reality of imagination is to embody *(tajassud)* that which is not properly a body *(jasad)*.[18]

Also, because imagination governs everything which can be perceived as existing, it is, says Ibn al-ʿArabī, "the absolute ruler" *(al-ḥākim al-muṭlaq)*:

> We only make this allusion to call attention to the tremendousness of imagination's level, for it is the Absolute Ruler *(al-ḥākim al-muṭlaq)* over known things.[19]

But for incorporeal meanings, embodied in dream images, to be grasped and become conscious, one needs to be able to interpret them. To understand the messages conveyed in visions and dreams, the dreamer or the dream interpreter has to have access, through a special intuitive talent and experience, to the World of the Imaginal *(ʿālam al-khayāl wal-mithāl)*. "Through the science of [dream] interpretation," writes Ibn al-ʿArabī,

> a person comes to know what is *meant* by the forms of images when they are displayed to him and when sense perception causes them to rise in his imagination during sleep, wakefulness, [mystical] absence, or annihilation.[20]

The interpreter, like imagination itself, is mediating, *crossing over*, among the dreamer, the dream images, and the *meanings* which lie behind these images. He is also mediating between his own imaginative faculty and that of the dreamer. This *mediation* is borne out by the Arabic term for interpretation: *ta'bīr* (from the root *'-b-r:* to traverse, to cross over). "This is because," says Ibn al-'Arabī,

> the ... interpreter 'crosses over' ... by means of what he says. In other words, ... he transfers his words from imagination to imagination, since the listener imagines to the extent of his understanding. Imagination may or may not coincide ... with imagination.... If it coincides, this is called his "understanding" *(fahm)*; if it does not coincide, he has not understood.... We only make this allusion to call attention to the tremendousness of imagination's level, for it is the Absolute Ruler *(al-ḥākim al-muṭlaq)* over known things.[21]

For Ibn al-'Arabī, basing himself on the Qur'ānic tradition, the archetypal dream interpreter—he who symbolizes the mediating nature of the realm of the imaginal—is none other than Joseph. In the opening lines of the chapter dedicated to Joseph in his *Bezels of Wisdom (Fuṣūṣ al-ḥikam)*, Ibn al-'Arabī gives a lengthy description of this realm, embodied in Joseph, which holds the key to the existential doubleness characteristic of dreams, of divine images revealed to prophets and mystics, of the meaning of dreams, and ultimately of existence *(wujūd)* itself. He writes:[22]

> The light of this luminous wisdom [symbolized by Joseph] expands to [embrace] the plane of imagination. This is the beginning of Divine inspiration granted to the people of Assistance *(ahl al-'ināya)*.

> [This is supported by a *ḥadīth* transmitted in the name of] 'Ā'isha: "The first inspiration [granted to] the Prophet was a veridical dream. Every dream he had was [as clear as] the breaking of dawn.... " She did not know that the Prophet had said, "Men are asleep; when they die they wake up."[23]
>
> ⁘
>
> [Dreaming] is sleep within a sleep. Everything which comes about in this manner is named the plane of imagination. This is why it requires interpretation *(wa-lihādhā yu'abbaru)*. In other words, something which in itself has one form appears in a different form, and [the interpreter] *crosses over ('ābir)* from the form seen by the dreamer to the form which is pertinent to the matter; for example, knowledge appears as milk.[24]
>
> ⁘
>
> Later on, when the Prophet was granted inspiration, he was transported away from his ordinary senses ... and became "absent" from those present with him. What took him over was the plane of imagination, though he was not in a state of sleep.
>
> In the same way, when the angel appeared to him in the form of a man, this too was from the plane of imagination. Although he was an angel and not a man he appeared to him as a human being.[25]
>
> ⁘
>
> The observer who possesses knowledge transmutes this [form] until he arrives at the true form and says, "This is Gabriel.... " Both perceptions are true: there is the truth of the sensual eye and the truth of this being Gabriel.

The inquiry into the nature and essence of imagination leads Ibn al-'Arabī to explain, in his own way, the idea, current in medieval philosophies, that the only *real* existence belongs to God alone. He writes:

> Know that whatever is referred to as "that which is not God" *(siwā allāh)*, in other words, the world, relates to God as shadow to man. It is God's shadow. This is the essence of the relation of [real] existence *(wujūd)* to the world....
>
> The world is *imagined*, it does not possess a real existence, and this is the meaning of imagination, namely, you imagine that [the world] is a thing in itself outside God, but this is not so.... Know that *you are imagination* and whatever you perceive as not-you is also imagination. Existence is imagination within imagination, and real existence is nothing but Allāh from the point of view of His essence, not from the point of view of His names.[26]

But this relativistic approach does not imply that Ibn al-'Arabī criticizes or undervalues the function of imagination. On the contrary; he emphasizes imagination's all-encompassing role in erecting the double, relativistic nature of existence and consciousness. Whatever we think, whatever we know, whatever we experience, he implies, is like a dream. But a dream is not an ephemeral figment devoid of its own relative type of reality. A dream—a *true dream*—is a formal incarnation of supernal, archetypal *meanings* which, when correctly understood, can change one's life entirely. Moreover, a dream—together with prophecy and mystical visions—is an extraordinary means whereby man can attain the plane of Divine messages and attributes. And at the same time it is, like everything else, a mere *reflection*, a shadow of *al-Ḥaqq*, the only *Real Existent*, which is totally and absolutely unmediated and unreachable.

Part Three: Dreams and Experiences of an Early Sufi Couple

Whatever the theoretic, epistemological aspect of dreaming, the literary evidence shows the great attention with which dreams have been listened to in the Sufi tradition. Some of the earliest evidence comes from the further reaches of the Islamic world. There, in Tirmidh, a town on the shores of the Oxus river (the Amu Daria), a 9th-century seeker went in search of inner knowledge. Abū ʻAbdallāh Muḥammad ibn ʻAlī al-Ḥakīm at-Tirmidhī has left a personal document which describes his search, a document which is, to the best of my knowledge, the first autobiographical work written, or at least preserved, in Sufi literature, and probably also in Muslim literature at large.[27]

In the Sufi tradition at-Tirmidhī's name has become associated with the doctrine, fundamental to his teaching, concerning the *awliyā'*, the friends of God, the holy men of Islam.[28] According to this doctrine, one of the routes by which God communicates with his elect is through dreams. This is based on the understanding of a Qur'ānic verse which reads:

> Surely God's friends—no fear shall be on them, neither shall they sorrow.... For them is *good tidings (bushrā)* in the present life and in the world to come (10: 62-4).

"Good tidings," at-Tirmidhī writes in his *The Way of the Friends of God (Sīrat al-awliyā')*, "is a veridical dream.... The dream of the faithful is God's word spoken to him in his sleep."[29]

In his autobiography, which is entitled "The Beginning of the Matter" *(Buduww sha'n)*, at-Tirmidhī recorded a series of dreams, as well as mystical experiences, and key events in his life. Most of the dreams recorded were dreamed by his wife. Since at-Tirmidhī does not disclose her name, I shall refer to her simply as Umm 'Abdallāh, in the same way that he is called Abū 'Abdallāh. Although the dreams were given to her as Divine messages for her husband, the document makes it clear that she is not just a mediumistic messenger. The dreams reflect also her own inner development. Significantly, at-Tirmidhī's record ends with Umm 'Abdallāh's own mystical experiences.

This, then, is a document which describes the inner journey, through dreams and experiences, of a mystical couple united in marriage as well as in the spiritual quest, whose inner and outer lives are closely knit together. In this respect, I think, it is not only a rare document, but also a rather rare and precious human experience.[30]

In his autobiography at-Tirmidhī tells how for years, after his initial spiritual awakening which took place during a pilgrimage to the Ka'ba, he kept searching on his own, with no teacher, and without companions. He writes:[31]

> The love of solitude came into my heart. I would go out into the wilderness and wander in the ruins and graveyards around my town. This was my practice, and I kept it tirelessly. I was looking for true companions who would support me in this, but I found none. So I took refuge in ruins and in solitary places. One day, while in this state, I saw, as if in a dream, the Messenger of God, peace be upon him. He entered the Friday mosque of our town and I

> followed him closely step by step. He walked until he entered the *maqṣūra* (the section reserved for the dignitaries) and I followed, almost cleaving to his back, stepping upon his very footsteps.... Then he climbed up the pulpit, and so did I. Each step that he climbed, I climbed behind him. When he reached the uppermost step he sat down and I sat down at his feet, on the step beneath him, my right side facing his face, my face facing the gates which lead to the market, and my left facing the people [in the mosque]. I woke up in this position.[32]

This is the first auspicious dream which Abū 'Abdallāh records. At-Tirmidhī does not find it necessary to interpret the dream. Its symbolic meaning is, to him, apparent. Traditionally, seeing the prophet in a dream is understood as a true, real event and must be taken at face value and not interpreted away.[33]

The period which preceded this dream is described as intense, filled with ascetic and devotional practices. He talks of his determination and zeal, but also of his aloneness and confusion. In spite of his inner conviction, he needs some external validation and guidance. The dream reflects an exceptionally close adherence to the Prophet, a *physical* closeness which symbolizes and heralds support, direction, and spiritual attainment.

The second dream which at-Tirmidhī records again speaks for itself and does not require him to indulge in interpretation. He writes:

> A short time after this, while praying one night, I was overtaken by deep tiredness, and as I put my head on the prayer rug, I saw a huge and empty space, a wilderness unfamiliar to me. I saw a huge

> assembly with an embellished seat and a pitched canopy the clothing and covering of which I cannot describe. And as if it was conveyed to me: "You are taken to your Lord." I entered through the veils and saw neither a person nor a form. But as I entered through the veils an [overwhelming] awe descended upon my heart. And in my dream I knew with certitude *(ayqantu)* that I was standing in front of Him *(bayna yadayhi)*. After a while I found myself outside the veils. I stood by the opening of the [outer?] veil exclaiming: "He has forgiven me!"[34] And I saw that my breath relaxed of the fear.

This, no doubt, is more than a dream; it is a mystical experience. The dream is told in a laconic brevity which stands in contrast to the intensity conveyed. Alongside the depth of the personal experience, the dream imagery links at-Tirmidhī with the ancient tradition of mystical encounters with the Lord who sits upon the Throne. "Certitude" *(yaqīn)*—inner mystical knowledge—and the mystic's overwhelming awe in the proximity of God are themes which recur in many of at-Tirmidhī's descriptions of the *awliyā'*, the friends of God.[35]

At a certain point in at-Tirmidhī's spiritual journey his wife starts having dreams which contain a clear message for him. This is a phenomenon for which I don't know a parallel in Sufi literature. It is made clear that Umm 'Abdallāh herself becomes involved in the transformative process initiated through the dreams, and is told in one of them that she and her husband are on the same rung. At-Tirmidhī writes that, while he was going through a period of great hardships, being harassed and persecuted by certain religious and political groups, his wife said to him:

> I saw in a dream, as if standing in midair, outside the house, on the path, an image of an old man, curly-haired, wearing white clothes, on his feet sandals, and he was calling to me from the air (in the vision I was standing in front of him): Where is your husband? I said: He has gone out. He said: Tell him, the prince commands you to act justly, and he disappeared.

This is clearly a teaching dream. In spite of the persecution he encounters, at-Tirmidhī's position amongst his own companions has become that of a spiritual guide. He tells how people of his hometown started gathering in front of his door beseeching him "to sit in front of them" *(al-qu'ūd lahum)*. He himself, however, does not have a spiritual teacher to turn to. His authorization, or license to teach *(ijāza)*, comes by means of dream messages. Through the dreams of his wife he is being prepared for the role of a master. The old man, white-haired, clad in white, is none other than Khiḍr, that teacher from the angelic plane of those seekers who do not have a flesh-and-blood guide.[36]

A similar figure appears also in Umm 'Abdallāh's second dream. Al-Ḥakīm at-Tirmidhī writes:

> Now my wife kept dreaming about me, dream after dream, always at dawn. It was as if she, or the dreams, were messengers for me. There was no need for interpretation, because their meaning was clear. This was one of her dreams:
>
> I saw a big pool in a place unknown to me. The water in the pool was as pure as spring water. On the surface of the pool there appeared bunches of grapes, clear white grapes. I and my two sisters were sitting by the pool, picking up grapes from these bunches and eating them, while our legs were dangling upon

the surface of the water, not immersed in the water, only touching it.

I said to my youngest sister: Here we are, as you see, eating from these grapes, but who has given them to us? And lo, a man came towards us, curly-haired, on his head a white turban, his hair loose behind his turban, his clothes white. He said to me: Who is the owner of a pool such as this and of grapes such as these? Then he took me by the hand, raised me, and said to me at a distance from my sisters: Tell Muḥammad ibn 'Alī to read this verse: "We shall set up just scales on the day of resurrection [so that no man shall in the least be wronged....]"[37] On these scales neither flour is weighed nor bread, but the speech of this will be weighed—and he pointed to his tongue—and it will be weighed with these and these—and he pointed to his hands and legs. You don't know that excess of speech is as intoxicating as the drinking of wine.

I said: Would you, please, tell me who you are? He said: I am one of the angels; we roam the earth, and our abode is in Jerusalem. Then I saw in his right hand [a bunch] of young green myrtle [branches], and in his other hand two branches of fragrant herbs. While he was talking to me he was holding them in his hands.

Then he said: We roam the earth and we call on the worshippers. We place these fragrant herbs on the hearts of the sincere [worshippers] *(al-ṣādiqūn)*, so that by them they can carry out acts of worship. And this myrtle we place upon the hearts of the just *(al-ṣiddīqūn)* and those who possess certitude *(yaqīn)*, so that by them they can discern what is just. These herbs in summer look like this, but the myrtle is evergreen, it never changes, neither in summer nor in winter.

Tell Muḥammad ibn 'Alī: Don't you wish that you could have these two? And he pointed to the myrtle and the herbs. Then he said: God can raise the piety of the pious to such a stage that they will need no piety. Yet He had commanded them to have piety, so that they should [come to] know it.

Tell him: Purify your house! I said: I have small children, and I cannot keep my house completely pure. He said: I don't mean from urine. What I mean is this—and he pointed to his tongue. I said: And why don't you tell him so yourself? He said: ... [What he does] is neither a grave sin nor a minor sin. In the eyes of people it is a minor sin, but for him this is a grave one. Why should he commit it? Then he moved the hand which was holding the myrtle and said: Because this is [as yet?] remote from him.

Then he plucked out of the bunch which he was holding some of the myrtle and handed them to me. I said: Shall I keep it for myself or shall I give it to him? He laughed, and his teeth shone like pearls. He said: This is for you, and as for these which I am holding, I myself shall take them to him. This is between the two of you, because you are both at the same place together. Tell him: This is my last counsel to him. Peace be with you!

Then he added: May God bestow on you, oh sisters, 'green gardens' (joy and fruitfulness), not because of your fasts and prayers, but because of the purity of your hearts.... I said to him: Why don't you say it in front of my sisters? He said: They are not like you and they are not your equal. Then he said: Peace be with you, and went away. I woke up.

As in the previous dreams, here too one is struck by the allusions to ancient traditions, teachings, and archetypal images: the clear pool of water, the bunches of grapes, the messenger clad in white. The myrtle, a central image in Umm 'Abdallāh's dream, is an ancient symbol for the just, the righteous, the *ṣiddīq* (and in the Jewish tradition: the *zaddīq).* In the book of Zechariah (1: 8-11), the prophet is shown a vision which is in many ways reminiscent of Umm 'Abdallāh's dream images:

> I saw by night, and behold a man riding upon a red horse, and he stood among the myrtle trees that were in the bottom.... Then said I, O, my lord, what are these? And the angel that talked with me said unto me, I will show you what these be. And the man that stood among the *myrtle trees* answered and said, These are they whom the Lord has sent *to walk to and fro through the earth.* And they answered the angel of the Lord that stood among the myrtle trees, and said, We have walked to and fro through the earth, and behold, all the earth sitteth still, and is at rest.

The Arabic for myrtle—*ās*—derives from a linguistic root which denotes "healing." In the East myrtle has been known for millennia to possess healing qualities. For certain religious groups it had special holy connotations. Umm 'Abdallāh's dream alludes, through the symbolism of herbs and myrtle, to two levels of spiritual healing or instruction: the level of ordinary good worshippers *(aṣ-ṣādiqūn)*, who are symbolised by the fragrant herbs, and the level of the just *(aṣ-ṣiddīqūn)*. The latter, who in at-Tirmidhī's teaching are synonymous with "the friends of God," are symbolized by the myrtle. Both types of worshippers are *sincere*—as is indicated by the linguistic root *ṣ-d-q*, common to their respective designations. Nevertheless, they represent a hierarchical distinction between those who worship God externally and those who worship Him both externally and internally. The nature of the worship of the first group is not altogether firm; it's rather fickle, since the herbs which symbolize them "in summer... are like this," namely, withered, "and in winter... are green." As for the *ṣiddīqūn*, the mystics, "those who have attained certitude," they are symbolised by the evergreen myrtle which never withers, neither in winter nor in summer.

The hierarchy which distinguishes the *ṣādiqūn* from the *ṣiddīqūn* is one of the main themes in at-Tirmidhī's vast literary corpus. A clear relationship exists therefore between his, or his wife's, dream-experiences and the development of his mystical teaching. Thus the dreams indicate a process of inner integration, whereby the symbolic messages become truly directive and instructive. The dream brings good tidings also for Umm 'Abdallāh. She is distinguished from her sisters and is told in unambiguous terms that she and her husband "are together in the same place," and she too is given a branch of myrtle. Thus through the dream both wife and husband have become prepared for the next phase of their spiritual journey.

The next stage is inaugurated by a dream in which Umm 'Abdallāh is shown the spiritual transformation which is going to take place in her husband and in the world around him through his teaching. The dream points to her own deep involvement in this process: she becomes, or pledges to become, the custodian and protector of her husband's work. Without her his mission cannot be complete. Here is the dream:

> [In her dream] she was in the open hall of our house.... There were several couches there, upholstered with brocade. One of the couches stood next

to the family mosque. She said: I saw a tree growing by the side of this couch, facing the mosque. It grew up to a man's height, and it looked very dry, like a withered piece of wood. It had branches, similar to a palm tree, but the branches were all dry, like wooden pegs or filings. Now from the bottom of the trunk new branches emerged, about five or six, and they were all green and moist. When these branches reached the middle of the dry tree it started stretching and extending upwards to about three times a man's height, and so did the branches too. Then from amidst the branches there appeared bunches of grapes. I heard myself saying: This tree is mine! No one from here to the other end of the world has a tree like this!

I came closer to the tree and heard a voice coming from around it, although I could see no one there. I looked at the trunk and saw that it had grown out of a rock, a big rock. By the side of this rock I saw another big rock which had a hollow, like a pool. From the trunk of the tree a brook emerged and its water, which was pure, flowed into the hollow of the rock and gathered there.

Again I heard a voice calling me from the bottom of the tree: Can you pledge to protect this tree so that no hand would touch it? Then this tree is yours. Its roots have stood in sand and soil; many hands have touched it, and its fruit became worthless, then rotted and dried up. But now we have placed the rock around it, and we have nominated a bird over it, to watch over the fruit of this tree. Look!

I looked, and saw a green bird, the size of a pigeon. It perched on one of the branches, not on the green moist ones which grew from the bottom of the trunk, but on a dry one.... The bird hopped upwards, climbing from branch to branch; whenever it perched on a dry branch, which looked like a dry peg, it became green and moist, and bunches of grapes hung down from it. The voice said: If you

> protect this tree faithfully the bird will reach the top of the tree and the whole tree will become green; if not, the bird will stay here, in the middle. I said: I will; indeed, I will protect it! But there was no one to be seen.
>
> The bird flew to the top of the tree, branch after branch, and the whole tree became green. When it reached the top of the tree I exclaimed with amazement: *lā ilāha illā 'llāh!* ("There is no god but God"). Where are all the people? Can't they see the tree and come nearer? And the bird answered from the top of the tree: *lā ilāha illā 'llāh!* I wanted to pick up a tender grape from the tree, but a voice said to me: No! Not until it has ripened! And I woke up.

This dream carries a prophetic message for both husband and wife. Its images, as those of the previous dream, are ancient and archetypal. Discourse on the meaning of tree, rock, brook, the bunches of grapes (again), the green bird could take up many pages. But Abū 'Abdallāh is content to let the dream speak for itself. The magical transformation of the withered tree which takes place in front of Umm 'Abdallāh's eyes, the clear, authoritative messages which are conveyed to her through a hidden messenger, the green bird—a touch of Khiḍr?—which calls out the formula of faith and surrender from the top of the tree—all these images carry a lucid numinosity that touches the reader as it touched the dreamer. For her, who has a complete and utter faith in her husband's mission and destiny, the dream speaks with prophetic truth. She understands and accepts her role in his mission with enthusiasm and joy. Though the time is not yet ripe, the "tree" is destined to grow to immense dimensions and be protected by the "angelic" bird which is nominated upon it.

Umm 'Abdallāh continues to dream, and her new dreams reveal deeper layers of the extraordinary nature of her husband's mission. "On another occasion," Abū 'Abdallāh writes,

> she dreamed that she was sleeping with me on the roof. She said: I heard voices coming from the garden, and got anxious, because I thought that there were guests whom we had neglected. I'll go down and feed them, I thought, and went to the edge of the roof in order to climb down, when the edge of the roof, where I was standing, descended until it reached the ground and stopped.
>
> I saw two dignified persons sitting. I approached and apologized. They smiled. One of them said: Tell your husband: Why do you bother with this green [grass]? Your task is to give strength to the weak and to be their support. And tell him [also this]: You are one of the pegs of the earth, and to you is assigned a section of the earth.
>
> I said: Who are you? One of them said: Muḥammad Aḥmad, and this is 'Īsā (Jesus). Tell him, he added: You are saying, Oh, King, oh, Holy One, have mercy on us! [It is you who should] become sanctified! Every piece of land which you bless will grow strong and mighty, and that which you do not bless will become weak and worthless.
>
> Tell him: We have given you the Inhabited House: "[I swear] in the name of the Inhabited House."[38] May you have success! Then I woke up.

In this prophetic dream, which heralds a destiny far beyond the boundaries of Tirmidh or the 9th century, at-Tirmidhī is assigned, by no less than Muḥammad and Jesus, the role of a *peg*, one of the *pegs (awtād)* of the earth.

The spiritual hierarchy of the *awliyā'* consists of a fixed number of evolved human beings, without whom the existence and well-being of the world cannot be maintained. At the top of this hierarchy stands the *pole (quṭb)*, who is referred to by at-Tirmidhī as "the Master of the Friends of God" *(sayyid al-awliyā')*, or as their Seal *(khātam al-awliyā')*. Under the *pole* come the seven *pegs*, below which come the forty *successors (al-abdāl)*.

This hierarchy has become central to Sufi teaching and terminology.[39] Although it was not originated by al-Ḥakīm at-Tirmidhī—in fact, this is a very ancient teaching—he was its main and earliest exponent in the Sufi tradition. In this extraordinary and highly auspicious dream Abū 'Abdallāh is assigned no less than "the Inhabited House"—an allusion to the Holy House, the heart and center of Islam—by none other than two of the great spiritual authorities of his tradition. The dream is thus more than a message; it is an assignment from the highest source to a mission of cosmic proportions.

Information about Sufi women does not exist in abundance. We are fortunate to have access to this unique record which tells about a loyal, sincere, prophetic woman, whose dreams have been carefully and lovingly recorded by her husband. This unnamed woman from Central Asia became awakened, through her deep empathy with her husband's destiny, to her own inner quest. Alongside her dreams for him, at-Tirmidhī's autobiography records also Umm 'Abdallāh's own spiritual ripening through dreams. In one of these dreams she sees herself and her husband sleeping together in bed. The Prophet comes and lies down with them.

In another dream, one of the last dreams in the document, and one which—the record says—is meant for her alone, she sees the Prophet enter their house. She wants to kiss his feet, but he does not allow it. "He gave me his hand," she told her husband,

> and I kissed it. I did not know what to ask of him. One of my eyes had been badly inflamed, so I said: Messenger of God, one of my eyes has been infected with inflammation. He said: Cover it with your hand and say *lā ilāha illā 'llāh*, the One without partner, His is the kingdom and His is the praise, He revives and He kills, He holds the good in His hand, He is the omnipotent one. I woke up, and since then, whenever anything befalls me I repeat these words and the obstacle is removed.

The final passages of at-Tirmidhī's autobiography record Umm 'Abdallāh's own mystical experiences. He writes:

> After these dreams she felt an urge to search for truth herself. The first experience that she had, which confirmed the veracity of her dreams, was this: while she was sitting one day in the garden, five or six days after she had had this last dream, the following phrases descended upon her heart: The light and guide of all things! You are He whose light pierces all darkness!
>
> She said: I felt as if something penetrated my chest, circled within my heart and enveloped it. It filled my chest up to the throat; I almost choked from its fullness. Heat spread through the cavity of my body, my heart was aflame, and all the sacred

names appeared to me in their glory. Anything upon which my eyes fell, on the earth or in the sky, anyone whom I looked at, I saw as I have never seen before, because of the beauty and joy and sweetness [which filled me]. Then a verse in Persian descended upon my heart: We have given you one thing!

Again I was filled with joy, elation, and great energy. The next day (she said) another verse descended on my heart: We have given you three things: Our glory, Our might and Our beauty!

Then, she said, I saw a glow behind me, and it stayed above my head as if in a dream, and in this glowing light these three things were revealed to me: the knowledge of the Divine Glory, the knowledge of the Divine Might, and the knowledge of the Divine Beauty.

Then I saw something shimmering and moving, and it was conveyed to me: These things are going to take place. All that moves is from Him; the might and the high rank are from Him, and so are the beauty and the merit. This fire that I first saw in the sky is from Him, and now I see it as sparks of emerald and silver, blown and kindled.

On the third day these words descended on her heart: We have given you the knowledge of past and future.

She remained in this state for some time, and then the knowledge of the names of God was revealed to her. Each day new names opened up to her, and the glowing light was upon her heart, and the inward meaning of the names was revealed to her. This lasted for ten days. On the tenth day she came to me and said that the [Divine] name the Gracious *(al-laṭīf;* also: the Kind, the Gentle, the Subtle) was revealed to her.

With these experiences at-Tirmidhī's autobiographical record, seemingly abruptly, ends. But finished or unfinished, this is a unique document. From the care with which these, as well as the rest of the dreams contained in the document, were recorded, it is clear how seriously dreams were taken as heralds of destinies by the early Muslim mystics. In particular, at-Tirmidhī's record of his and his wife's dreams gives an insight into the importance assigned to dreams as instruments of spiritual teaching. In this respect, at-Tirmidhī's autobiography stands out not only as an ancient personal dream journal, but also as a testimony of the *practical* function of dreams in the processes of inner transformation on the mystical journey.

4

Where the Two Seas Meet: The Story of Khiḍr

We will take upon's the mystery of things
As if we were God's spies
Shakespeare, *King Lear* V, iii

The Masters are the spies of the hearts.
'Abdallāh Ibn 'Āṣim al-Anṭākī

The story of Khiḍr is the story of a meeting, the meeting between the two planes of existence in which seekers live out their mystical quest. It is the story of how this meeting becomes possible and real in the midst of day-to-day life. Khiḍr, whose name is usually translated as "the Green Man," is always there, where the two planes meet. He is there, "where the two seas meet," the sea of life and the sea of death, the space-bound and the spaceless, the time-bound and the timeless. Khiḍr comes to us in legends and stories as a mythical figure, as an archetypal image rather than as a concrete person. But for us to be able to navigate between the two planes freely, he has to be realized *concretely* in our lives. It is Khiḍr, by whichever form he chooses to reveal himself, who makes the passage between the two worlds possible. But first he has to be sought out, to be recognized. The meaning of the message that he carries with him has to be grasped.

I wrote the first version of this chapter in London, on a bleak January morning. There was not much movement in the air. A lifeless scene lay in front of my eyes: red, uniform roof-tiles, wet and immobile; blind, sealed windowpanes with opaque curtains; inanimate TV aerials sticking out aimlessly in a metallic, hostile sky. Naked trees spread their crooked arms and spiky fingers ominously. Birds had forsaken this place, had migrated to warmer, more hospitable regions. Only the cries of ravens and the shrieks of a few seagulls now and then pierced the immobile silence. Not a leaf to be seen on that January morning, not much green. A gloomy, wintry suburban landscape. A world which had grown old and tired: *'ālam-e pīr*, "an old world," in the words of Ḥāfeẓ, the 14th-century Persian poet from Shiraz. Yes, the world has grown old. And yet, very soon, he promises (and his words have been taken as oracles for all these centuries by lovers of Sufi poetry), only a pace away, a turning point, a change; the world will be turned upside down: spring will burst forth and everything will become alive and green. Here are Ḥāfeẓ's words:

> The breath of the morning wind will soon spread the
> fragrance of musk,
> And the world will become young again;
>
> The narcissus will soon wink at the anemones,
> And scarlet lilacs to white lilies a fragrant cup will
> soon display,
>
> The nightingale, who endured so long the pain of
> separation
> Will soon burst into the rose's chamber in joyous
> noise and clamorous array....
>
> If I leave the mosque and go to the tavern, don't fuss,
> For the preaching has taken too long, and time will

soon be on its way.
O, heart, what will assure the wealth of *baqā'*
If you put off for tomorrow the joys of today?...

The rose is precious, enjoy her company now,
For into the garden she came this way, and soon she
will go that way....

O, poet, this is a gathering of friends; read a ghazal,
sing a love-song,
How long will you say: "it came this way, soon it will
go that way?"

It is for your sake that Ḥāfeẓ has come to the plane of
existence,
With a firm foot bid him farewell, because soon he
too will be passing away.[1]

In these verses Ḥāfeẓ has captured the transition point between the dying old world and the young new budding world. He has conveyed the transitory state of the new as well as the old. Everything "comes this way and soon will go that way." But between the old and the new there is a meeting point, an ephemeral place where what *was* meets that which *is about* to take its place. This meeting point is the realm of Khiḍr, the green one, the hidden one, the remover of obstacles, the timeless Pole.

As I prepare now the second version of this chapter, Ḥāfeẓ's wisdom comes to life for me. It is mid-April. I am not in London, but on the West Coast of America. Everything around me is lush and bursting with life. Even Ḥāfeẓ's poetry is no match for the living, vivid experience of Chimney Rock. Walking there I experience the deep joy, colorfulness, versatility, and sacredness of Nature in its most ravishing appearance. Yet I also experience the transient nature of everything around me, including myself, the brief moment in which this experience can be captured in time:

> The rose is precious, enjoy her company now,
> for into the garden she came this way, and soon she
> will go that way....

The experience of the "now" *(waqt, ḥāl)*, of the timeless moment, so fundamental to Sufi teaching and so different from everything to which we have become conditioned—this experience too belongs to the realm of Khiḍr.[2]

The name Khiḍr is Arabic and it comes from Muslim sources. Yet the figure of this keeper of the secret of immortality is echoed, in various names and forms, in some of the oldest recollected stories of the human race. When Gilgamesh, the great hero of ancient Mesopotamia, discovered that every living thing must die, he resolved to seek out the wise old man of his time, Utnapishtim, who lived at the mouth of the rivers *(ina pi narati)* on an island across the Sea of Death, in order to learn from him the secret of immortality.[3]

In a similar way, but with different names and protagonists, a famous yet enigmatic Qur'ānic passage tells how Moses, the great prophet and law-giver of the Children of Israel, sets out to search for the source of Divine knowledge.[4] Moses pledges to search for a certain mysterious, unnamed man, upon whom God has bestowed His Divine knowledge *(al-'ilm al-ladunī)*. This knowledge is superior to the knowledge and wisdom given to Moses. According to Muslim commentators, this unnamed man, whom the

Qur'ān describes simply as "one of Our servants unto whom We had given mercy from Us, and [whom] We had taught ... knowledge proceeding from Us,"[5] lives, like Utnapishtim in the Gilgamesh epic, on a green island abundant with lush vegetation in the heart of the sea. This island is marked by a rock, and it is located "where the two seas meet" *(majma' al-baḥrayn)*. It is at this place that Moses, according to the Qur'ān, is to meet the mysterious figure identified as Khiḍr.

The Qur'ānic story of Moses and Khiḍr is told in a fragmented and enigmatic way. It is obvious that the audience to whom the story was related was familiar with the main story lines. But for later readers, many details which are missing in the Qur'ānic version have been added by Muslim commentators. Here are the opening lines of the story as told in the Qur'ān:

> And ... Moses said to his page,
> "I will not give up until I reach
> *the meeting of the two seas*,
> though I go on for many years."
> Then, when they reached their meeting,
> they forgot their fish, and it took
> its way into the sea, burrowing.
> When they had passed over, he said
> to his page,"Bring us our breakfast;
> indeed, we have encountered
> weariness from this our journey."
> He said, "What thinkest thou? When we
> took refuge in the rock, then I
> forgot the fish ...
> and so it took its way into
> the sea in a manner marvellous."
> Said he, "This is what we were
> seeking!"And so they returned

> upon their tracks, retracing them.
> Then they found *one of Our servants,*
> *unto whom We had given mercy*
> *from Us, and We had taught him*
> *knowledge proceeding from Us.*[6]

Apart from the rock, there is another sign by which Moses and his servant are able to recognize the place where the two seas meet: the miraculous revival of the cooked fish which Moses' servant has prepared for their breakfast. Although the Qur'ān does not say it explicitly, it is evident that the way in which the cooked fish finds its way into the sea is connected with the special quality of the water in this extraordinary place: it is the water of eternal life. Everything it touches is revived and becomes alive forever.

This is yet another ancient motif. It is found in myths and legends about the great king Alexander. Alexander the Great left such a deep impression on the peoples of the East in Antiquity that for centuries, well into the Middle Ages, legends circulated about his superhuman personality and deeds. According to some legends, the great Alexander became disillusioned with all his conquests and achievements when he contemplated the temporary nature of every living thing. He decided to search for the spring of eternal life. He embarked on his search with a companion, a cook named Andreas. After many years of wandering unsuccessfully they decided to part ways. Andreas, on his way, happened to take a pause for food by a river. He opened the basket where he had stored a cooked fish. A few drops of water splashed accidentally on the fish, and immediately it was revived and leaped into the water. Andreas jumped after the fish, and became inadvertently blessed—or cursed, as it was sometimes implied—with immortality.

In some Islamic versions of the Alexander legends it is related that, on diving into the water of immortality, Alexander's companion became green (in Arabic *khaḍir)*, hence the attribute *al-khaḍir*, "the green one," from which derives the somewhat colloquial form *al-khiḍr*, which means "the color green," or simply "greenness."[7]

Khiḍr is sometimes described as living in rivers and riding a fish, and therefore he is also known as *Dhū an-Nūn*, "he who possesses the fish."[8] Khiḍr is believed to be walking on the skin of the earth, and wherever he steps green shoots come forth. His touch and presence bring things to life. He is endowed with the power of finding water which is hidden in the depth of the earth. He can be present in many places at one and the same time. He materializes in many disguises and forms. He is the one who appears in desperate situations to the "constrained" *(al-muḍṭarr)* and removes all obstacles. He is therefore the *mushkil gushā* of all times.[9]

Moses is motivated to make the journey to the place "where the two seas meet" in order to find the teacher who has been given direct knowledge from God. This is the sacred knowledge *('ilm ladunī)* after which mystics seek. He takes a vow to search for this meeting point for as long as it takes. It has been revealed to him that only in this mysterious place do the two planes of existence come together; only there can the mystical knowledge be truly transmitted.

What are the “two seas”? Many interpretations have been offered by Muslim commentators. Some made great effort to try to locate them geographically. Sufis, however, have understood it to indicate the place where the sea of life and the sea of death meet, where the state of *fanā’* and the state of *baqā’* meet. This place is marked by a rock and by the miracle of resurrection and transformation symbolized by the revival of the cooked fish. The cooked fish itself represents the anguished soul of the seeker in search of the water of mystical immortality.

The rock is a symbol of God’s Mercy: it is a refuge, a stronghold, a place of rest for the weary travelers on the path. But there are many rocks along the seashore and in the sea. How is this one to be recognized? By what special mark? There is no obvious demarcation line between the two zones. Even Moses with all his eagerness and wisdom, and in spite of his special rank as the prophet to whom God had spoken “mouth to mouth”—even Moses did not recognize this meeting point when he reached the place where the two seas meet. How much more so “ordinary” seekers?

But Moses does not give in to despair or self-blame; he is determined to go on for as long as it takes. And this is the true moral of the story for travelers on the mystical path. Rūmī has captured the meaning behind Moses’ humility and determination to go in search of the mysterious teacher regardless of his unique closeness to God. This is how Rūmī has conveyed this lesson in his *Mathnawī:*

> Learn from him with whom God spake, O noble sir! See what Kalīm (Moses)[10] says in his longing!
>
> “Notwithstanding such a dignity and such a prophetic office, ... I am a seeker of Khiẓr ... quit of self-regard.”

> ... "O Moses, thou hast forsaken thy people; thou hast wandered distraught in search of a blessed man.
>
> Thou art an emperor delivered from fear and hope: how long wilt thou wander? How long wilt thou seek? To what bound?
>
> (He that is) thine is with thee, and thou art conscious of this. O, (thou who art exalted as the) sky, how long wilt thou traverse the (low) earth?"
>
> Moses said, "Do not make this reproach....
>
> I will fare as far as *the meeting-place of the two seas*, that ... I may be accompanied by the Sovereign of the time.
>
> I will make Khiẓr a means to (the achievement of) my purpose: (either) that, or *I will go onward* and journey by night *a long while*.
>
> I will fly with wings and pinions for years: what are years? For thousands of years."
>
> (He said) "I will fare," meaning,"Is it not worth that (toilsome journey)? Do not deem the passion of the Beloved to be less than the passion for bread (worldly goods)."[11]

Moses, then, is going in search of the mystical teacher. And the teacher is there, "where the two seas meet," at the meeting point of past and future, light and darkness, the transient and the eternal. The mystical journey is *always* a search for this meeting point. This is one of the deep meanings of the "union of opposites," the *coincidentia oppositorum*.[12] It is a journey to an altogether different plane from the one with which we are familiar. At the same time the search is not a flight; it is not an escape from this familiar, ordinary plane: it is a meeting of the two.

In order to reach the water of mystical immortality, which is marked nowhere geographically or spatially, the mystic too, like Gilgamesh, Alexander, Andreas, Moses, and his page, must take up a journey in the course of which he shall have to traverse the Sea of Death. The Sea of Death is the plane of illusion. When consciousness and self-identity are held bound by the spell of impressions and sense perceptions, one is deemed dead.

Gilgamesh, Alexander, and Moses all embarked on their journey because they came to realize that on this plane of existence everything is bound to perish. All three stand for some grand achievement: there was no hero in ancient Mesopotamia mightier than Gilgamesh; there was no conqueror in Antiquity more powerful than Alexander; there was no prophet in the Biblical tradition superior to Moses. Yet all three, attaining the summit of man's efforts, had to realize that all their achievements were transient, ephemeral, without real substance. In essence they were null and void, and their duration, from the vantage point of sacred eternity, less than a mustard grain of measured time. This is the realization behind any spiritual quest:

> All that dwells upon the earth is perishing *(fānin)*,
> yet still abides *(fa-yabqā)* the Face of thy Lord,
> majestic, splendid.[13]

This Qur'ānic verse is the source for *fanā' wa-baqā'* ("annihilation" and "permanence"), the pair of opposites which lies at the core of Sufi perception of Reality. Sufis have applied this pair to designate the highest stage on the path of inner transformation: *fanā'* indicates the annihilation of the psychological identification with the lower self, the ego *(nafs)*, while *baqā'* indicates the permanence of the higher Self, the soul, man's everlasting core of being. *Fanā'* is understood, therefore, not as the liberation of soul from body in the afterlife, but as its liberation from the confinement of ego-bound consciousness in this life. It is the liberation from the blurred, restricted vision of ordinary sense-perception, of conventional values, of the collective sense of right and wrong, good and evil. To "traverse the Sea of Death" means to go through a long and painful process in which self-centeredness falls away, in which delusions of the ego's omnipotence fall away. When the *nafs,* the seat of ego-consciousness, steps aside in recognition of its appropriate place within the scheme of things, then can the soul abide with the Beloved, "majestically, splendidly."

Our three heroes, men of great achievements and of huge egos, become humbled when they realize that in the end everything perishes. Embarking on the journey is in itself a sign of a new attitude, an attitude of humility, poverty, and longing for true fulfillment. Every spiritual journey can be traced back to this starting point. When the feeling of want, of inner poverty, of missing something essential—like air for breathing—takes over, and especially when it takes over after a life of great achievements, then a turning of the heart, a sincere *tawba* occurs.[14] We are told that as soon as Moses and his page, Joshua bin Nūn, discovered that they had missed the meeting place with the teacher, they at once "returned upon their tracks, retracing them." To retrace one's steps, to recognize one's errors, is a crucial point on the path. This is when the real transition takes place. In Sufi terms this stage is named *tawba,* repentance, a conversion of the heart. From this point on, the mystical quest is in essence a "retracing" of one's steps, a "regression" from the point of view of ordinary life.[15]

One's sense of achievement must die so that the Sacred can radiate within the heart. The point of death for the *nafs* is the point of revival for the soul. At this point Khiḍr is waiting. He is both the undertaker and the midwife. He shatters illusions and delusions, and then gives meaning and direction to the soul's search. If, like Moses, Alexander, and Gilgamesh, the seeker vows to keep up the journey even if it takes a lifetime, even though he has to retrace his steps many times, then, at the right place and time, he will encounter Khiḍr who will guide him from station to station.

Khiḍr lives on a green island by the source of the Water of Immortality. He is the life force behind all natural phenomena. Nothing can be alive and vital without Khiḍr's touch or presence. When a seeker goes through times of emptiness and depression, in an inner wilderness where nothing seems to grow, he has seemingly lost touch with Khiḍr. Khiḍr has veiled himself. But he is there, hiding behind the thorny, barren branches, or in the empty waterholes. When friends gather and there is no feeling of intimacy and empathy, when words sound empty and meaningless, Khiḍr seems to be absent; he keeps himself in hiding. When things become mechanical, repetitive, unconscious, then, too, Khiḍr is veiled. But if companions gather with a sense of purpose, if there is something meaningful in their lives that has brought them together, *here, now*, and if that which happens in that "here and now" has vitality, then they know: this is the imprint of Khiḍr.

When the eyes glimmer and shine, when Eros is in the air, then Khiḍr is around.

But also when old idols are smashed, when the traveler experiences states of rage and frustration, when he cannot go on with his routine, with idly surrendering to the tyranny of circumstances, when he has reached a point of no return, when he feels the time has come to risk that which has been taken for granted, then, provided the time is right, Khiḍr is at work. When despair becomes greater than fear, it is Khiḍr who intervenes and comes to his help as the "remover of obstacles," as the *mushkil gushā*. This ever-present life force gives the seeker strength to change the direction of his erring life.

In the following poem inspired by a dream, the inner Khiḍr is lost and then found. When he is re-found, he becomes the primordial, green energy of becoming and creativity:

> Once there was a man,
> a green man, ancient man.
> He lived before time was,
> he wove creation out of the green,
> the evergreen green planes of his interiors.
>
> I lost him.
> Transformation of the color green
> to light and vice versa ceased.
> There was no hope:
> the future stopped becoming,
> I lost my man of green,
> I lost my man of light.
>
> I dreamed.
> I dreamed a circle.
> I dreamed myself a circle,

and there I was, and he,
and many men like him,
men and women of green
weaving threads of golden rays of green
to be my daughter's hair,

my red-haired, blue-eyed daughter,
so young that she can hardly know her name,
so tender she can hardly speak
the sounds that have formed her,
the primal notes of her and my becoming.[16]

When the mysterious way in which we are connected inwardly to Khiḍr reveals itself in a dream, or an insight, in relationships, or in an art form, then the deep meaning of his evergreen life force becomes evident. It is then that obstacles which had blocked the process of transformation are miraculously removed.

In the Sufi tradition the link with Khiḍr comes often through dreams. Khiḍr-dreams come from the deepest, most ancient recesses of the soul. Khiḍr in dreams is a sign of a shift, a tremendous inner movement in the psyche. Here is a dream of inner transition dreamed by a modern seeker:

> I go to a funeral. I am just arriving and my mother is there taking off her dripping silver-grey coat. I take off my own coat and realize that I am wearing the same silver-grey coat as wet and dripping as my mother's. There are many coats hanging on coat stands but I do not see anyone else. The funeral takes place in a hall which looks like a lecture hall.

> Then the scene changes.
>
> A few of us are sitting on the floor. We call for Khiḍr. It is like a ceremony. He appears without shape and I tell him to materialize. Suddenly I am pulled into the center as if on a skateboard and he grows out of myself. I cannot watch myself and feel possessed. The only thing I can see of Khiḍr is a golden-green light. What remains of myself is the old potato when you dig out the new ones.
>
> Then I wake up with a terrible fear. The wind outside is strong and roaring and I try to calm down, which is difficult and takes time. I feel hot like an immersion heater.

"The wind outside is strong and roaring." How tremendous is the energy of transformation: in the brief moment of a dream one dies like an old potato and is reborn anew. A funeral is about to take place in the opening scene of the dream. The dreamer and her mother are the only persons there, but there are many coats hanging on coat stands, as though there were many invisible participants in the funeral. Many indeed: the multitude of relationships, conditionings, and patterns which have shaped the lives of mother and daughter. They have gathered there to witness the death and burial of the primary bond between the two. This bond which is so essential to us when we are small becomes too narrow, too constricting, too suffocating when we grow up. The relationship with the mother is the most subtle, the most obstinate and long-lasting of all our relationships. Before the colossal transformation heralded by Khiḍr can take place, the dreamer has to grow out of the uroboric relationship with her mother.

In the dream both mother and daughter wear the same silver-grey coat. They both take their coats off. The coats are dripping wet. It is raining. Rain is grace; rain carries the touch of Khiḍr; rain *is* Khiḍr, the water of compassion which is present at every new creation.[17] In the ritual of the funeral both mother and daughter die and are born anew. The funeral symbolizes the crossing of the Sea of Death.

Then another ritual takes place in the dreamer's inner chambers: a group of companions is sitting in meditation, performing a very particular *dhikr*: they invoke Khiḍr. This is not a practice in which the group normally engages. It symbolizes something deeply unique to the dreamer. It is her own mode of *dhikr*. The group invokes him, and he comes. This is the rule: "He appears by whichever name you call Him." Khiḍr is shapeless, formless, as is the teaching, as all teachers are: they have neither a name nor a face, only a golden-green light. This is the light of *baqā'*, the light of eternal life—after the dark night of *fanā'*, the golden-green light of *baqā'*.

The dream preserves an ancient quality, a sense of mystery, of the otherworldliness which lies at the opposite side of the outer life. The dreamer is a woman who puts a lot of effort in her search. The intensity of her quest-energy is tireless, and yet in her dream she is pulled to the center as if on a skateboard; she is gliding, *effortlessly*. After the practice of invocation, which symbolizes the effort she puts into the process, she is now moved effortlessly into the center of her being. And there, *out of herself,* Khiḍr materializes. We search for a teacher out there, but the outer teacher always points to the inner teacher. Ultimately, the search is for the Khiḍr within, and the meeting point of the two seas is where the two planes converge within the core of our being.

A powerful dream-experience such as this equals many years of outer tribulations. But the dream does not promise a tranquil outer life. Khiḍr symbolizes the realm of possibility, opportunity, potentiality. The meeting of the two seas means that, through the efforts of a sincere search, this realm comes alive. What the dreamer has encountered in the dream she will have to live out in the unfolding patterns of her new life, blessed by the expansive grace of her inner Khiḍr. The field—in which old, dead potatoes are the sole reminders of the past—will yield a new crop.

Such a dream is often initiated through the grace of a living teacher in whom the mystical tradition is perpetuated. This is yet another way in which Khiḍr reveals himself to seekers. The Water of Life which flows from the Source of All Being becomes manifested *concretely* in the living teacher. If Khiḍr is the archetypal life force behind the spiritual journey, then the contemporary, living teacher is the earthly manifestation of this life force. Without a link with a teacher, real transformation may not come about easily. Or if it does come about, it might dwindle after a while. But when one becomes connected to a living teacher, life cannot continue along its former routes. Things start changing. All those who have been seriously interested in spiritual life know this from their own experience. Most difficulties on the path arise because, although the seeker craves change, he does not really want to give up anything. The teacher, like Khiḍr, has therefore a twofold aspect: he comes across as a merciful, nourishing benefactor; but he can also appear as a ruthless, uncompromising demolisher of habits and thought-forms. *He first seduces, then executes, then revives.* Again and again on this never-ending journey one returns to the point where the two seas meet, where life and death converge. The contact with a teacher, according to all mystical traditions, assures that the seeker does not fall back into the sleep of unconsciousness and mechanical existence. The teacher, like Khiḍr, is both the reviver of dead souls and the destroyer of illusions. Like Khiḍr, he too stands at the meeting point of the opposites within oneself.

In the foreword to her book, *Daughter of Fire*, Mrs. Tweedie describes the way in which her teacher, Bhai Sahib, forced her "to face the darkness within" herself. She writes:

> He made me "descend into hell," the cosmic drama enacted in every soul as soon as it dares to lift its face to the Light. It was done very simply, by using violent reproof and even aggression. My mind was kept in a state of confusion.... I was beaten down in every sense till I had to come to terms with that in me which I kept rejecting all my life.... Only a heart which has become non-existent can resurrect, pulsate to the rhythm of a new life.
>
> "...Ye have to die before you can live again.... "[18]

The Teacher, like a finely tuned compass, always points to the "mystical North." North symbolizes death. There is something ominous about the sunless, esoteric North, like the ominousness of a black hole. But this is how it's seen by a limited, three-dimensional perception. Viewed from the dimension of the teacher, or of Khiḍr, this black hole, the void symbolized by the North, is a pathway to a higher level of consciousness, a door to the beyond.[19]

The teacher, then, points to a direction which is both ominous and auspicious, frightening and exciting, warning and promising. In deep states one may experience a chilling awe *(hayba)* coupled with the sweetness of intimacy *(uns)*. We are terrified of letting go, and are scared stiff of the teacher. And at the same time we are attracted, helplessly, hopelessly, like Ulysses' sailors, beyond and against our will, to become annihilated in the killing grace of the teacher.

The deeper we penetrate into the story of Moses and Khiḍr, the more wondrous it becomes. This unnamed man who carries the everlasting grace of God behaves in a bizarre and obnoxious way. Once the encounter takes place and Moses finds his teacher, he is in for a big surprise, because everything Khiḍr does is against the deepest convictions, the deepest sense of morality which Moses exemplifies. Who is Moses and what does he represent? In the Sufi tradition, nourished by Islamic prophetology, Moses is a law-giver messenger *(rasūl)*, the highest rank of prophecy. As a giver of Divine law he represents the highest values of justice and morality.

But the teacher robs Moses of these values. The teacher points out to Moses that his understanding of the values of justice are based on human shortsightedness and on a mistaken interpretation of appearances. Khiḍr acts three times in a way that leaves Moses and all conscientious listeners to this story in a state of shock. First, he drills a hole in the boat of some poor fishermen, and they cannot go out to sea to fetch in their daily catch. Then he comes to a place where he and Moses are graciously invited into some people's house, and the next morning he kills their young son. Third, he comes to a place where people are offensive to both him and Moses, but he helps them build a wall. At all these points Moses cannot contain himself; he protests and demands an explanation. But this is contrary to the deal which he has made with Khiḍr.

When Moses, after his long journey of quest, finally found Khiḍr at the meeting point of the two seas, he asked Khiḍr's permission to follow him wherever he went. Khiḍr agreed, but on one condition, that Moses should not ask any questions, should not demand any explanations. Moses accepted this condition, but in the face of the teacher's acts, he could not keep quiet.[20]

In *Daughter of Fire* Mrs. Tweedie protests time and again against her teacher Bhai Sahib's behavior which, from her angle, does her injustice. The disciple will be pushed to rebel and protest against things he witnesses which go against his convictions and values. The teacher will tell the disciple, at times quite literally, that day is night and night is day, will deliberately create situations of confusion and misunderstanding. Khiḍr's story must not be taken on its mythical, symbolic level only. The meeting with the teacher is about a concrete process of emptying, total emptying, with no reservations. This is a difficult test of endurance. It is also a crucial test of discretion.

It is said that at the beginning of their encounter, the disciple has the right to test the teacher. What does it mean? How can the disciple, at the beginning of his journey, when he is losing his grip on discrimination based on former values, and when he has not yet acquired the teacher's values—how can he possibly make a congruous judgment? A big paradox! But the disciple *knows*. Something in the disciple knows. Not the rational mind, which becomes more and more useless, but something else. When the heart finds out, as Moses did, that this is its meeting point, that this is its *homecoming*, then it can let the teacher take over, and a season of tests and hardships begins for the disciple. A genuine teacher will never act without the implicit consent of the disciple, which the teacher, the spy of hearts, intuitively knows. Yet, archetypally, part of the deal for the disciple, when confronted with the teacher's trickstery, is to refrain from asking "why."

One of the long-lasting tests is this: whatever happens around the teacher is never what the disciple expects. Like Moses, who has to watch Khiḍr commit atrocious acts without being allowed to ask for an explanation, so the disciple. He must learn to acquire a new eyesight, to see things with a new perception, from a new vantage point. Because Khiḍr's acts only *seem* arbitrary and mean. Behind them lies a deeper vision of all three situations he and Moses have encountered together.[21]

At the meeting point of the opposites, in life-and-death situations, the teacher is present and waiting. At the level of a real meeting with the teacher, the discrimination between the opposites falls away. Life and death do not stand apart anymore. One implication of this is that teachers do not really die. Their energy is immortal, since they drink water from Khiḍr's source. Teachers who belong to the same path *(ṭarīqa)* create a living lineage *(silsila)* which persists beyond their physical death. Sufi tradition has preserved many anecdotes of meetings between past and present generations of teachers. Such a communication, which defies physical death, is made possible through the link with Khiḍr. The Naqshbandi path in particular has become known for the fact that its teaching has been transmitted regardless of historical connections.[22] Hundreds of years sometimes separate teacher and disciple. That such timeless meetings are possible is the hallmark of Khiḍr. Through Khiḍr's work at the meeting place of the time-bound and the timeless, communication is vertical rather than linear. In the image of Khiḍr all teachers become one; in the image of Khiḍr the teacher and the teaching become one.

The Sufi tradition has distinguished a special group of seekers: those whose *sole* link with the teaching is through Khiḍr himself. There are those rare Sufis who do not have a teacher in the flesh. Their only teacher, as in Moses' case, is Khiḍr. They have been given a special name: *uwaysiyyūn*. They are named after Uways al-Qaranī, a contemporary of the Prophet Muḥammad, who lived in Yemen and, due to his mother's illness, could not make the journey to Medina to join the companions of the Prophet. And yet he had a direct link with Muḥammad. The Prophet said that the sweet scent of Uways wafted all the way from Yemen to Medina, and thus their spirits had been at all times together.[23] Such meeting in the spirit takes place also in the case of seekers and teachers whose link with the mystical tradition is via Khiḍr.

Of the many anecdotes transmitted by the Sufi tradition in which the Divine Knowledge is passed on to the seeker through Khiḍr, here are two. They tell of the special relationship between Khiḍr and two early mystics: the 11th-century Khurāsāni master Abū Sa'īd ibn Abī al-Khayr, and the 9th-century master from Tirmidh, al-Ḥakīm at-Tirmidhī.

In his youth Abū Sa'īd committed himself to a very austere and ascetic way of life. For days he would wander alone in harsh and lonely places. His father, who was concerned about him, would go after him and bring him back home. And the Sheikh, to please his father, would come home with him. But after he had stayed there a few days, he desperately needed seclusion. Again he would run away and hide in the mountains and the deserts. The people of Meyhana, his hometown, would sometimes catch sight of him wandering in those remote areas; they would see him in the company of an "awesome old man dressed in white." Later, when Abū Sa'īd had attained his high mystic rank, people asked him:

> "O, Shaikh, those days we saw you, who was the awe inspiring old man you were with?"
>
> [Abū Sa'īd] replied, "That was Khezr—*peace be upon him!*"[24]

In *Lives of Muslim Saints and Mystics* Farīd ad-Dīn 'Aṭṭār tells how al-Ḥakīm at-Tirmidhī, who did not have a link with a living teacher, was trained by Khiḍr. At-Tirmidhī, 'Aṭṭār writes, wished to join some friends of his who went on a journey in quest of knowledge. But his mother fell ill, and since she was a widow, she pleaded with him to stay with her. He did, but was very distressed. He spent long hours alone in the cemetery weeping. Then a luminous old man appeared in front of him one day, and said:

> "Would you like me to teach you a lesson daily? . . . "
>
> "I would," Termedhi replied.
>
> "So," Termedhi recalled, "every day he taught me a lesson, till three years had gone by. Then I realized that he was Khezr, and that I had attained this felicity because I pleased my mother."[25]

This legendary version told by the 13th-century poet does not necessarily tally with biographical data which can be compiled through other sources. Its importance nevertheless lies in the fact that it shows how the teaching is transmitted via Khiḍr when a physical link does not materialize for the sincere disciple.[26]

The link with Khiḍr alludes also to the *esoteric* nature of the mystical teaching. What is related in books or transmitted orally is not the complete teaching. There are things which belong to the realm of the unspoken. That Khiḍr is also he who guards the true esoteric aspect of the tradition can be gleaned from the following mysterious story. This story, too, is told by 'Aṭṭār. He relates it in the words of Abū Bakr al-Warrāq, allegedly at-Tirmidhī's closest disciple. Leaving his readers with a feeling of mystery and awe, 'Aṭṭār alludes here to the affinity of Khiḍr and fish. Here is Abū Bakr's account retold by 'Aṭṭār:

> Every Sunday ... Khezr would visit Termedhi and they would converse on every matter.... One day Termedhi handed over to me many volumes of his writings to cast into the [river] Oxus. I examined them and found they were replete with mystic subtleties and truths. I could not bring myself to carry out his instructions, and instead stored them in my room. I then told him that I had thrown them in.
>
> "What did you see?" he asked.
>
> "Nothing," I replied.
>
> "You did not throw them in," he concluded. "Go and do so."
>
> ... I went back and threw the books into the Oxus. I saw the river open up, and an open chest appeared; the volumes fell into it, then the lid closed and the river subsided. I was astonished.
>
> "Did you throw them in this time?" Termedhi questioned me when I returned to him.
>
> "Master, by God's glory," I cried, "tell me the secret behind this."
>
> "I had composed something on the science of the Sufis, the disclosing of ... which was difficult for human minds to grasp," he replied. "My brother Khezr entreated me. The chest was brought by a fish at his bidding, and Almighty God commanded the waters to convey it to him."[27]

5

Eros and the Mystical Quest

Go, and love first.
Then come to me and I will show you the way.
Jāmī[1]

In reality, that which attracts is a single thing,
but it appears multiple.
Rūmī[2]

There is a part in us which feels that love is something too intimate, too tender to be exposed. Love wants to hide, to withdraw into its sacred shrine in the innermost of the soul. It's difficult to talk of love because love is a state of melting. It's an experience in which opposites merge with one another without boundaries, without differentiation, like colors in a potter's furnace. Words, on the other hand, are clear-cut, differentiating, isolating. The sensitive words of a poet-friend echo in my ears:

Put away your hands.
A bud cannot be opened
by a man.[3]

But love desires also to be revealed, to share its beauty, to freely pour itself out into the open. This is why men and women, young and old, modern and ancient, have given expression to their experiences of love in poetry, in art, and in relationships. I am surrounded by books which are the evidence of the need men and women have to express their most concealed desires, their most agonizing longing, in the language of love poetry. Between the wish to remain silent and the urge to make verbal love to love, the heart oscillates no end. It's the same on the path of mystical quest: love seeks to express itself. "Love cannot be hidden," Bhai Sahib, the Sufi teacher from Kanpur, says to his disciple Mrs. Tweedie:

> What is in the heart becomes expressed outwardly. The exterior reflects the inner attitude; it cannot be helped.... It is like love; it cannot be hidden.[4]

This is the way of love: between the silences it tries to communicate, to say *I love you, I am overcome by you, I melt when I hear your name, I dissolve remembering your nearness when you're far.* It wants to sing the praises of the loved one as does the lover in the Song of Songs, that tender, sensuous biblical love poem which mystics have identified as a dialogue between God and the soul:

> Behold, thou art fair, my love;
> behold, thou art fair;
> thine eyes are like doves.

And it wants to hear the same enchanted words echo back,

> Behold, thou art fair, my beloved,
> yea, pleasant (1:15-16).

The male lover can't help exclaiming,

> As the lily among thorns,
> so is my love among the daughters.

while the female lover can't help responding,

> As the apple tree among the trees of the wood,
> so is my beloved among the sons (2:2-3).

Love wants a dialogue. In its very essence it's an experience between two, the lover and the beloved, an experience in which the lover is also the beloved, the beloved also the lover. But who loves? And who is loved? Between whom does the love-dialogue take place? "In the whole of the universe there are only Two," Bhai Sahib says to Mrs. Tweedie:

> In the whole of the universe there are only Two: the Lover and the Beloved. God loves His Creation, and the Soul loves God. In order to be able to create, the One Being had to become two, and logically there had to be a difference between the two. The creation was only possible because of the two opposites; everything in creation responds either to positive or to negative forces, or vibrations. There is the Sound and the Echo, the Call and the response to it, Light and Darkness; without the opposing forces, how could the world exist?[5]

Bhai Sahib's words reflect a vision, a vantage point, from which love is seen as a Divine quality that *transcends* as well as *includes* the whole range of human experience. Our separate, isolated experiences of love are included within the all-encompassing love between God and creation. This all-encompassing quality is reflected in the Qur'ānic verse, "My Mercy encompasses all things" (7:156). In this vision, God, by virtue of His all-encompassing Mercy, is a lover; we are beloved. It is love, the ultimate faculty of Divine expression, which brings all there is into existence. Existence then becomes *seemingly* polarized between God *(al-ḥaqq)* and creation *(al-khalq)*.[6] Thus the most sublime—while also the most fundamental—attraction of opposites is between God and creation. The attraction that arises between any other pair is but a reflection of this fundamental attraction which lies, whether we know it or not, at the root of our existence. This vision goes beyond the understanding of some Greek philosophers and their medieval followers, who saw Love, Eros, as the divine power which attracts to each other the two severed halves, male and female, which in a primordial state of being constituted a whole, a hermaphrodite.[7] In the Sufi vision of love, the two polarized entities which agonizingly desire one another are God and creation, God and the human soul, not one half of a human being and its complementary half.

Bhai Sahib's words also imply that the love between God and man is not to be taken on a metaphoric level. It is not a mere poetic metaphor, nor an allegory, nor a symbol alluding to something ineffable, unspeakable. It is substantial, potent, and real. Sufis have lived and realized, consciously and with surrender, the burning, living reality of the love between God and the human soul: "In the whole of the universe *there are* only two: the Lover and the Beloved."

The mystical vision of the all-embracing love was formulated by the 13th-century mystic Ibn al-'Arabī in all its boldness and magnitude. He says,

> The Breath of the All-Merciful made the cosmos manifest in order to release the property of love and relieve what the Lover found in Himself. So He knew Himself through witnessing in the Manifest.[8]

> God is qualified by love for us, and love is a property that demands that he who is described by it be merciful toward himself.... So nothing emerges from Him except the mercy "which embraces all things" (7:156). It extends to the whole cosmos, that which is and that which has not yet come to be.[9]

What does it mean "to release the property of love and relieve what the Lover found in Himself?" First and foremost it means that love is primary. At the beginning there is love; then, consequently, there are lovers. We can attempt to understand it from the level of our human experience of love: when we carry love within us we will ultimately need to project it into something, into someone, into another. This is the only way by which we can be *relieved* of the burden of carrying this love, all coiled and hidden, alone. The most obvious instance is erotic, sexual love, when a powerful urge forces us to release the surge of libido. This act is always heightened by being reciprocated, by conveying a "dialogue." The erotic drive, by its very nature, desires to find a release in another. Through the activation of love-desire, human lovers too become procreators. New creations come into being. But the need to "release" the love in us reveals itself also in other creative manifestations. A mother knows that during the nine months of pregnancy she becomes a container for a new life which grows inside the darkness of her womb in suspension, until the time is right for it to push itself into the outer world in a cry and a sigh of relief. Everything we produce —a piece of furniture, an architectural structure, a drawing, a letter, a book—emerges from an initial drive, an initial idea, initial love.

This is the natural scheme of things, but the lower reflects the higher; as above so below. The relationship between God and creation springs from the same erotic-creative principle. The externalization of Divine love is seen by Ibn al-ʻArabī as an *exhalation—nafas*—as a "breathing-out" of God's uroboric love into an "other." This is how creation comes into being. The universe and all that exists come into being in an explosive Divine exhalation which is alluded to in orgasmic terms. God's love which was folded within itself pours out in a tremendous, potent *sigh of relief* which releases His creative energy. Ibn al-ʻArabī writes:

> "Giving relief" is to eliminate ... constriction *(ḍīq)*.... When the possible thing knows its possibility while in the state of nonexistence, it is distressed, since it yearns for the existence allowed by its reality.[10]

As long as God's attributes, names, and actions are in a state of potentiality—"possibility"—Mercy *(raḥma)*, which is the keynote of all there is, cannot be activated, has not been "breathed out." But then, in an act of merciful out-breath, the creative energy contained in God's powers, or names, comes into manifestation: "Through the Breath of the All-merciful God gave relief to the divine names."[11] The "black hole," to use a contemporary image, in which everything was held in constriction, exploded into the myriad of life forms which make the created, "breathed-out" universe:

> Through the All-merciful Breath God relieves every distress in His creatures.[12]

> The All-Merciful relieves this [constriction] through His Breath, since He brings the possible thing into existence. Hence His "giving relief" is His elimination of the property of nonexistence within the possible thing.[13]

Creation is not a singular event which took place in some distant past time. It goes on all the time, on many levels. Each breath is a new creation; each breath is a new creative force. An out-breath, a sigh, is also the exclamation which comes out spontaneously at the climactic point of the erotic act without which nothing can come into existence. The breath of the All-merciful *(nafas ar-raḥmān)* is thus seen by Ibn al-'Arabī as both an orgasmic sigh of relief and as that which breathes life. Creation, therefore, is at one and the same time the *act* and the *product* of the Divine erotic energy. God created the universe as a product of the primordial love contained in His essence. Creation, God's love-child, is the manifestation of God's hidden powers, as expressed in the tradition "I was a Treasure but was not known. So I *loved* to be *known*, and I created the creatures and made Myself known to them. Then they came to know Me."[14]

Ibn al-'Arabī makes explicit the analogy between God and man by reiterating that the merciful breath of love through which everything comes into existence is all-encompassing:

> Since man comes into existence upon the Divine Form, he finds confinement intolerable. So God relieves that in him through this All-merciful Breath, inasmuch as His breathing is a property of the Love by which He described Himself in the saying, "I loved to be known." God makes man manifest through the All-merciful Breath. Hence this Divine Breathing is identical with the existence of the cosmos, and the cosmos comes to know Him as He desired. So the cosmos is identical with mercy, nothing else.[15]

Mercy, *raḥma*, derives from a root in Arabic which connects it with the word for womb, *raḥim*. Womb, as also the linguistic form for *raḥma*, is feminine. The thrust and the outpouring of the erotic energy are male. In an Islamic myth which derives from more ancient mythologies, the creative, cosmic male energy is envisaged as the primordial "Pen," *qalam*, with which God "writes" the destinies of all created beings in the Book of Creation, in the Mother of Books *(umm al-kitāb)*.[16] The undifferentiated Being, which *was* when *nothing* was, has been envisaged as holding in the confinement of Non-being both feminine and masculine within Its unmanifested essence. It holds within Itself both Mother and Father, both womb and pen. This analogy, by reflection, stretches down also to our human experience. We, too, hold this polarized pair within our being. We, too, before differentiation takes place in us, hold both masculine and feminine together in a coil. By loving another we become liberated—in the same way that God, by creating us, releases Himself from His uroboric "aloneness"—from holding these powerful opposites alone, in ourselves. The direct experience of these opposites in us—*in differentiation*—has an explosive, ecstatic momentum. Here is a record of a personal experience which helped me to understand the potency of these inner opposites:

> I was sitting in a small, quiet room with a loved one. Suddenly, in front of me, to the left, my eye caught an ink bottle on a book-shelf. For some reason the sight of the innocent ink bottle aroused in me a strange state of agitation. All of a sudden I couldn't breathe. I started trembling. I was overcome by a powerful emotion which had surfaced without warning from within. In this emotional state—which I could assimilate only in hindsight, when I cooled down—I *was* the ink bottle, concave and full of a dark, mysterious fluid, in a state of waiting, openness, and receptivity in an immobile silence. Then, right above the ink-bottle, I "saw" a quill—one-pointed, sharp, purposeful, slowly coming down towards "me" to dip itself in my ink. And all at once I *was* the ink bottle, waiting in still suspension, I *was* the ink, and I *was* also the pen. And in the split-second when the quill in my free-flowing phantasy dipped its tip into the ink, in that split-second, I experienced a shattering upheaval on many levels. I was on the brink of losing consciousness.

Only after many days could I understand the meaning and numinosity of this experience. Beyond its obvious sexual interpretation there lay for me the real experience of the pure, differentiated male and female identities in me. This state of polarity, of total *separation of the opposites*, created such a yearning each for the other that its outcome was far beyond the capacity of the body to hold together. It created an inner explosion.

This archetypal experience, in hindsight, clarified for me also the powerful symbolism of writing, words, letters, sounds, verbal expression—an important aspect of many mystical systems—as the mysterious product of this inner intercourse.[17]

Thus I was given an insight into the mystery alluded to by the vision of creation by word, by the *Divine Logos*, so intrinsically interwoven into the fabric of the three religions which have made our culture—Judaism, Christianity, Islam. I also understood why the Sufi tradition is full of Eros, why it revolves ceaselessly around love, referring to itself as the Religion of Love (in Persian *kīsh-i mehr).* It became clear to me, from the living reality of my own experience, why for Sufis the mystery of love has always included a strong element of passion, *'ishq*; why all great Sufi poets and teachers have implied time and again that *'ishq*, love-desire, passionate love, is not a mild pietistic affection or ideal, nor a dreamy, sentimental, poetic metaphor, nor a refined, philosophic concept. It is a crude, ruthless, and glorious reality which pervades all levels of being, body and soul, and demands complete receptivity, sincerity, attention, and responsibility. *'Ishq* cannot be taught, cannot be preached; its potency can only be experienced. This is why one finds many allusions to the virility of prophets. The following passage by al-Ḥakīm at-Tirmidhī illustrates this point:

> The prophets, peace be with them, have been given a greater amount of sexual potency [than ordinary men] due to [the power of] their prophecy. This

> is because when the chest becomes filled with the light [of prophecy] this light overflows to the veins, and the psyche *(nafs)* and veins become aroused, and they awaken desire with all its potency. The energy of desire becomes potent through [the joint activity of] the heart and the psyche.[18]

And Bhai Sahib, in an answer to a question of a disciple, explains:

> A man who is impotent can never be a Saint or a Yogi. Women too can be impotent. The Creative Energy of God which manifests itself in its lowest aspect as procreative instinct is the most powerful thing in human beings, men and women alike.[19]

It is from the level of my experience that the words of Ibn al-'Arabī have become meaningful to me:

> The Breath of the All-merciful bestows existence upon the forms of the possible things, just as the human breath bestows existence upon letters. Hence the cosmos is the words of God in respect to this Breath, as He said, "His word that He cast in Mary" (Qur'ān 4:171), a word which is the very entity of Jesus. God reported that His words will not be spent, so His creatures will never cease coming into existence and He will never cease being a Creator.[20]

Breath, sound, letters, words, prophetic messages, poetry—all these expressions reflect the mystery of existence within nonexistence, of manifestation within Nothingness, of the unspeakable and the spoken. "The root principle of all things is speech and words," writes Rūmī. "Speech is the fruit of the tree of action.... God most High created the world by a word.

> *His command when He desires a thing, is to say to it 'Be!' and it is.*"[21]

At the same time, facetiously, Rūmī says also this:

> When you say, 'In this present age words are of no account,' you negate this assertion also by means of words. If words are of no account, how is it that we hear you say that words are of no account? After all, you say that also by means of words.[22]

Yet in the same vein, Rūmī says also this:

> These words are for the sake of that person who is in need of words in order that he may understand. But as for the man who understands without words, what need has he of words? The man ... who hears a low sound, what need has he of shouting and screaming?[23]

The polarity of male and female, abstention and action, nonexistence and creation, silence and utterance, essence and form reflects a mystery which pervades our lives. To hold these opposites together means to live a paradox, to touch the *Mysterium Coniunctionis*, to bring about a coincidence of opposites.

Love between two human beings, or for that matter between any pair in which the attraction of opposites is constellated, reflects the love between God and creation. When manifested, this attraction is activated by the beauty of the created form and revolves around it: "Contemplation of the Reality without formal support is not possible," says Ibn al-'Arabī.[24] Rūmī, too, has pointed out that the seeker must not ignore, nor deny, the physical, sensual side of his being. He says:

> The physical form is of great importance; nothing can be done without the consociation of the form and the essence. However much you may sow a seed stripped of its pod, it will not grow. Sow it with its pod and it will become a great tree. From this point of view the body is fundamental and necessary for the realization of the divine intention.[25]

And Maḥmūd Shabistarī, a 14th-century Sufi poet from Herat in Afghanistan, explains the nature of this mysterious conjunction between God and man, essence and form, in *The Secret Rose Garden*:

> ... From the unseen world descends
> Heavenly beauty,
> And plants its flag in the city
> Of earthly fairness,
> Throwing the world's array into confusion;
> Now riding the steed of comeliness,
> Now flourishing the sword of eloquence,
> And all alike bow down,
> Saints and kings, dervishes and prophets,
> Swayed by the charm of Beauty's fascination.[26]

This conjunction may create confusion and bewilderment in the heart and psyche of the seeker who has been touched by human beauty and affection and yet feels that these are not the real objects of his search. This confusion is, in fact, one of the main problems on a mystical path which emphasizes *'ishq*. Passion is an energy necessary for the journey, but it can also become a test, the cause of misunderstandings, abused in relationships. Like any energy it can be conserved or wasted. This is how a modern seeker tenderly expresses her bewilderment:

> How shall I know when we meet?
>
> You will open your mouth to speak,
> words will become birds and fly
> directly to heaven
> but that is not the sign.
>
> Your voice will run over me like honey
> enter through the pores of my skin
> till each cell opens
> a sweet-centred flower
> but that is not the sign.
>
> Nor is the drum-beat
> at the source of the waterfall,
> nor the flame
> at the source of the drum-beat.[27]

Rūmī addresses precisely the same bewilderment, which has beguiled so many seekers after truth, in the following revealing quatrains:

> They try to say what you are, spiritual or sexual?
> They wonder about Solomon and all his wives.
>
> In the body of the world, they say, there is a Soul
> and you are *that*.
>
> But we have ways within each other
> that will never be said by anyone.[28]

You say you have no sexual longing any more.
You're one with the one you love.

This is dangerous.
Don't believe that I have a love like that.

If one day you see a picture of how you think,
you'll hate yourself, openly.[29]

At night we fall into each other with such grace.
When it's light, you throw me back
like you do your hair.

Your eyes now drunk with God,
mine with looking at you,
one drunkard takes care of another.[30]

Yet if it's the heart's destiny to become open through love, it has first to be ready to bleed in the operation.

In one of the most profound and moving love stories in Sufi literature, an old man falls desperately in love with a young woman. The man is not only old in age (in Arabic *shaykh)* but, due to his wisdom and religious devotion, has become the spiritual guide *(Sheikh)* of many. In *The Conference of the Birds* 'Aṭṭār tells the story of this poor Sheikh, Sheikh Ṣan'ān, in order to demonstrate how the quest after Truth requires a genuine, uncompromising, at times shattering experience of love. The seeker must traverse the Valley of Love, the second of the seven valleys of the mystical journey. This experience overrides all previously accumulated knowledge and convictions. The love of the Sheikh, who has been steeped in Muslim lore, for a Christian girl, an impossible, unrequited love, ruins the Sheikh. It robs him of everything he has gained, has stood for, everything he has cherished, has believed in, has devoted his life to. It robs him of his status, of the respect others hold for him. It leaves him with nothing, a poor old man on the brink of insanity, on the threshold of death. But there is no way he, a sincere seeker, can take a short-cut, can avoid passing through this terrible valley. Nothing can open the heart and make it bleed but a true experience. Nothing can unravel the secret of the rewardlessness of earthly love but an unreciprocated, failed love. In his agony the old man casts away his home, his beliefs, his religion, his customs, his friends, his disciples, and throws himself abjectly on the doorstep of his beloved. Here are some verses which tell his story:

> When gloomy twilight spread its darkening
>   shrouds—
> Like blasphemy concealed by guilty clouds—
> His ardent heart gave out the only light,
> And love increased a hundredfold that night.
> He put aside the Self and selfish lust;
> In grief he smeared his locks with filth and dust
> And kept his haunted vigil, watched and wept,
> Lay trembling in love's grip and never slept.
> "O Lord, when will this darkness end?" he cried,
> "Or is it that the heavenly sun has died?
> Those nights I passed in faith's austerities
> Cannot compare with this night's agonies;
> But like a candle now my flame burns high
> To weep all night and in the daylight die....
> Love consumes me through this endless night—
> I yield to love, unequal to the fight."[31]

Through the sincere prayers of a friend (an allusion to a *walī*, the friend of God) and through the grace of the Prophet Muḥammad, the Sheikh is redeemed. A new vision of truth and meaning is revealed to him and restores his composure. He experiences a true *tawba*, a true repentance. And now his counterpart, his *anima*, his ruthless beloved, at last awakens. At last, through a dream-vision, his ardent love finds an echo in her heart. She wakes up to the depth of her own love and starts her own wandering in the desolate wilderness in search of him. Here are 'Aṭṭār's verses:

> She woke, and in her heart a steady light
> Beat like the sun, and an unwonted pain
> Throbbed there, a longing she could not restrain;
> Desire flared up in her; she felt her soul
> Slip gently from the intellect's control....
> She had no friend and found herself alone
> In an uncharted world; no tongue can tell
> What then she saw—her pride and triumph fell
> Like rain from her....
> Her frame was weak, the heart within her bled,
> But she began the journey to her sheikh,
> And like a cloud that seems about to break
> And shed its downpour of torrential rain
> (The heart's rich blood) she ran across the plain.[32]

But the story ends with a twist. This is not a romantic poem. The human experience of love rends open the lover's heart for that *other, transcendent* love, which is as passionate and uncompromising as the earthly one—love for the Divine Beloved. As she meets the Sheikh, she realizes that her true desire is not for earthly gratification of love. She discovers that it's her soul which has awakened. And it's this yearning of the soul for God that lovers—*'āshiqūn*, men and women seeking after essential truth—must in the end realize, a realization which the poet expresses through the last words of the dying woman:

> ... Then, as her comely face
> Bent to his words, her heart began to feel
> An inexpressible and troubling zeal;
> Slowly she felt the pall of grief descend,
> Knowing herself still absent from the Friend.
> "Dear sheikh," she said, "I cannot bear such pain;
> Absence undoes me and my spirits wane.
> I go from this unhappy world; farewell
> World's sheikh and mine—further I cannot tell ... "
> And saying this the dear child ceased to live.
> The sun was hidden by a mist—her flesh
> Yielded the sweet soul from its weakening mesh.
> She was a drop returned to Truth's great sea;
> She left this world, and so, like wind, must we.[33]

When the orientation of transcendent love dawns in the seeker's soul, it calls for responsibility in behavior. From a youth possessed by erotic, overflowing ecstasy, the seeker grows into manhood *(rujūliyya)* which knows how to contain the erotic energy. In the old Sufi circles which existed all around the Mediterranean, in Mesopotamia and in Central Asia, where women were mostly kept from associating with men, erotic love manifested itself very often among men. Beardless, effeminate youths *(murd)* were deliberately made part of the scene within Sufi groups in order to awaken the hearts through the contemplation of the Divine beauty reflected in the face of a human being. Love-desire for these angelic, probably quite lustful youths became a predominant theme in Sufi poetry, and the boundaries between earthly love and divine love, at least on the poetic level, became blurred. Conventional poetic allusions to the beloved's ravishing beauty through physical imagery, and the erotic verbal playfulness between lovers are apparent in the following quatrains by Ḥāfeẓ, the prince of Persian Sufi poets:

> Like on lute, my fingers stray over your curls and play,
> my heart and your lips are tuned in harmony all day;
> your mouth, this sweet pistachio nut, is my daily food;
> Lord, my wounded heart in a state of hunger does stay.[34]

Yūsuf, the Biblical Joseph, the youth whose beauty is proverbial in both the Jewish and the Muslim traditions, became the symbolic manifestation of God's Beauty—*jamāl*, the Divine attribute which is attested to in the tradition "God is beautiful, and He loves beauty."[35] Joseph, a prophet in Muslim prophetology, has been endowed with many spiritual virtues. At the same time he is also described as possessing such physical beauty that every man and woman who set eyes on him was overcome to the point of self-oblivion.[36] In Egypt, where he was sold as a slave, Yūsuf was taken into the household of Zulaikha, a willful Egyptian princess. When she saw him, Zulaikha's passion was kindled, but in the face of his pious abstention, she became inconsolable. Countless versions and couplets, mainly in Persian, use the love-story of Zulaikha for Yūsuf—a story of frustration, tribulation, perseverance, abstention, and triumph—as an allegory of the human passion for God. Here, for example, is how 'Abd ar-Raḥmān Jāmī, a 15th-century poet from Herat affiliated with the sober (!) Naqshbandi path, describes the first appearance of Yūsuf in Zulaikha's life. It happens in a dream which foretells future events:

> Closed fast in sleep [Zuleikha's] outward eyes may lie,
> Yet from her heart looks out another eye.
> Sudden a youth comes to her from the door;
> A spirit 'tis, I say a youth no more....
> The cypress tall his slave in dignity.
> As chains his ringlets, falling him around,
> Both wisdom's hand and foot of counsel bound.
> Shone from his brow a light of brilliant ray,
> The moon and sun before him prostrate lay....
> Smiles shedding sweets upon his lips abode,
> And from his mouth speech mixed with sugar flowed....
> A dimpled apple from his chin was hung,
> Or like a quince upon an apple strung.
> With moles of musk was his cheeks' rosebed dressed,
> As crows that in the garden build their nest....
> Silver his side and arms, a mighty pair,
> Not so his loins, thin drawn out as a hair.
> Upon his face Zuleikha cast one look....
> To his fair form and pleasing traits as well
> She with a hundred hearts a captive fell.[37]

In view of the power of *'ishq*, the literal consummation of erotic passion within Sufi groups presented one of the gravest pitfalls for the mystical quest. Therefore the masters were strict and explicit: no "acting out," no consummation of the love-desire was allowed between adepts. Celibacy has never been advocated in Sufi etiquette, but neither has promiscuity. Most Sufi adepts have been married men and women who have maintained their erotic relationships within the warmth of the marital container.

From the point of view of spiritual attainment, erotic "acting out" was considered severe and dangerous, not only for young disciples, but also for those on higher stages of the spiritual journey. *'Ishq* had to be contained; drunkenness *(sukr)* had to be held in check within mature sobriety *(ṣaḥw)*. In his *Epistle*, al-Qushayrī, the 11th-century master from Nishapur, writes unequivocally,

> One of the gravest tests on this path is the company of young men *(aḥdāth, murd)*. He who is tested in this way is considered by the consensus of the Masters as one who has fallen out of God's grace ... even if he is endowed with a thousand wondrous experiences.... *The heart must never be attached to the created*.... Someone is quoted as saying: "I stayed in the company of thirty sheikhs who had all attained the stage of substitutes *(abdāl)*, and all of them, upon my taking leave of them, admonished me and warned me of indulgence in the company of young men.[38]

Such seems to be the final word with regard to Eros. In the end, here is where the crucial test lies: not in the denial of erotic passion and human sensuality and physicality, but in the understanding of the deeper nature of the erotic energy, and consequently in the voluntary effort that seekers make to use the earthly to open a door to the transcendent, the created to the Non-created. Where weakness lies, there strength is to be found. This is why according to Sufi understanding the complete man—*al-insān al-kāmil*—stands on a higher level in the hierarchy of being than the angels. Angels worship God with devotion; they are pure; they are devoid of lusts and temptations, which are the effect of the physical clay-nature of man. As for mankind,

"In their natures I have mixed together the crudeness of earth with the fire of emotions," God is purportedly saying in a tradition recorded by al-Ḥakīm at-Tirmidhī. "But in spite of this they find in the depths of their hearts the light of love, compassion, and remorse, and this is their greatest merit. In spite of their lower selves, in spite of temptations which constantly surround them, they remember Me with fear, adoration, and longing. In their repentance they cry their hearts out to Me and plead for My Mercy. They are the ones who truly deserve My nearness and loving intimacy."[39]

To learn how to live within the power of desire for the created and yet yearn for the Non-created means to make the heart, which has become intoxicated with love, a doorway to the Infinite.

6

Dhikr: The Experience of the Remembrance of God

I sleep, but my heart is awake.
The Song of Songs 5:2

The heart is healed by the permanent remembrance of God.
Al-Ḥakīm at-Tirmidhī

Dhikr, remembrance of God, is both a practice and a mystical state. As a mystical state it conveys a paradox: although *dhikr* means "remembrance," the ultimate experience which the practice of *dhikr* points towards is of a forgetfulness, of forgetting everything but God. In a state of complete absorption in the invocation of God's name, everything disappears from the orbit of perception, imagination, or comprehension. The mystic is absorbed in an all-encompassing nothingness.

Dhikr is experienced on many levels. On the outermost it's a repetition of a Divine name, a mantra. Repetition is basically a mechanical practice which is performed either audibly, pronouncing the sacred name or a sacred formula with the tongue *(dhikr al-lisān)*, or soundlessly, focusing inwardly on the name without articulation. But this is only a preliminary stage of *dhikr*.

The mechanical repetition of God's name prints a "groove" upon the *heart*, the mystical vehicle of consciousness. This groove is an antithesis to the grooves which mechanical thinking creates upon the mind. Thus permanent practice of *dhikr* helps the practitioner to silence the ongoing process of circular thinking and focus the attention on one point.

The heart, as we have seen in detail in chapter one, is envisaged as a vehicle of consciousness which consists of layers within layers, each layer deeper and finer than the one which envelops it.[1] When *dhikr* is practiced continuously, it penetrates into the deeper layers of the heart and they, like a bud, open and unfold. Through this practice a process takes place in which the heart expands and is refined, or polished, to enable it to become the place within man in which the mystical secrets are witnessed. "The Sufis," says Rūmī, "polish their breasts with invocation and meditation so that the heart's mirror may receive virgin images (from the Unseen world)."[2]

Sufis name this inner practice of *dhikr* "the remembrance of the heart" *(dhikr al-qalb)*. Due to its depth, ordinary, mental consciousness is often excluded from the awareness of the "inner *dhikr*," and the practitioner may become conscious of it only when the *dhikr* surfaces again onto the outer planes. Thus a devotee may wake up from sleep or from anesthetic to find himself repeating the *dhikr*. The power of *dhikr* to penetrate such deeper levels of the practitioner's being is demonstrated by the following story, which has been told in many versions:

> Sahl [ibn 'Abdallāh at-Tustarī][3] said to one of his disciples: Strive to say continuously for one day: "O Allah! O Allah! O Allah!" and do the same the next day and the day after that—until he became habituated to saying those words. Then he bade him to repeat them at night also, until they became so familiar that he uttered them even during his sleep.

> Then he said: "Do not repeat them any more, but let all your faculties be engrossed in remembering God!" The disciple did this, until he became absorbed in the thought of God. One day, ... a piece of wood fell on his head and broke it. The drops of blood which trickled to the ground bore the legend "Allah! Allah! Allah!"[4]

In addition to the articulation of a sacred formula (or text), *dhikr* means also the sacred formula or text as such, in particular a sacred text which should be carefully listened to and committed to memory. It is in this sense that Sufis understand the first *dhikr* to be God's address to mankind, "Am I not your Lord?" *(alastu bi-rabbikum)*, to which the uncreated souls responded with an affirmative "Yes" *(balā')*.

This "moment" before time, before creation, when the souls of all human beings were held within the all-encompassing embrace of the Totality of Being, with no differentiation, without boundaries, lies at the roots of the Sufi tradition. It is nourished by a Qur'ānic verse which states the primordial relationship between mankind and God:

> And when thy Lord took from the Children of Adam, from their loins, their seed, and made them testify touching themselves, 'Am I not your Lord?' They said, 'Yes, we testify' (7:172).

The vision which speaks through this verse is universal and timeless. It has become known in the Sufi tradition as "the Day of the Covenant" *(yawm al-mīthāq)*. In this covenant a relationship is established between God and mankind, a relationship built upon a bi-polar foundation: the acceptance of God's Lordship *(rubūbiyya)* and human servanthood *('ubūdiyya)* on the one hand, and the experience of God's nearness on the other. Sufi mystical knowledge *(ma'rifa)* is based on the *memory* which awakens in the heart through contemplating the message conveyed in this verse.

Al-Junayd, the master of the 9th-century Sufi circle in Baghdad—probably the first circle *(ḥalqa)* of mystics named Sufis—writes:

> In this verse God tells you that He spoke to them at a time when they did not exist, except so far as they existed in Him. This existence is not the same type of existence as is usually attributed to God's creatures; it is a type of existence which only God knows.... Embracing them He sees them in the beginning when they are non-existent and unaware of their future existence in the world. The existence of these is timeless.[5]

For the mystic, all that unfolds in life bears the stamp of this moment. Life's goal becomes simply this: to return to the very beginning (in Arabic *al-ma'ād ilā -l-mabda'*), to return to the dawn of existence, to return to the Source of Being, to return *home*. The goal and purpose of the mystic *(al-'ārif)* is to return to the state in which he was before he was created. Al-Junayd formulates this statement in the following classic passage:

> What is the unity *(tawḥīd)* of the mystics? That the servant be as a lifeless body in front of God... in a state of annihilation *(fanā')* from the self *(nafs)* and from people's expectations ..., devoid of sense-perception and bodily movement, so that Truth *(al-ḥaqq)* may fulfil what It had willed for him, namely: *that his end will return to his beginning*, and *that he*

> *be as he was before he was*.... Unity means to come out of the confinement of temporality into the spaciousness and the expanses of timelessness *(sarmadiyya)*.[6]

The primordial *dhikr* pronounced in that timeless time became imprinted on the hearts of all men and women, and in the practice of *dhikr* it is remembered repeatedly. Ruwaym Abū Muḥammad, a 9th-century Baghdadi Sufi of al-Junayd's circle, sums this up in the following passage:

> The people heard their first *dhikr* when God addressed them, saying, "Am I not your Lord?" This *dhikr* was hidden in their hearts even as their testimony [of God's Lordship] was hidden in their intellects. So, when they heard the [practiced] *dhikr*, the things hidden within their hearts appeared, and they were ravished, even as the things hidden in their intellects appeared when God informed them of [His Lordship] and they believed.[7]

Thus the path, or rather the soul awakened through remembering, demands of the seeker an uncompromising commitment to re-enact the unequivocal "Yes" with which it testified to God's Lordship on the Day of the Covenant.

In the practice of *dhikr*, seekers have been given a tool whereby the inner layers of the heart gradually open and a new state of consciousness is tasted. This state differs from the linear, horizontal perception of time, space, and logical sequence. A modern seeker who has committed herself to a traditional forty-day retreat *(khalwa)* comments on the effect of repetitive *dhikr* which she practices as an integral part of her experience:

> I should do a lot of zhikrs, but what is a lot? My usual approach to life is intellectual and cognitive, whereas zhikrs work on a completely intuitive level. Here we are dealing with other dimensions in which "reason is bondage" and where the idea is to leave it behind.[8]

Dhikr and meditation *(murāqaba)*, two interrelated practices, produce an experience of timelessness free of the change and variegation *(talwīn)* which are the effect of time. This experience is echoed in the following verses by Rūmī:

> At the time when in the company of that selected
> group I began to meditate,
> Stepping out of myself,
> The soul got rid of all time that turns youth into age.
> All change arises out of time:
> He who gets rid of time gets rid of change.
> Oh, my heart, for a while be out of time, get rid of change.
> Oh, my heart, for a while be out of time to be free
> from "how" and "why."
> Time does not know the nature of Timelessness,
> Because only Wonder can lead to it.[9]

A repeated experience of the timeless and spaceless dimensions through *dhikr* develops a realization, intrinsic to any mystical experience, that there exist more planes or spheres of being than the ordinary mind can recognize. Such an awareness explains why in the literature of most mystical traditions one finds an abundance of visions and poetic descriptions of the ascent of the soul through heavenly spheres, or its descent into the depth of the underworld. These visions and images reflect the wonder and awe with which mystics have experienced the timeless travel through the manifold planes of existence.[10]

The archetypal experience of ascent which lies at the foundation of the Sufi tradition is the "night journey" of the Prophet Muḥammad, alluded to in the Qur'ān, sūra 17:1, and known as the *mi'rāj* (ascent) of the Prophet. Experiences of ascent are recorded also by Sufis. One of the earliest and best-known records of an ascent which surpasses the ordinary sense of time and space is attributed to Abū Yazīd al-Bisṭāmī. In *The Book of Scintillating Lights*, a 10th-century compilation, the compiler, Abū Naṣr as-Sarrāj, devotes several chapters to the commentary of al-Junayd upon Abū Yazīd's baffling utterances and descriptions of timeless and spaceless travels. The following passage which is culled from this classic Sufi source is one such description:

> The first time I attained His Aloneness *(waḥdāniyyatihi)* I became a bird whose body was of Oneness *(aḥadiyya)* and its wings of Permanence *(daymūmiyya)*. Then I kept on flying in the air of "howness" *(kayfiyya)* for ten years, till I arrived at an air [which surpassed] the former a hundred thousand thousands fold. And still I kept flying until I arrived at the space of Eternity *(azaliyya)* and there I saw the Tree of Oneness *(shajarat al-aḥadiyya)*.... And I looked and knew that all this was deception *(khud'a)*.[11]

The unexpected twist at the bottom line of that extraordinary experience, a twist which in blatant irony turns its magnitude on its head, means, according to al-Junayd's interpretation, that notwithstanding such altitudes as those attained by Abū Yazīd, the ultimate goal of the mystic is to surpass concern for *any* conscious recognition of the experience, since "attention to and occupation with the observation of existence and the Kingdom appear as deception when [the mystic] realizes the realities *(ḥaqā'iq)* of [God's] Singularity and absolute Unity."[12] Or, in other words: "The men [who have reached] the ultimate goal [know that] heeding to anything but God is deception."[13]

Such an attitude, which tends to relativize mystical experiences regardless of their numinous quality, is typical of the Sufi tradition. It is congruous with the attempt to direct the seeker towards an experience of *dhikr* so introverted that it leaves behind almost no cognitive traces. Since *dhikr*, when practiced correctly, penetrates one by one the numerous *inner* layers of the heart, Sufi literature accordingly enumerates also many degrees of *dhikr*. The innermost recess of the heart, as has already been indicated, is called *sirr*, "secret," alluding to the introverted, interiorized nature of true mystical experiences: they are kept *secret* even from the conscious mind; they are the place of intimate communication between the soul and God, where nothing else has access. Such a multiple-storied *dhikr* bears the stamp of the mystical, vertical, one-to-one relationship of the soul with God.

Nevertheless, in most Sufi circles *dhikr* has been practiced overtly. The circle of disciples *(ḥalqa)* would be exposed to a "listening" *(samā')* to a reciter *(qawwāl)*, or a musician, reciting or playing evocative passages or melodies. The impact of this listening would then stir up the emotions to such a degree that the body too would, involuntarily, be forced to move and participate in the inner experience. Or else the group would practice the invocations of divine names and formulae together, pronouncing the syllables in certain breathing rhythms, and this too would produce strong emotional and physical vibrations which would result in rapturous, ecstatic movements, sometimes to the point of loss of consciousness. Classical compilations such as *The Book of Scintillating Lights* report even death due to the impact of *samāʻ* and *dhikr*, especially in the case of novices *(mubtadiʾūn, murīdūn)*. Here is an example:

> A certain youth used to accompany al-Junayd. Whenever he listened to a *dhikr* he would cry and yell. One day al-Junayd told him: "If you do it once more you won't be allowed to accompany me." Ever since, when al-Junayd spoke words of [esoteric] knowledge, the face of this youth would alter, but he would contain himself to such a degree that drops of water would drip from every hair on his body. One day he uttered a shriek, burst open, and expired.[14]

Rūmī, who mastered, structured, and taught the art of ecstatic dance, sees rapture as the response of the mystic to an encounter with the bliss that emanates from the proximity of the Beloved. In his *Dīwān* he exclaims ecstatically:

> It is a day of joy. Come, let us all be friends! Let us take each other by the hand and go to the Beloved.
>
> When we become stupefied in Him and are all one color, let us keep going, dancing, toward the bazaar.
>
> It is a day for all the beauties to dance—let us close down our shops and all be idle.
>
> It is a day for the spirits to wear robes of honor—let us go as God's guests to the mysteries.[15]

Yet a group of 9th- and 10th-century Muslim mystics from Nishapur, one of the major cities of Khūrāsān, emphasized at an early stage of the development of Sufism a more rigorous interiorization of the mystical experiences in general and of *dhikr* in particular. These mystics became known as the *Malāmatiyya*, or *ahl al-malāma*—those who follow the Path of Blame. The Malāmatīs were concerned with the fact that the lower self, the *nafs*, wants to own every human experience, and thus claims ownership of any accomplishment, including mystical states.[16] When this happens, they maintained, and it happens virtually all the time, a one-to-one relationship with God is blocked. In the attempt to eliminate the control of the *nafs*, they pursued a path of "blame" *(malāma)*, incurring constant blame upon their "selves." This is why they were named Malāmatīs. The Malāmatīs tried to eliminate any exposure to external honor, which brings about conceit *('ujb)* and pretense *(iddi'ā')*. They chose therefore to conceal not only their spiritual attainments but also the fact that they were pursuing a path leading to mystical states. They attempted such "concealment" in two arenas: the public and the private. Thus—unlike most other contemporary Sufi groups—the Malāmatīs refrained from wearing any clothes which would distinguish them from other local Muslim citizens, and avoided public auditions of *dhikr* known as *samā'* (often translated as "spiritual concert," since it included music, recitation of verses, and ecstatic dance) which were practiced with great relish among other Sufi circles. In this they laid the foundation for two rules which were later implemented by the Naqshbandi path: first,"solitude in the crowd" *(khalwat dar anjuman)* and second, "silent—or hidden—*dhikr*" *(dhikr khafiy)*.[17] The Malāmatīs tried to practice *dhikr* in such a way that it would be hidden not only from the public eye, but also from their own inner eye!

The sayings and principles of the Malāmatī teachers of Nishapur were lovingly recorded by a later Nishapuri teacher, Abū 'Abd ar-Raḥmān as-Sulamī (d. mid-11th century). Through his maternal grandfather, as-Sulamī was a direct descendant of the early Malāmatīs. In a short treatise in Arabic entitled *The Malāmatiyya Epistle (Risālat al-malāmatiyya)*, he wrote down dicta attributed to the early Malāmatī teachers. The following passage is a challenging statement. It focuses on the layers of the heart which are awakened, activated, and refined through the practice of *dhikr*, while emphasizing the almost unattainable dimension of a fully interiorized *dhikr*:

> One of their principles maintains four levels of the remembrance of God: the *dhikr* of the tongue, the *dhikr* of the heart, the *dhikr* of the "secret" *(sirr)*, and the *dhikr* of the spirit *(rūḥ)*. When the *dhikr* of the spirit is sound, the heart and the "secret" are silenced: this is the *dhikr* of contemplation *(mushāhada)*. When the *dhikr* of the secret is sound, the heart and the spirit are silenced: this is the *dhikr* of awe *(hayba)*. When the *dhikr* of the heart is sound, the tongue is silenced: this is the *dhikr* of Divine Grace. When the heart is heedless to the *dhikr*, then the tongue takes over, and this is the *dhikr* of habit.
>
> Each of these levels has a blemish. The blemish of the *dhikr* of the spirit is that it be perceived by the secret. The blemish of the *dhikr* of the heart is that the lower self might take notice of it and admire it, or that it might gain by it the reward of attaining a spiritual rank.[18]

In this short and highly condensed passage the author lists the levels of *dhikr* from the most interiorized outwards. By way of paraphrasing this statement, I find it more convenient to look at the practice starting with its most external, mechanical, habitual aspect. Thus in the practice of *dhikr* prescribed by the Malāmatīs, one starts by pronouncing the sacred name *Allāh*. This level is practiced either audibly or by a silent inner repetition of the external form of the name as it is imagined by the mind. This is the habitual or mechanical aspect of *dhikr*. Then comes a stage in which the heart takes over. In this stage, awareness of syllables and forms may become silenced to allow an experience of bliss. This deeper, blissful level of *dhikr* emanates from Divine Grace. Deeper and beyond the boundaries of ordinary consciousness is the stage when *dhikr* takes place in the "secret," the innermost *sirr*, the heart of hearts. This is an "experience" of numinous awe, emanating from the Divine *Tremendum*. Then a deeper level is reached which is identified as the level of *spirit*. According to the Qur'ān, the spirit *(rūḥ)* belongs to God alone—"The spirit is of the bidding of my Lord"(17:85). "Bidding" renders the Arabic *amr*, an elusive term which may mean also "business." The spirit, the verse implies, is God's business, it is in God's hands. It lies deeper even than *sirr*. Its relationship to God is the most profound mystery, never revealed either to prophets or to angels; yet it seems to be available, in some sense, to sincere practitioners of *dhikr*. This, we are told, is the *dhikr* of "contemplation" *(mushāhada)*. At this level, it seems, the *spirit* within the one who is remembering—that counterpart within man of the Divine Spirit—contemplates God in total cognitive silence. It is also probable that by using *mushāhada*, which derives from the same root as *shahidnā*—"we testify" (allusion to Qur'ān 7:172)—the Malāmatī teachers wished to point to the Primordial Covenant, in the realization of which man returns to *the state he was before he was.*

The Malāmatī teachers also say that all these stages of *dhikr* have blemishes, are imperfect; in other words, it's hardly possible to achieve them in perfection. The "blemish" of each of these levels is that the more external one should perceive or register the *dhikr*. A total silencing down of all outer and inner perceptions is very difficult to achieve. Nevertheless, the ultimate goal of the practice is formulated, or at least hinted at, by the Malāmatīs' structural design of *dhikr*.

Dhikr (or in its Persian term *yād kard)* is one of eleven principles which were laid down in the 13th and 14th centuries by the Naqshbandi masters of Central Asia, and which have distinguished the Naqshbandi path from most other Sufi fraternities. Khwāja 'Ubaidallāh Aḥrār, a venerable 15th-century master from Samarqand, has said that "the real meaning of *dhikr* is inward awareness of God."[19]

The origin of the first eight principles laid down by the Naqshbandi masters is linked with the name of 'Abd al-Khāliq al-Ghujduwānī. So also is the teaching of *dhikr*. Al-Ghujduwānī, from a village near Bukhara, was one of the four successors of the 12th-century master Yūsuf al-Hamadhānī. It is from the latter that the lineage *(silsila)* of the Masters of Central Asia, the *Khwājagān*—the forerunners of the Naqshbandi path—originated. Al-Ghujduwānī taught his disciples the silent *dhikr*, the hidden *dhikr* of the heart *(dhikr khafiy)*. In manuals describing the Naqshbandi path it is related that through his "spirituality" *(rūḥāniyyatihi)* 'Abd al-Khāliq transmitted this teaching to Bahā'ad-Dīn Naqshband, the eponym of the path, although there are more than a hundred years between them: al-Ghujduwānī died in 1220, while Bahā' ad-Dīn was born in 1318. Although five generations of masters separate them, this "spiritual" link represents a legitimate aspect of the Naqshbandi lineage where a master-disciple relationship is not bound by contemporaneity. A deceased master may work, after his physical death, through his "spirituality." 'Abd al-Khāliq himself was taught the silent *dhikr* by Khiḍr, God's unnamed servant who waits "where the two seas meet" *(majma' al-baḥrayn)*, and who is the master of those who may not have a flesh-and-blood teacher.[20]

The Naqshbandi sources tell how 'Abd al-Khāliq hit upon a Qur'ānic verse which he could not understand: "Call upon your Lord humbly and secretly" (7:54).[21] Sensing that a deep mystery lurked behind these words, he was nevertheless at a loss to grasp their meaning, until Khiḍr appeared to him and made him invoke the name of God while under water. "If you want Truth as a drowning man wants air, you shall get it in a split second." Submerged in water, 'Abd al-Khāliq must have tasted what a drowning man tastes. Yet at that moment he was immersed in the remembrance of God, in total surrender, not minding death. What he had experienced he sought to perpetuate by teaching his disciples the silent *dhikr*—*adh-dhikr al-khafiy*—

as one of the principles which from then on became the hallmark of the path which followed on from him.[22]

The image of a man or a woman practicing *dhikr* while totally immersed in the water of love reverberates also in Mrs. Tweedie's instruction for silent meditation, based on her master Bhai Sahib's teaching:

> We must suppose that we go deep within ourselves, deeper and deeper into our most hidden self. There in our innermost being, in the very core of ourselves, we will find a place where there is peace, stillness and, above all, love....
>
> After having found this place, we must imagine that we are seated there, immersed into, surrounded by the Love of God. We are in deepest peace.... All of us is there, physical body and all; nothing is outside, not even a finger tip, not even the tiniest hair. Our whole being is contained within the Love of God....
>
> Nothing will remain. [23]

Indeed, 'Abd al-Khāliq's authority with which he had "spiritually" instructed Bahā' ad-Dīn to perform the silent *dhikr* was so strong that the latter had to deviate from the way *dhikr* had been practiced around his living teacher, Amīr Kulāl:

> Shortly before Amīr Kulāl died, he instructed his companions to follow Khwāja Bahā' al-Dīn. When his pupils and friends protested on the grounds that Khwāja Bahā' al-Dīn had not practised public *dhikr*, the Amīr said: "In all his actions he is guided by the Exalted Truth and not by his own will."
>
> Khwāja Bahā' al-Dīn Naqshband said:
>
> "A special awareness arose in me when I began to practise silent *dhikr*. That was the secret I sought."[24]

A passage in an old text book which I found years ago in an Arabic bookshop in Jerusalem explains the esoteric way by which the silent *dhikr* and the name *Naqshband* are associated:

> The meaning of *naqsh band* is "to seal the imprint"—*naqsh* means to engrave, to make an impression, to imprint; *band* means to tie, to bind, to seal. Its esoteric meaning is "to seal the impression of the Form of Perfection upon the seeker's heart."
>
> Up until the time of the Master Bahā' ad-Dīn, who was named Naqshband, the followers [of the Path of the Masters] used to practice the *dhikr* silently in solitude and audibly in groups. But the Master ordered that they should practice it [at all times] in silence. This he did because of an order he had received from the "spirituality" of the Master 'Abd al-Khāliq al-Ghujduwānī who was the [deceased] master of [Bahā' ad-Dīn's] masters in the world of the journey [to God]. ['Abd al-Khāliq] and his companions used to practice *dhikr* silently, whether alone or in a group. Practiced in this way their *dhikr* produced a deep impression on the hearts of the disciples, and this impression was called *naqsh*....
>
> *Naqsh* is the form (i.e., the blueprint) of that which is impressed upon wax or any similar matter, and *band*, namely the binding, is the permanent subsistence of the impression without effacement.

The text then goes on to describe how the *naqsh* of God's Essence and Names was stamped upon the heart of every man and woman in the day of creation, and explains the efficacy of the silent *dhikr* in sealing it and in protecting it from fading away:

> It is said that, when Adam and his progeny were created, God's Forms were looked upon by the *tawajjuh* of the Supernal Divine Essence without "how" or "when."

Tawajjuh—sitting face to face—is the esoteric method by which the mystical teaching is transmitted from teacher to disciple directly, by reflection, rather than through speech.[25]

> Thus Adam and his progeny came into being with a special Form which bears the names of the Divine "observer," and which is predicated by His attributes. It is by the essence of this Form that their relationship [with God] is realized: as He has actions, so they have actions; as He has laws, so they have laws imposed on others. It is in this way that the impression *(naqsh)* of the Essence, the Attributes, the Names, the Actions and the Laws were manifested in the coming into being of Adam and his progeny.
>
> Some of Adam's progeny, due to the predominance of the lower self upon the perfected Self within them, have allowed the impression to fade away. Others, however, have perfected the *naqsh;* they are called *Naqshbandis*.[26]

Thus, the silent *dhikr* is the means whereby the *naqsh*—the primordial impression imprinted on the soft, receptive matter of the heart—becomes perfected. The text implies that within the heart of every human being there reside not only the counterparts of God's Attributes, Actions, and Laws, but also the counterpart of the Divine Essence "without how and when." These archetypal counterparts which have been imprinted on the human heart from its very inception have their blueprint in God's Forms: "as He has actions, so they have actions; as He has laws, so they have laws imposed on others." Moreover, not only the "Forms"—attributes, names, actions, laws—are imprinted, but the Essence too.

This is a bold idea which holds the key for the possibility of union between God and man: "It is by the Essence of these Forms that [man's] relationship with God is realized." This relationship is meant to be realized not in the afterlife but in the hearts of *living* men and women. But it requires of them a commitment to permanently practice the *dhikr* in the way in which it was taught by Khiḍr to 'Abd al-Khāliq al-Ghujduwānī and by the latter to Bahā' ad-Dīn. For during man's lifetime these divine impressions can be either effaced or perfected and sealed forever. Perfecting and sealing the divine images by which the hearts were made is achieved through the practice of the silent *dhikr*.

This understanding of the efficacy of *dhikr* explains why Sufi teachers have repeatedly said that there is nothing of permanent value in a person's life except the remembrance of God. In the same vein they have also said that every moment that passes, every breath which is breathed without remembering God is wasted. Sufis are taught to be constantly in the state of remembering God. From the vantage point of the ordinary mind such achievement seems impossible: how can the mind remember to remember God in the midst of the multitude of tasks which it has to perform? How can the mind fix its attention on more than one thing at a time?

The key to this question may lie in the connection which is made between *dhikr* and breath. The breath is the most instinctive, and thus the most fundamental, manifestation of the remembrance of God, since with the breath the sound "hhhh"—which alludes to the Divine Hiddenness, and which is articulated at the end of the sacred name *Allāh*—is instinctively aspirated. The repetition of the sacred name or formulae is connected with the waves of the breath, with the perpetual sequence of exhalation and inhalation in conjunction with which the *dhikr* is performed. Bahā' ad-Dīn Naqshband used to say: "The foundation of this path is the breath" *(mabniyy hādhā aṭ-ṭarīq 'alā an-nafas)*, and 'Ubaid Allāh Aḥrār reiterated that "Most important on this path is observing the breath."[27] Observing the flow of the breath prevents the inner attention from falling into a state of heedlessness *(ghafla)*, and keeps the heart at all times present with God.

An early mystic whose name is linked both with the Naqshbandi masters, especially Bahā' ad-Dīn, and with the Malāmatīs of Nishapur is al-Ḥakīm at-Tirmidhī. A contemporary of the latter, he knew and corresponded with several of the teachers of Nishapur, although he did not belong to their circle. He is linked with Bahā' ad-Dīn Naqshband in the same way that Bahā' ad-Dīn is linked with 'Abd al-Khāliq al-Ghujduwānī, namely, through his "spirituality." The 9th-century mystic from the town of Tirmidh, on the shores of the Oxus River in Transoxania, lived five centuries before Naqshband. Yet Bahā' ad-Dīn acknowledged his link with at-Tirmidhī, asserting: "The encounter face to face *(tawajjuh)* with the spirituality of

Muḥammad ibn 'Alī al-Ḥakīm at-Tirmidhī brings about featurelessness *(maḥw aṣ-ṣifa)*.... For the last twenty-two years I have been following in the footsteps of al-Ḥakīm at-Tirmidhī; as he was featureless so am I now featureless. He who knows it, knows."[28]

Similarly to the Malāmatīs and the Naqshbandis, at-Tirmidhī too taught that the true mystical *dhikr* is the silent *dhikr* of the heart. Here, to end, is how he describes the stages of *dhikr* and its effect on different types of practitioners:

> *Dhikr* is the food of mystic knowledge. Mystic knowledge is sweet and pure, and the heart is its vessel and its treasure-trove.... In its essence *dhikr* emanates from the realm of Divine Joy, and therefore, when it descends upon the heart it awakens joy. If it hadn't mingled with the joy of the lower self, *dhikr* would have been complete and pure, but when the self mingles with it, Divine Assistance which flows from the Remembered is cut off, and the *dhikr* is stranded in the turbid, murky joy of the self.
>
> Those who aspire to purity find pleasure in *dhikr* alone, since their self has become the captive of their heart. Their lower self is besieged, as it were, by the mystical knowledge and is unable to move freely in the pursuit of its own pleasure....
>
> Outwardly, the mingling of self and *dhikr* may appear as bodily movement: the performer of the *dhikr* may be stirred to dance, or clap his hands, or shake his head, or wave vigorously from side to side—all these involuntary bodily movements point to the fact that the agitated self has mixed its joy with the *dhikr* of the heart.

Inwardly the mingling of the self with *dhikr* may result in the heart contemplating its own remembrance. This too points to an impure *dhikr* in which the self is mingled, since remembrance is not the same as the Remembered.

When the *dhikr* is performed by one who has a "seat" and communion in the higher realms, then the heart will stop contemplating the *dhikr* and its eyes will contemplate the Remembered alone.

When the heart is absorbed in the Remembered there is no room in it for contemplating remembrance.

Hearts vary in their ranks and stages: the hearts of ordinary worshippers are imprisoned in midair. They cannot soar very high because their earthly desires pull them down.

The hearts of seekers soar and then stop, according to their ranks. Where they stop, there is their rank. They too are held captive by their earthly inclinations and are weighted down by desires.

The hearts of those who arrive stop by the Throne. They too are held back by the residue of desires in them, and they too cannot attain God's Place in His Kingdom.

But the hearts of the pure and the chosen reach Him where He sits—they are the ones who have perfect communion and pure *dhikr*. They are those of whom Moses, peace be with him, spoke when he said: "O God, are you near so I could commune with you, or are you distant so I would call you?" God said: "I sit with those who remember me" *(anā jalīs man dhakaranī)*.[29]

7

The Color of Water

There is great joy in darkness. Deepen it .
Sanā'ī[1]

The lovely forms and colours are undone,
And what seemed many things is only one.
Farīd ad-Dīn 'Aṭṭār[2]

In Sufi terminology "color" signifies a state: a state of mind in general, or, more specifically, a mystical state. Water is an elusive element; its essence is fluidity; it cannot be captured or held in time and space. Color and water come together in an intriguing image by which the mystic is described in Sufi literature.

Very early on in the history of Sufism, Sufis in the various centers meditated upon the meaning of mystical knowledge, *ma'rifa*, and the qualities of the mystic, *al-'ārif*. The early Sufi compilations of the 10th and 11th centuries contain many sayings on the nature of both. In *The Book of Scintillating Lights*, compiled in the 10th century by Abū Naṣr as-Sarrāj, the following description of the mystic is attributed to Abū Yazīd al-Bisṭāmī, the 9th-century master celebrated for his ecstatic visions and utterances:[3]

> When asked to describe the characteristics of the mystic, Abū Yazīd said: *The color of water is the color of his receptacle*. If you pour [water] into a white receptacle you will imagine it to be white. If

> you pour water into a black receptacle you will imagine it black, and so also with yellow, red, and the other colors. States shift the mystic between one another, but his Lord is He who shifts the states *(muḥawwil al-aḥwāl)*.[4]

This description of the mystic as someone whose color is the color of water has always fascinated me. It presents a kind of Sufi *koan,* a riddle worth pondering. What are the different receptacles whose colors are reflected in the water of mystical knowledge? And what, indeed, is the color of water?

Imagine a world in which the only color is as undistinctive and indescribable as the color of water—in other words, a colorless world. As soon as I close my eyes, colors rush forward in defiance. From the treasure-trove of forms my imagination conjures up a kaleidoscope of images in many shades: a peacock's tail with its brilliant royal blues and turquoises; a rainbow majestic over a greyish-purple sky in a shimmering landscape; the dance of oranges, pinks, crimsons, blues, and greens in a Matisse painting. Or the haunting numinosity of colors in a dream; the tender lilacs, pinks, mauves, whites, and greens of cherry trees in blossom; the volcanic explosion of a field of blood-red poppies; the hundred shades of russet in autumn. Or the dazzling yellow of a sea of sunflowers stretching out for miles and miles in the flesh-pink soil of Andalusia.

Forms and colors are the primal matter of our visual experiences whether sensory or imagined. Colors enrich us. They shape and express our moods. My language dwindles in the face of the richness of color, and when I recall that there exists a myriad of shades and colors above and below the range of our ordinary visual perception, I become dumbfounded.[5]

One of the most ravishing experiences of forms and colors that I have ever had was watching sea life in the Red Sea. Climb down a few steps into an underwater chamber surrounded by glass walls, choose a point from which to watch the spectacle which comes into view behind the glass walls, or wander around peeping out from different vantage points—an amazing parade of multifarious life-forms passes silently by: multi-colored, bizarre fish, sea urchins, eels, water snakes, jellyfish, huge cauliflower-like sea creatures extending long arms ready to devour whatever comes into their orbit, tiny sea-horses, petrified stars, the coral reef which houses this abundance—all defy ordinary perception and description. I became drunk, transported, by this silent, kaleidoscopic, hallucinatory procession. All that glory, vivacity, inventiveness, gaiety, ugliness, ruthlessness, playfulness, and solemnity which floated along the glass walls gave me a unique and unforgettable glimpse into the realm of Divine Beauty and Majesty.

In contrast, consider a feather of a jay, so minute that you have to take great care not to damage it when holding it in your palm. Brownish-grey, rather ordinary looking on one side, but on the other side such an unexpected exquisite pattern of lavender and white stripes. Even the minutest design reflects the singular craftsmanship of the Divine Creator.

Colors not only reflect the beauty of the outer world, but can also manifest as inner perceptions. Even blind people can "see" colors. The following testimony is both moving and enlightening. It was written by Jacques

Lusseyran, a hero of the French Resistance, who had become blind at the age of seven and henceforth developed an inner perception of color which had become no less, perhaps even more, vibrant and gratifying than the lost sensory perception. He writes:

> Sighted people always talk about the night of blindness. But there is no such night, for in every waking hour and even in my dreams I lived in a stream of light....
>
> Colors, all the colors of the rainbow survived. For me, the child who loved to draw and paint, colors made a celebration so unexpected, colors of things and of people. My father and mother, the people I met or ran into in the street all had their characteristic color which I had never seen before I went blind....
>
> It was the same with love.... The summer after the accident my parents took me to the seashore. There I met a little girl my own age.... She came into my world like a great red star, or perhaps more like a ripe cherry. The only thing I knew for sure was that she was bright and red.... How natural that people who are red should have red shadows. When she came to sit down by me between two pools of salt water under the warmth of the sun I saw rosy reflections on the canvas of the awning; in the sea itself the blue of the sea took on a purple tone. I followed her with a red wake which trailed behind her wherever she went.[6]

In the Sufi tradition color is viewed in a special way. To put it in a nutshell, the oscillating inner states of the wayfarer on the mystical path are seen as "colors." In the idiom of Sufi literature, the process which is activated on the mystical journey is sometimes referred to by an Arabic word which means "variegation," "changing colors": *talwīn*. This term derives from the Arabic word for color, *lawn* (or, more colloquially, *lōn)*. Variegation denotes the fluctuation of the heart from one state to another. Thus *lōn* is sometimes synonymous with *ḥāl,* which means a mystical state.[7] The term *lōn* in this sense has even found its way into colloquial language; in some modern Arabic dialects, the question *ēsh lōnak,* which literally should be rendered "What is your color?" means, in fact, simply, "What is your state? How are you?"

In mystical terms, color *(lōn)*, like state *(ḥāl)*, indicates the restless, unstable, fickle, and fluid experiences, extensively explored in this book, which the seeker undergoes—experiences which, in spite of their mystical and revelatory nature, are still to a large extent subjective and ego-bound. The mystical journey is a dynamic process in which the states and stations of the heart unfold. Each state has its own mood, its particular form, its own color. The fluctuation of the heart is, as has been indicated above, probably the major theme in Sufi literature. The lamenting reed which accompanies the caravan of wayfarers in the desert of mystical bewilderment repeats this theme endlessly. "Nothing stays forever," moans a Persian poet, "everything moves on, oscillates, changes: *ū mīrāwad*, he (or she?) is walking away." (The Persian language, in which so much of Sufi literature has been written, does not distinguish between the genders; hence there is no telling whether the beloved who is walking away is male or female.)

Talwīn relates not only to the oscillation of psychological or emotional states encountered on the mystical journey. Also those experiences which belong to the realm of the *imagination ('ālam al-mithāl wal-khayāl)*[8]—the colors and the visions which come up in dreams, in spontaneous or voluntary fantasies, in deep states of meditation, or in intuitive flashes—experiences which have been identified by a long tradition of visionaries as mystical—all come under the law of change and variegation. This is a point worth highlighting, since it is frequently overlooked by adepts and scholars of mysticism: essentially, according to the Sufi outlook, it is not the mystical experiences which are of the highest importance, but *transcending* them.

Many mystics, however, have left accounts of experiences in which colors have been seen as the reflection of their inner states. The late-12th-century mystic Najm ad-dīn Kubrā, to take one example, one of the greatest visionaries in the Sufi tradition, is well-known for his experiences of colored lights. His book *Whiffs of Beauty and Revelations of Majesty (Fawā'iḥ al-jamāl wa-fawātiḥ al-jalāl)* is full of descriptions of visions of colors. These are not physical colors; they are perceived, he says, by the organs of inner sight, not by the sensory eyes. Henri Corbin, whose *The Man of Light in Iranian Sufism* is an analysis of the visionary experiences of Kubrā and other Sufi mystics, explains that these visions are "no illusion but a real visualization,... the coloration of *real* objects and events whose reality ... is not physical but suprasensory, psycho-spiritual."[9]

Here are some passages which portray Kubrā's teaching of the meaning of visionary colors:

> You come to gaze with your own eyes on what you had until then only known theoretically, through the intellect....
>
> ... When you see before you a great wide space, an immensity opening onto the far distance, while above you there is clear pure Air and you perceive on the far horizon the colors *green, red, yellow, blue,* know that you are about to pass, borne aloft through this air, to the field of these colors. The colors are those of the spiritual states experienced inwardly. The color *green* is the sign of the life of the heart; the color of ardent pure *fire* is the sign of the vitality of spiritual energy, signifying the power to actualize. If the fire is dim, it denotes in the mystic a state of fatigue and affliction following the battle with the lower ego and the Devil. *Blue* is the color of this lower ego. *Yellow* indicates a lessening of activity. All these are suprasensory realities in dialogue with the one who experiences them in the twofold language of inner feeling *(dhawq)* and visionary apperception. These are two complementary witnesses, for *you experience inwardly in yourself what you visualize with your inner sight, and reciprocally you visualize with your inner sight precisely what you experience in yourself.*[10]

The realm of the imagination, the *mundus imaginalis* (*'alam al-mithal*), is the realm the seeker tunes into when, in the practice of "active imagination," he frees his imaginative faculty from sense perception and the thinking process. It is also the realm of archetypal dream images. It has many levels, and it can be cultivated so that it becomes finer and subtler as the inner organs of perception become finer and subtler. On its finest, subtlest level, we are told by

Kubrā, the realm of the imagination touches the realm of real mystical visions and true prophecies. Through his intense visual experiences, Kubrā discovered, according to his own testimony, the spiritual reality of, for example, the color green. He writes:

> *Green* is the color that outlasts the others.... This green may be absolutely pure or it may become tarnished. Its purity proclaims the dominant note of the divine light; its dullness results from a return of the darkness of nature.[11]

> Know that to exist is not limited to a single act.... On the mystic journey there is a *well* corresponding to each act of being. The categories of being are limited to seven.... When you have risen up through the seven wells in the different categories of existence, lo and behold, the Heaven of the sovereign condition *(robūbīya)* and its power are revealed to you. Its atmosphere is a *green light* whose greenness is that of a vital light through which flow waves eternally in movement towards one another. This green color is so intense that human spirits are not strong enough to bear it, though it does not prevent them from falling into mystical love with it. And on the surface of this heaven are to be seen points more intensely *red* than fire, ruby or cornelian, which appear lined up in groups of five. On seeing them, the mystic experiences nostalgia and a burning desire; he aspires to unite with them.[12]

One of the main concerns of Sufi teaching is to map the fluctuations of the heart from state to state, from "color" to "color," to outline its never-ending variegation. Sufi manuals from the 10th century on, and a few earlier Sufi writers, have mapped for future travelers the bumpy terrain through which the mystical journey passes. They have named the states and stations the wayfaring heart undergoes when it embarks on the quest for its kernel. Sufi teaching, as has been reiterated, is focused on the stations of the heart *(maqāmāt al-qulūb)*, on the inner journey of the heart to God *(sayr al-qalb ilā allāh)* through extreme polar states. States of elation and ecstasy which Sufis taste on the path have been named "expansion" *(basṭ)*; states of anguish and despair—the dark night of the soul—have been named "contraction" *(qabḍ)*. Between these extremes the hearts are kept in constant fluctuation.

In the two following passages, Ibn 'Aṭā' Allāh, a 13th-century Sufi poet from Egypt, explains why the tossing and turning of the heart is needed as an experiential tool leading eventually to a *liberation* from the swing of the opposites, thus alluding to the secret of Oneness which transcends, and *includes*, polarity:

> Sometimes He makes you learn in the night of contraction
> What you have not learnt in the radiance of the day of expansion.
> "You do not know which of them is nearer to you in benefit" (Qur'ān 4:11) [13]

> He expanded you so as not to keep you in contraction.
> He contracted you so as not to keep you in expansion,
> and He took you out of both
> so that you not belong to anything apart from Him.[14]

The purpose behind the oscillation between the opposites, between states of elation and depression, *expansion* and *contraction*, is explained also by Bhai Sahib on a day when his disciple, Mrs. Tweedie, is experiencing happiness, when her "heart is full of such peace." He says:

> According to the System, the Shishya (in Hindi: disciple) is constantly kept between the opposites, ups and downs; it creates the friction necessary to cause suffering which will defeat the Mind.[15]

Thus, whether the records are old or new, whether they use traditional terminology, poetic language, or the direct form of a diary, they tell a similar story. They give reports of a system which is hardly interested in concepts and theories, but in the accumulation of inner experiences which will, if persevered in, transfer the seeker from the world of polarity and duality to the world of oneness.

But the mapping of the heart's journey is only a means to an end. What is this end? To point towards what is beyond all states and colors, towards a state which is a non-state, towards a color which is a no-color. Here is a thought-provoking statement made by Ibn al-'Arabī, the 13th-century Andalusian mystic:

> The people of perfection have realized all stations and states and passed beyond these to the station above both majesty and beauty, so they have no attribute and no description.[16]

What does it mean to pass "above both majesty and beauty"? What can it mean "to have no attribute and no description"? What is the Sufi after? What is the highest or deepest attainment of the Sufi who seeks after Truth? It is not esoteric knowledge, nor peace of mind, nor special powers, nor is it stoic, detached states of contemplation. Rather, it is the state of total *annihilation*, a state described as an absorption in nothingness, in colorlessness; to be annihilated in that nothingness which has no shape, which has no color, which is beyond color or state, which is absorption in the Totality of Being. This is the state known as *fanāʾ*, cessation, passing away, the end of all states, a non-state. A passage from one of the oldest Sufi compilations tries to describe this state:

> The mystic passes away from what belongs to himself, and persists through what belongs to God.... When "centred" he is also "dispersed." ... He is "absent" and "intoxicated" because his power of discrimination has passed away, and in this sense all things become one to him.[17]

But if this is the ultimate desired state, what are we to do with our love for nature, our love for color, for art and music, for craft and poetry? What are we to do with our love for beauty? This is a most perplexing question. And there are not only the sensory colors and experiences that the ultimate mystical experience demands transcending; there are also the imagined colors and experiences of dreams, of active imagination, of insights, intuitions, and revelations which have been identified by a long tradition of visionaries as mystical experiences. What will become of these when a state of nothingness takes over?

Sufi literature addresses these questions without qualms or perplexity. For example, in *The Conference of the Birds*, a unique Sufi epic, the poet, Farīd ad-Dīn ʿAṭṭār, speaks explicitly and relentlessly about that supreme desire of the individual soul to become absorbed within the Ocean of Totality, within the colorlessness of nothingness:

> The seventh [valley is] Poverty and Nothingness—
> And there you are suspended, motionless,
> Till you are drawn—the impulse is not yours—
> A drop absorbed in seas that have no shores.[18]

> First lose yourself, then lose this loss and then
> Withdraw from all that you have lost again—
> Go peacefully, and stage by stage progress
> Until you gain the realms of Nothingness.[19]

> Made one with his belovèd he became
> The Nothingness of an extinguished flame.
> True pilgrims fathom, even as they fight,
> The passion of annihilation's night.[20]

> All that I ever lost or ever found
> Is in the depths of that black deluge drowned.
> I too am lost; I leave no trace, no mark;
> I am a shadow cast upon the dark,
> A drop sunk in the sea, and it is vain
> To search the sea for that one drop again.
> This Nothingness is not for everyone,
> Yet many seek it out as I have done;
> And who would reach this far and not aspire
> To Nothingness, the pilgrim's last desire?[21]

> Then, as they listened to the Simorgh's words,
> A trembling dissolution filled the birds—
> The substance of their being was undone,
> And they were lost like shade before the sun;

> Neither the pilgrims nor their guide remained.
> The Simorgh ceased to speak, and silence reigned.[22]

An immense tension lies at the core of the mystical journey: the tension between shifting experiences and immutable silence, between mystical states and the ultimate non-state. I have quoted at length from *The Conference of the Birds* because I know of no other piece of literature which brings the two poles of the mystical quest into such stark juxtaposition: at the one pole the ever-changing, bewildering experiences the seeker *must* traverse in the process of variegation *(talwīn)*; and at the other pole, the still, black point of absorption in nothingness, beyond experiencing and beyond variegation. "'There is nothing but Nothingness,' he said yesterday," Mrs. Tweedie quotes her teacher Bhai Sahib in *Daughter of Fire*:

> "There is nothing but Nothingness." ... And the way he said it, repeating it with emphasis, and the echo it awakened in my heart, made me think that it was meant for me. It struck me as the most wonderful sentence and it made me glad.... Speaking of this astonishing state of nothingness, I said that at the beginning it was just Nothing; later there was like a sorrowful happiness with much longing in it, but now it was just wonderful. Why it was so wonderful I could not say; this feeling is too new and difficult to analyze.... When at home I realized that the answer is contained in his statement of yesterday: there is nothing but Nothingness, and it represents a perfect state—that's why it is so wonderful.[23]

A few months earlier, on April 10th, 1966, Mrs. Tweedie wrote in her diary:

> Our relationship to God is something entirely different from what we usually imagine it to be. We think that the relationship of God and man is of duality. There is God and there is the man who will pray to God... or who will worship, or love, or praise God. There are always two. But it is not so. I have found that our relationship to God is something quite different. It is a merging, without words, without thoughts even ... into something. Something so tremendous, so endless, merging in infinite Love.... And the physical body is under suffering; it is taut like a string in this process of annihilation....
>
> "What you have said," he nodded gravely, "is absolutely correct."[24]

The disciple may not always realize it immediately, but when a real connection is established between him and the teacher, and when he *willingly* becomes exposed to the energy of the teacher, then a process starts in which the disciple not only oscillates between conflicting, polar states horizontally, but much more intensely he is thrown between two different dimensions of existence *vertically*, two different levels of consciousness. The disciple may not be aware of the subtle and rapid transition between these different dimensions, and this unawareness may last for a long time. He may not understand why he suffers so much, why the journey involves so many difficulties, so many sacrifices and misunderstandings, and why every familiar value is falling away. The disciple may protest and challenge the teacher, even challenge God. Moses himself, as we saw, could not understand why Khiḍr committed certain unbearable iniquities, acts that seemed to Moses malevolent and totally unjust.[25] But gradually, imperceptibly, through being exposed to the energy of the teacher (as we have been exposed to 'Aṭṭār's verses), the disciple's consciousness may occasionally become attuned to both realms of being simultaneously. When this happens, everything on the ordinary level of existence is transformed and becomes revitalized.

This traveling, sometimes at the speed of light, between the two planes of existence causes bewilderment, intense resistance for the mind, pains of crucifixion for the body. Often the disciple prefers to shut his eyes and deny the agonizing movement between here and not-here. It is so confusing, so hard to accept, to understand, to explain. It is easier to indulge in the "yo-yo syndrome" (a contemporary term for *talwīn)*. But eventually, if he sincerely and trustingly perseveres, he will awake to the pull of another dimension, a different state of consciousness, another level of being. And then he will be thrown back—with a thump—onto the earth again, because he must not neglect his earthly business.

This is the main reason for the states of confusion and resistance which are so much a part of the mystical journey. The verses of *The Conference of the Birds* are meant to hammer into the reader's heart and mind, through the experiences and tales of the birds, that *other*, that truly mystical dimension in which the key phrase is *There is nothing but Nothingness*. In this dimension all colors disappear. All mystical experiences cease, *everything* ceases. This is very difficult to accept. It is perhaps the greatest demand that the mystical path claims of the wayfarer, the greatest paradox which cannot be reconciled, because this non-state, the ultimate state of merging in Nothingness, is meant to take place in the midst of life, within all the colors, shapes, and moods which life presents.

It is in the midst of life that the seeker encounters that place in himself where the two planes of existence meet, the two planes to which he becomes hopelessly exposed once he crosses the threshold of the teacher's door. This meeting point, as we saw, is traditionally described as "the meeting of the two seas," *(majma' al-baḥrayn)*. Here, at this inner meeting point, the sincere seeker will find Khiḍr, the eternal Guide. Khiḍr lives in the midst of the sea of death. In order to reach the water of eternal life guarded by Khiḍr, the seeker must traverse this sea. He has to experience successive deaths, and only when he dies to all that he has owned, *including his mystical experiences*, only when he inwardly renounces ownership of anything at all, only then is he revived and reborn into a timeless existence enfolded by the Ocean of Being.

Death and the state of utter inner poverty have been symbolized by the color black. The 15th-century Sufi Sheikh Shams ad-dīn al-Lāhījī, who was in the habit of wearing black only, recorded the following overwhelming experience of the black light of annihilation which absorbed all lights and colors:

> I saw myself present in a world of light. Mountains and deserts were iridescent with lights of all colors: red, yellow, white, blue. I was experiencing a consuming nostalgia for them; I was as though stricken with madness and snatched out of myself by the violence of the intimate emotion and feeling of the presence. Suddenly I saw that the *black light* was invading the entire universe. Heaven and earth and everything that was there had wholly become black light and, behold, I was totally absorbed in

> this light, losing consciousness. Then I came back to myself.[26]

Black light, a contradiction in terms. This is one of the deepest, if not *the deepest* of mystical experiences. At the core of our separate existences as individual human beings, as well as at the core of Existence as such, there is a void, a black point of nothingness. This is the edge of knowing, this is the edge of consciousness, the edge of experiencing. And yet, in some mysterious way, it *is* experienced. It *does* become known, and it has been reported and documented by many mystics of different affiliations. But at the moment of experiencing it, its totality takes over, and in the face of the black light everything perishes; the black light alone exists.

We have come full circle back to the image at the beginning of this chapter: the color of water. Abū Naṣr as-Sarrāj, the 10th-century Sufi compiler who quotes Abū Yazīd al-Bisṭāmī's description of the mystic, *The color of water is the color of his receptacle*, offers the following commentary to this image:

> Abū Yazīd's statement means, and God knows best,[27] that the water, to the extent of its purity, reflects the color of the receptacle, yet the color of the receptacle does not alter its state of purity. The observer imagines that the water is white or black, but the water in the receptacle is in one constant reality. Thus also are the mystic's features in relation to God. Notwithstanding the changing states

> which overtake him and shift him from one to another, his innermost heart, his *sirr,* is with God in one constant reality.[28]

The color of water. A simple image which captures the very essence of Sufi mysticism, and the nature of the paradox within which the seeker must live. Water symbolizes both the fluidity and the potential purity at the core of the mystical life. There is no rigidity, no self-opinionatedness, just the compassionate fluidity of empathy, tenderness, and melting substances.

When water is pure it reflects the color of the container in which it is held. We live within many "containers": the physical body with its organs and sense perception, the social fabric and relationships, our likes and dislikes, our profession, our opinions, our beliefs and principles, our fears and ambitions, even our spiritual life, our dreams, our aspirations, our deepest experiences. All these are different parts and aspects of the individuality within which we are contained. These aspects lend us color, distinction, and characteristics. We are distinguished from one another; we behave differently in different situations, with different people: we do not behave the same way when we are at work as when we are with friends in a social gathering, when we are ill as when we are healthy, when we are angry as when we are content, when we fall in love as when we fall out of love, when we meditate as when we watch a movie. Circumstances change constantly, yet at heart the mystic remains the same. Something deep within remains constant, silent, and without variegation. In his or her innermost, he, or she, has become free from identifying with any state or stage, with any object or person, with any project or aspiration, be it blameworthy or praiseworthy. When viewed from the heart of hearts, from "the secret of secrets," from the state of *'ayn al-jam'*, all is connected to the Source of Total Being.

To the extent that the water is pure, it has no color of its own. It has no character, no features. It reflects whatever passes on its way, whatever throws its reflection upon it. Ultimately, within its very depths, the water reflects the black light of the Absolute Darkness.

This is why the masters have prayed to become colorless and featureless. And it is in this vein that the master of the Naqshbandi fraternity, Bahā' ad-Dīn Naqshband, said: "*For the last twenty-two years I have been following in the footsteps of al-Ḥakīm at-Tirmidhī. As he was featureless so I am now featureless. He who knows it, knows.*"[29]

8

Sufi Ethics and Etiquette: The Path as a Way of Life

The Sufis are the sweepers of the dunghills of men.
A Sufi saying

There are many [Naqshbandis] still living in the city. But their dress shows nothing. They are like invisible ones! What matters is in the heart! It is only the heart that matters!
A contemporary Sufi from Bukhara[1]

The mystical path is usually lived in the context of a group. A Sufi group which gathered around a master used to be known as *ḥalqa*: a ring, a sphere, a circle. The members of a *ḥalqa* were closely affiliated to each other as companion-wayfarers on the path to God. In time the early circles joined together to form a *ṭarīqa:* a path, a fraternity. Life within Sufi groups required of the members full attention not only to their own needs but also to the needs of their fellow men and women. Each moment, each place, and each person created situations which required a particular act or attitude. Hence we find in numerous Sufi compilations whole sections devoted to ethics and etiquette. Some Sufi authors have even compiled special treatises devoted to the subject of *ādāb,* which is the Arabic term for etiquette. Lists of etiquette include prescriptions for the right conduct in different circumstances: what one should do and what one should not do, how one should act and when one should abstain from acting. These lists of *ādāb*, which were transmitted, either orally or in a written form, were laid down, taught, and watched over by the masters in order to maintain within the groups a solid social interaction based on service, and in order to cultivate a surrendering character. Abū ʻAbd ar-Raḥmān as-Sulamī, a 10th- to 11th-century master who had a Sufi "school" *(madrasa)* in Nishapur, sums up this approach simply: "Bring joy into the lives of your friends and meet their needs.... Do not find fault with your friends."[2] *Ādāb* lists have thus set out the norms of behavior within Sufi groups and have defined the commended way of living according to the Sufi tradition.[3]

What is the foundation upon which these didactic and practical aspects of the path are built? An old saying, attributed sometimes to ʻAlī ibn Abī Ṭālib, the fourth Muslim Caliph, states that Sufism is nothing but the possession of good nature: "Sufism is good nature; he who has the better nature is the better Sufi."[4] That this should be a definition of a mystical system may come as a surprise. There is no mention of ecstasy, revelation, miracles; simply "good nature." Al-Hujwīrī, the 11th-century Sufi from Afghanistan, records this saying in his *Kashf al-Maḥjūb (The Unveiling of the Veiled)*, one of the earliest manuals of Sufi lore. Like most Sufi compilers, al-Hujwīrī adds his own interpretation to the material which he records. This is how he comments on the saying, "Sufism is good nature; he who has the better nature is the better Sufi":

> Good nature is of two kinds: towards God and towards men. The former is compliance with the Divine Decrees, the latter is endurance of the burden of men's society for God's sake.[5]

Al-Hujwīrī's statement captures an essential aspect of Sufism. It implies that good nature, or "goodness of disposition" (to use the translator R. A. Nicholson's somewhat archaic idiom),[6] is the infrastructure of a sound mystical life. Good nature is a necessary asset not only in the arena of social relationships, but also in relation to God.

This fundamental facet of Sufism is encapsulated in an idiom, current in Sufi literature, which may be roughly translated as "to be of a good mind," "to have a good opinion," or simply "to think positively" *(ḥusn aẓ-ẓann)*. Sufi teachers constantly remind their disciples that they should apply "positive attitude" not only in their personal circumstances and social relationships, but also in relation to God. This may sound superfluous: can there be any other way of relating to God? What is this injunction about?

All too often even sincere seekers are prone to feel embittered over the hardships they encounter in life and on the path. They resent their recurring problems, their failures, the wrongs that have been done to them, the fact that the teacher rejects them, the injustice in the world, and so on. Bitterness, envy, a grudge—these emotions constellate a negative attitude, *sū' aẓ-ẓann,* which means "to think negatively" about that which God has decreed. When this attitude is predominant, the seeker becomes identified with his troubles and pains, and loses sight of the road ahead. This, according to Sufi etiquette, is a self-centered indulgence which is destructive to spiritual progress. The seeker, therefore, is called upon "to comply with God's decree" as well as "to endure men's company for the sake of God." The inner and outer struggles in the station *(maqām)* of endurance *(ṣabr)* build up trust in God *(tawakkul)*, and progressively lead to the state of resignation and content *(riḍā)*. Ibn 'Aṭā', a close companion of al-Ḥallāj, describes the station of content as follows: "[It is when] the heart observes God's primordial choice for man,[7] so that he comes to know that that which God has chosen for him is best, and so he resigns contented and lets go of anger."[8]

A group, relationships, family life, a failure, a loss, illness, and other difficulties which life presents—all provide opportunities for practicing the attitude of *ḥusn aẓ-ẓann*. The hardships and "tests" which confront the seeker can be very conducive to spiritual life, if he puts this attitude into practice. Bhai Sahib, the 20th-century Sufi master from Kanpur, used to say: "The greater the limitation, the greater the perfection."

According to Sufi tradition, two polar attitudes lead to the state of *riḍā*, contented resignation: the one is gratitude *(shukr)*, the other perseverance *(ṣabr)*. Sufis are taught to apply one or the other in joyful and painful situations respectively. When things run smoothly, the attitude of gratitude takes the seeker away from the delusional *nafs*, which tends to ascribe all good things to itself, and directs his attention towards the real source of bounty. In painful circumstances the attitude of perseverance creates an inner space clear of resentment in which the seeker waits for the tidal waves to subside. Here is how Rūmī paraphrases this teaching poetically:

> Why talk of night? For the lover displays a thousand signs, the least of which are tears, yellow cheeks, a frail body and failing health.

> In weeping he is like the clouds, in perseverance like the mountains, in prostration like water, in lowliness like dirt in the road.
>
> But all these afflictions surround his garden like thorns—within it are roses, the Beloved, and a flowing fountain.
>
> When you pass by the garden's wall and enter into its greenery, you will give thanks and prostrate yourself in gratitude:
>
> "Thanksgiving and praise belong to God! For He has taken away autumn's cruelty. The earth has blossomed, spring has shown its face!"[9]

Another Sufi tradition, which runs in a similar vein, has been attributed to the prophet Muḥammad. He says: "God has shaped the character of the *walī* on nothing but generosity" *(mā jabala allāh waliyyan illā 'alā as-sakhā')*. Generosity rests on the foundation of good nature that a Sufi should possess and cultivate before anything else. It implies giving spaciously, being of service, having consideration for the needs of another, visiting the sick, being hospitable, being wide and open without too many calculations, inhibitions, or conditions. "Care for your brethren more than you care for your own family," writes as-Sulamī; "Be satisfied with little for yourself and wish much for others."[10] And al-Qushayrī, citing a current dictum, describes Sufism as "an open hand and a good heart."[11] Other images of generosity are a bountiful tree, a wide flowing river, the abundance of the earth, the grace of rain.

One recalls how Bhai Sahib lived, how many people lived with him, lived off him. Mrs. Tweedie, who observed his way of life during her stay with him in Kanpur, often expressed indignation. To her Western eyes some of these people were simply parasites. But Bhai Sahib insisted that this is how a Sufi should live.

In the rules of conduct of certain early Sufi groups, one of the most prominent measures taught by the masters was *īthār,* roughly (and inadequately) translatable as "altruism." *Īthār* means to place the other in front, to give precedence to the other. It is the ultimate sign of Sufi chivalry *(futuwwa).* It is put into practice in gatherings (for example, in a gathering for prayer or for meditation) when disciples are content to sit in the back rows rather than in the front rows, or when they shy away from reserving a seat. During a meal the disciple does not attempt to get the best or freshest pieces. The Prophet Muḥammad, it is told, when he ate with his companions was always the last to start eating.[12] And Abū Sa'īd ibn Abī al-Khayr, in what is perhaps the first collection of rules of conduct prescribed to a Sufi group, writes: "Let them not eat anything save in participation with one another."[13]

Īthār means also to refrain from passing judgment on one's fellow men. Moreover, it means to justify the actions of the other, even though they may appear wrong. When Dhū an-Nūn was asked, "With whom shall I associate?" his answer was, "With him who ... does not disapprove of any state you happen to be in."[14] The followers of "the Path of Blame," the *Malāmatī*s of Nishapur, laid down the rule: "Respect others, regard others with favor, justify the wrong-doings of others and rebuke your own self."[15] And Abū 'Alī ad-Daqqāq, al-Qushayrī's revered master, said, perhaps provocatively: "[Sufism] is a path which is only right for people with whose spirits God sweeps the dunghills."[16]

The conduct of the masters is a model for the disciples to live by, but the disciple is required to develop also a sense of discretion. How far to extend giving or to withdraw from giving are issues which have to be faced daily within an interactive group. Awareness and discretion are called for so that giving should not be practiced for the wrong reasons—for example, in order to please, or in order to appease. And conversely, when giving is withheld, the disciple should avoid trying to self-righteously justify himself. Service, help, giving generously become natural, like the flow of water, when one is *there*, present, attuned to real needs, without asking too many questions or putting too many conditions.

Behind "giving" and "generosity" there lies an essential principle: *One is never given anything for oneself alone.* I have always found this a profound, far-reaching principle. When one realizes that he has been given something for which he has had a true need, he experiences gratitude and is released from being wrapped up in a self-centered state of need. When he experiences, at times to his surprise, that there is a "giver" out there and that his need has been met, then he can relax from fears, anxieties, and mistrust. His entire environment, inner as well as outer, changes. Gratitude breeds generosity. It is a modest, inconspicuous way of bringing about change. Sufis refer sometimes to the process of generously giving and gratefully receiving as "polishing the mirror of the heart." "Do not wear the garb of the Sufi," warns as-Sulamī, "before you have qualified for it by cleansing your heart."[17]

Another ancient saying comes to mind: "When you see someone whose heart is soft and warm, know that he is a Sufi." The name "Sufi" derives from the Arabic word for wool: *ṣūf.* The qualities required of a Sufi are, therefore, softness and warmth. This saying reflects an old tradition shared by the peoples of the Mediterranean since Antiquity. It can be found, for example, in pre-Islamic Jewish traditions, which describe the people of the South as possessing, collectively, soft and warm hearts. Early Muslim traditions too describe the people of Yemen (and *Yemen* means *South)* in the same way: their hearts are said to be soft and warm. Later on, it seems, Sufis adopted this tradition and linked it with the image of *wool.* Images of softness, warmth, abundance, non-rigidity have from time immemorial exemplified "Sufis" of whichever denomination. Thus, before any virtues or etiquette can be put into practice, the adept is called upon to acquire the warmth and softness of heart which breed generous giving, service to others, gratitude, and contentment.

But is the call "to acquire" not contradictory to the notion of "disposition," which implies an innate feature? Indeed, but when a sincere seeker enters the orbit of a teacher, he gradually assimilates with the teacher, and in the course of time "acquires" the teacher's qualities: one mirrors back the teacher's qualities. Sufi ethics go even further: they teach that to follow the path ultimately implies "to assimilate the qualities of God"—*al-takhalluq bi-akhlāq allāh.* As God is generous and bountiful, so should God's lovers be.[18] When the process of transformation takes place in the blessed environment of a teacher, a door opens; changes are at hand. The inner and outer transformation which disciples go through is said to be the true miracle accomplished by the friends of God. Bhai Sahib used to describe his own house thus: "This is a house of drunkards, this is a house of change."

There is a universal dimension to the ancient Sufi teaching which requires nothing more than "the goodness of disposition," a soft, warm heart, and the assimilation of the teacher's qualities. Such teaching seems free of the rigidity and self-righteousness that moralistic systems tend to acquire. It is not bound by any theological teachings. Fundamentally, it transcends denomination, ethnicity, and religious identity. True, Sufism has been formulated and lived out by a long line of Muslim teachers and disciples. The love and respect for the Prophet Muḥammad and for the Islamic religious law have been part and parcel of this tradition for the last twelve hundred years. The Naqshbandi path in particular has been known for its strict adherence to the Sunni *sharī'a.*[19] But this may have changed according to the needs of the time. Bhai Sahib, the 20th-century Naqshbandi-Mujaddidi from Kanpur, was given the "license" *(ijāẓa)* to teach by Guru Maharaj, his Muslim teacher, who had never demanded that he relinquish the Hindu tradition. And Mrs. Tweedie was sent by Bhai Sahib to the West as his successor, regardless of her Russian-Orthodox origins.

The universal dimension is highlighted by Bhai Sahib's saying, recorded by Mrs. Tweedie in one of the earliest entries of her diary,

> "Sufism is a way of life. It is neither a religion nor a philosophy. There are Hindu Sufis, Muslim Sufis, Christian Sufis—My Revered Guru Maharaj was a Muslim." He said it very softly with a tender expression, his eyes dreamy and veiled.[20]

A few days later, on October 12, Bhai Sahib elaborated:

> A System is a School of Yoga, or a Path of Self-Realization—the meaning is the same. We are called Saints, but it is the same as Yogis—in Wisdom there is no difference. The color of our Line is golden yellow, and we are called The Golden Sufis or the Silent Sufis, because we practice silent meditation. We do not use music or dancing or any definite practice. We do not belong to any country or any civilization, but we work always according to the need of the people of the time. We belong to Raja Yoga, but not in the sense as it is practiced by the Vedantins. Raja means simply: Kingly, or Royal, the Direct Road to Absolute Truth.[21]

Goodness of disposition, generosity, adherence to the ways of the teacher, a universal system which is based on gratitude, perseverance, service, and inner silence—this is the framework of Sufi ethics and etiquette.

"Sufism is violence (*'anwa*), there is no peace in it" is a startling saying, especially when attributed to al-Junayd, this celebrated master of the Baghdadi circle, who left a lasting impression on the Sufi tradition.[22] Indeed, the encounter with a Sufi teacher creates for the disciple a restless, forceful situation in which he is mercilessly taken into the sway of the opposites: often he will find himself in a whirlpool of inner conflicts, on a merry-go-round, with his nose in the mud. In spite of the inner and outer disturbances which the teacher and the path will create for him, the disciple is also required to live a grounded, responsible outer life. This is because the mystical quest is lived, and must be lived, in the midst of life. Extreme inner upheavals may rise within the disciple when he earnestly tries to bring the two worlds together. He loses his grip on previous notions of right and wrong, while at the same time he is trying to maintain a footing in the world of outer concerns and appearances.

Sufi teachers have taught that on the path one has to give up the notion that what one sees is in fact the way it is. A passage from Rūmī's *Discourses,* which were written in prose with a clear didactic purpose, poignantly makes this point:

> If everything were in truth as it appears to be, the Prophet, endowed as he was with a vision so penetrating, so illumined and illuminating, would never have cried, 'Lord, show me things as they are.' 'Thou showest a thing as fair, and in reality it is ugly; Thou showest a thing as ugly, and in reality it is lovely. Therefore do Thou show us every thing just as it is, that we may not fall into the snare and that we may not go astray perpetually.' Now your judgement, however good and luminous it may be, is certainly not better than the Prophet's judgement. He used to speak in this fashion; so do you now not put your trust in every idea and every notion. Be ever humble and fearful before God.[23]

From the same relativistic approach, Abū Najīb as-Suhrawardī, a celebrated 12th-century Sufi master from Persia and the author of one of the earliest Sufi works on etiquette, writes in his *Sufi Rule for Novices* :

> The answers to questions about Sufism vary according to the spiritual station of the enquirer: the novice *(murīd)* is answered with regard to the external aspect of Sufism, that is, concerning mutual relations (ethics). The Sufi of the middle rank *(mutawassiṭ)* is answered with regard to the inner states *(aḥwāl)*, and the knower *(al-'ārif)* is answered with regard to the reality *(al-ḥaqīqa)*. The beginning of Sufism is learning *('ilm)*, the middle is praxis *('amal)* and the end is grace.[24]

The teacher will create confusing and frustrating situations for the minds of the disciples when similar questions are answered in diametrically opposed ways. Many a time did Mrs. Tweedie accuse Bhai Sahib of contradicting himself. He always expressed surprise at these accusations, as she recorded in *Daughter of Fire*:

> No contradictions here, only your mind makes it so. In the morning one says something which belongs to the morning; at midday one says things which belong to this time; in the afternoon and in the evening one will say what is suitable to that particular time. There is no contradiction. We speak according to the time, the place, and the state of the progress of the disciple.[25]

One can clearly see how confusing and disconcerting life can be around a Sufi teacher, where ethics and the proper manners are *infused* into the *murīd* rather than directly taught. Not only is there no certainty or assurance in the outer situations which life presents, but one never knows with certainty what the teacher requires of him, or how the teacher looks upon him. Confusion is deliberately built into the system of Sufi education, until one learns, through being beaten up by repeated experiences, to adopt a new perspective, a new outlook on things. One learns not to trust anything but the subtle indications, or hints, which arise spontaneously in the heart. Then the outer situations, including the provocative and confusing behavior of the teacher, do not matter in the same way as before. One can lead then the most ordinary life or become a prominent leader; the ethics do not get contaminated by ego-driven desires. To put it in the words of as-Suhrawardī:

> The Sufi of the middle rank *(mutawassiṭ)* is in the process of ascending from one state to the next, but the consummate Sufi *(muntahin)* is in a position of stability, and he is immune to the effects of the changeful states of mind or harsh circumstances.... This is also attested to by the example of the Prophet, who at first had practiced solitude but afterwards mingled with people. Likewise, the "people of the portico,"[26] when they had reached the state of stability, became commanders and administrators, and mixing with the people did not damage their spiritual position.[27]

"Time," says al-Qushayrī, "is where you are in the moment," namely, where you are *now*.[28] Therefore, one of the first rules that the seeker has to endorse is how to live in the moment and according to the requirements of the moment. This principle has been articulated in different ways. Most inspiring is the way in which it was formulated by the *Khwājagān*, the Masters of Wisdom, the spiritual ancestors of the Naqshbandi path.

Initially, in the 12th century, eight rules were laid down by the masters. Later on, in the 14th century, Bahā' ad-Dīn Naqshband added three more. All these rules emphasize various aspects of "living in the moment." The masters have articulated them in short, pithy, and somewhat enigmatic formulae.

"Watch your step" (in Persian: *naẓar bar qadam)* is one of these formulae. How is it to be understood? There are many ways of interpretation. It may mean, simply, that one should have one's feet on the ground. This basic, down-to-earth rule often has to be restated within groups of spiritual aspirants. It may be desirable to aspire to the highest, but one must not forget where one is, or where one is going. Looking after one's daily affairs, fulfilling one's responsibilities in the right attitude, is as spiritually demanding as going off into deep mystical states. Quoting Bhai Sahib, Mrs. Tweedie has often reiterated: "We are not idle drones, nor lotus-eaters; we have our feet firm on the ground, while our heads carry the vault of the skies."

"Watch your step" can be understood also as "ponder your step," ponder the meaning and purpose of the steps you take in the transitory phases of life. In *The Alchemy of Happiness* al-Ghazzālī, a famous 11th-century teacher, addresses the need to remember constantly the purpose of life and of the spiritual journey. He writes:

> Real self-knowledge consists in knowing the following things: What art thou in thyself, and from whence hast thou come? Whither art thou going, and for what purpose hast thou come to tarry here awhile, and in what does thy real happiness and misery consist?[29]

Pondering these existential questions may lead to yet deeper realizations. The wayfarer on the path must learn to be at all times watchful, as a cat at a mousehole, not to become sidetracked by the landscape of the terrain in which the journey takes place. Sidetracking may arise from outer as well as from inner phenomena: one can become sidetracked by paying too much attention to experiences, dreams, psychological problems, the longing, the next stage on the path, as much as one can be distracted by paying too much attention to casual, mundane attractions which come and go. It is useful to observe that the aspiration for spiritual life can sometimes become an opaque veil. Therefore, in every step the seeker is advised: Be aware! Don't be complacent! Watch your steps!

One can then proceed and ponder: where do I stand in relation to the tradition to which I belong? Am I able to live up to the model of my spiritual ancestors? Can I live by their standards? Am I aware that I belong to a "tradition"? Do I accept its guidelines, its authority? Do I resent it? Are there any conflicts in me about it?

These as well as other levels of interpretation of this rule relate to the different orbits in which seekers live their lives. Clearly, each generation, each era, each group, each individual—all inject their own meanings into the formula. It is tersely phrased, so that it can become a seed-thought, a focus for inner contemplation which may lead to a deeper self-awareness and greater honesty and authenticity.

In *Kashf al-Maḥjūb*, al-Hujwīrī quotes a saying of a somewhat obscure 10th-century Sufi from Nishapur, Abū Muḥammad Murta'ish, who says: "The Sufi is he whose aspiration keeps pace with his foot." This saying adequately sums up what has been conveyed so far. Appending his own commentary, al-Hujwīrī writes:

> That is to say, he is entirely present: his soul is where his body is, and his body where his soul is, and his soul where his foot is, and his foot where his soul is. This is the sign of presence without absence.[30]

Another rule formulated by the masters is "awareness in breathing," or "conscious breathing" (in Persian: *hūsh dar dam)*. What does it mean to "breathe consciously"? Sufis have always maintained that each moment which passes in which God has not been remembered is a wasted moment. The breath connects us with the Divine. In the constant flow of inhalation and exhalation, *and especially in the almost imperceptible pause between the two,* a vibrating model of the two worlds in which we live presents itself to us: we withdraw, and then we re-emerge; we introvert into our inner recesses in order to extravert again and share life in its external fullness. Life, the complete life, consists of the polar states of "in" and "out." What lies in between belongs to the realm of silence and nothingness, the true esoteric aspect of the path to God.

J. G. Bennett, in his *The Masters of Wisdom*, sums up the commentaries to this formula which he found in Naqshbandi sources:

> Breathing is the nourishment of the inner man. As we breathe, we should place our attention on each successive breath and be aware of our own presence. For this, it is necessary to be in the right state because if the breath is taken inattentively, it will not go to the right place. Mawlana Saad ad-din Kashghari explained that *hosh dar dam* requires that from one breath to another we should keep our attention open to our goal. Inattention is what separates us from God....
>
> Khwaja Baha ad-din Naqshbandi said: "In this path, the foundation is built upon breathing. The more that one is able to be conscious of one's breathing, the stronger is one's inner life." He added that it is particularly important to keep awareness of the change from in-breathing to the out-breathing....
>
> Mawlana Jami, the great poet of central Asia, said that *hosh dar dam* is the absolute moment when personal identity is merged into the One. This, he said, is the ultimate secret of breath.[31]

This description may raise many questions. What kind of "awareness" is required here? Is it a mental awareness, in which one is still confined within the mind, and therefore is most unlikely to be in a state of "merging" with the One? Or is there another state of awareness which the above passage alludes to, and to which this practice may lead? What does "absolute moment" mean?

These are not theoretical, academic questions. Seekers have struggled with them for centuries in their quest for "the final goal of liberation." More than fifteen hundred years ago the same question was raised by the bewildered, yet inspired, St. Augustine, who wrote in his *Confessions*:

> As I rise above memory, where am I to find you? ... If I find you outside my memory, I am not

> mindful of you. And how shall I find you if I am not mindful of you?[32]

> In recalling you I rose above those parts of memory which animals also share … I came to the parts of my memory where I stored the emotions of my mind, and I did not find you there. I entered into the very seat of my mind … since the mind also remembers itself. But you were not there.[33]

Struggling and stumbling, seekers learn that there are indeed many levels of consciousness. But this struggle cannot be confined to the mental level alone, since on that level it's bound to tumble into a dizzying, bottomless pit of confusion. On the other hand, when consciousness is approached from the level of the breath, it may result in a sense of liberation from mental disorientation. But whether or not "the secret of breath" really points to "the annihilation of self and union with the absolute being which is the final goal of liberation," this the seeker will not find out unless he plunges *practically* into the mysteries of *hūsh dar dam*.[34]

The moral foundation upon which Sufi ethics are built is not the dichotomy between good and evil, right and wrong. Rather is it based on the dichotomy between the world of illusion and imaginary needs, in which the ego reigns in collaboration with the three-dimensional sensory perception, and the world of Reality *(ḥaqīqa)*. The world of Reality belongs to a dimension free from the limitation of sense perception, psychological needs, and wishful fantasies. Llewellyn Vaughan-Lee has put this idea in an interesting context, saying that relationships within a spiritual group are essentially vertical, not horizontal. The image of a vertical rather than a horizontal axis of friendship and companionship reflects the mystical orientation towards the Sacred. Deep in the collective psyche of the Sufi tradition lies this one-pointed orientation which *at all times* aligns the heart of the seeker with the Divine, with the Beloved. This alignment dictates the outlook with which a Sufi seeker views his entire life, which includes his moral and ethical life. This is how Abū 'Abd ar-Raḥmān as-Sulamī of Nishapur expresses the attitude which arises from such an orientation:

> God has spoken to this community with hints, and they have responded with mystic expressions. Who can know the inner stations of these people? Only the Friends of God, the pure of heart and those who know God. They are the lovers of God.... Their hearts are of the [heavenly] Throne while their bodies are of wild instincts. The tree of love has been planted in their hearts and their subtleties, like spies, secretly spread among people.... They worship God with love while people worship God with practices. This community looks to God from God, while people look to God from their worship. They don't take notice of anyone but God, and they love naught but Him.[35]

Sufis have always existed and worked within groups; the group has always been needed as a social container. In spite of the vertical orientation, horizontal relationships within the group have great validity and value. The Sufi manuals stress that the so-called "vertical" orientation has to be grounded by "horizontal" relationships. The "community," to use as-Sulamī's idiom, lives within a larger social container: the family, the town, the land, the culture of the age. All these are never ignored. In the scheme of Sufi ethics all have their rights: the right of the father, the right of the mother, the right of the spouse, the right of the children, the right of the extended family, the right of the neighbor, the right of the guest,[36] the right of civil servants, the right of the ruler, and so on. Yet all these horizontal social rights stem from the single central point from which one is at all times aligned vertically with the heart of the path, with the Beyond.

It is in this context that I find the following saying, attributed to Abū Yazīd al-Bisṭāmī, both intriguing and stimulating: "What is the most wondrous sign of the mystic? That he eats with you, drinks with you, jests with you, buys from you, sells to you, while his heart is in the Holy Kingdom. This is the most wondrous sign."[37] The wondrous thing is the coming together of the two dimensions within which the mystic lives. Outwardly he is not distinguished from any ordinary man or woman. He performs his duties and functions in the world in an ordinary manner. Nothing proclaims his real state. But inwardly he is attentive and attuned to a different realm of being.

A wonder this may be, but one that the path prescribes for all its seekers. In the rules laid down by the *Khwājagān*, the practice of this way of being in the world is known as "Solitude in the Crowd" *(khalwat dar anjuman)*. Such inner "solitude" in the midst of the hubbub of life with all its transactions becomes a profound experience when the vertical and horizontal alignments cross each other. It is then that the opposites meet; it is then that one becomes liberated from the unconscious or semi-conscious process of "identification" with the other, without losing the sense of true care and empathy. In other words, it is then that one becomes detached and humble at one and the same time.

It is said that even before the seeker consciously chooses to follow a certain path or a certain teacher, he has been inwardly *programmed* to align with this path or that teacher. Being "programmed," or "branded," (like sheep by their master) is innate—it is stamped upon the seeker's heart of hearts. This is his secret destiny which unfolds in his life day by day, stage by stage. It pulls him to gravitate, without clearly knowing why, towards a particular path or a particular teacher, and through this gravitation he changes. Sufis have named this attraction *jadhb,* and those who are attracted *majdhūbūn.* It usually takes a long time to reconcile outer life with the inner quest. It takes a long time to realize that joining a spiritual group, or setting time for the silent *dhikr*, is not in itself the goal of the journey. It takes time to realize that walking on the path is a twenty-four-hour-a-day job and it includes all the trivialities and pettiness of life. It includes "horizontal" relationships as well as the "vertical" experiences, visions, or big dreams that the seeker may taste from time to time.

But then there comes a point when the seeker becomes more or less aware, more or less awakened to the impact of the inner impression, the *naqsh*, which has been engraved (as the word *naqsh* implies) upon his heart and soul. It is then that his life *in its totality* becomes clustered around the path and cleaves to it as iron cleaves to a magnet. From that point on, whether he knows it or not, the innate "programming" becomes an outer reality. The inner law of the path shapes everything he does, everything he says, everything he becomes. From that moment on the seeker lives his everyday life, as well as his inner, spiritual life, in the presence of the path. The path then becomes for him a living entity, not a mere concept, nor an image, nor sets of rules, nor a futuristic anticipation. At this point, whether semi-consciously or fully conscious, he makes a commitment to follow the path. And from that point on, whether he knows it or not, he is *guided* by the path. If he is attentive enough, he shall find that in states of confusion and unknowing, which are the rule on a mystical journey, a hint will spring up from the innermost of his soul; an indication will arise, an urge, a dream, a direction. They emerge from the place in which his "secret" *(sirr)*, his heart of hearts, meets the heart of the path.

If he trusts this hint, he will be guided by it to act upon its indication. This is the very *essence* of the ethics and etiquette which have passed on to seekers from generations of earlier travelers on this path. This "code" helps the seeker to conform unruffled to the laws of the land and culture in which he lives; it also shows him how to blend within the social fabric in which life is lived without losing sight of the inner direction. By following the model of behavior which the path has set, the seeker learns how to live in both worlds at one and the same time. "A Wali (saint) is a balanced person," Bhai Sahib told Mrs. Tweedie,

> he knows that this world is not a bad one, and he has to live in both worlds, the spiritual and the physical, the life on this earth. There is nothing good or bad for him; good or bad are relative concepts.[38]

This is a description of a *walī,* one might argue, an enlightened being, a "complete human being" *(al-insān al-kāmil)*; what about novices, seekers, *murīdūn*? Yet in essence there are no two laws. As the seeker gravitates towards the teacher, the teacher becomes for him a model of the path; he becomes a mirror in which the seeker contemplates his own heart of hearts, his own innermost soul. In the mirror of the teacher the seeker sees his soul in her most ravishing, scintillating beauty which the Beloved has bestowed on her from eternity. Contemplating the reflection of his inner form in the mirror of the teacher, the seeker falls in love with this beauty, and vows to nurture it and look after it forever. Through this bond of love, the laws of the beloved teacher become also his laws, his qualities the seeker's qualities. On this level of attunement there are very rarely any significant confusions or muddle-ups. The seeker simply lives in a state of reciprocal love, which is felt when the heart expands and becomes forever softer and warmer.

9

"It Is the Function Which Creates the Organ."

Irina Tweedie

The poor of heart offers nothing to God but his poverty.
Abū Ḥafṣ al-Ḥaddād[1]

Woe unto thee, if by thy country thou meanest Damascus, Baghdad, or any other city of the world .
Shihāb ad-Dīn Suhrawardī[2]

Mystical systems vary; some spring from an unquenched thirst for knowledge, for *gnosis*; some revolve around the need to worship and revere; some strive to gain power over men and demons while others promote the concept and practice of service; and some come out of a longing to be absorbed in the Totality of Being. But regardless of typological differences, mystical systems share in common a *memory*, sometimes dim and opaque, of an existence in a previous, pre-earthly state of fullness. This memory gives birth to a nostalgia, to a painful restlessness, because in a life which is experienced as only partially lived, nothing can compare with the taste of blissful fullness *(sa'āda)* which this memory carries in its fold. The Valley of Quest is sought out because of this restless state of want, because of the desire to fill up an existential emptiness, because of an urge, hidden in the recesses of the soul, to become whole, to live wholly. This feeling lies at the core of man's efforts towards completion and fulfillment, and this is the bedrock of the mystical quest.

Mysticism is often identified with unusual experiences and supranatural phenomena. It is often thought that mysticism is about mysteries of the beyond, but in fact it is about the mysteries which lie hidden within man's own being. As we have repeatedly seen, Sufism teaches that that which lies within the center of man's being is the *heart.* "The word *heart* has two meanings," wrote al-Ghazzālī at the end of the 11th century in his monumental *The Revival of the Religious Sciences,*

> the cone-shaped [piece of] flesh which is located at the left side of the chest, ...and a divine and spiritual subtlety *(laṭīfa)* connected with the physical heart. This subtlety is the true essence of man. *It is this in man which perceives and learns and knows.*[3]

The backbone of the mystical path is the quest for a primordial wholeness. In order to become a *whole* human being the seeker has to discover his true nature. This is why, from a very early stage in its development, the Sufi tradition has developed a "mystical psychology," a science of the self *('ilm an-nafs),* built upon two interrelated principles. The first principle states that *man is created in the image of God,*[4] and the second that *the knowledge of the self leads to the knowledge of God.*[5] In its deepest sense, therefore, man's self-knowledge is the key which opens the door to his mystical goal, to the end which is also the beginning: the experience of a life lived fully, wholly, as a complete human being.

The man who has achieved the state of wholeness through self-knowledge is a true man. In Sufi terminology "man" *(rajul)* is not a gender denomination. It is an indication, regardless of gender, of a stage and a state in the seeker's inner development, be he man or woman. What, or who, is a true human being? Jalāl ad-Dīn Rūmī, in one of his discourses, offers the following definition:

> The man who can do without God and makes no effort is no man at all; whilst if he were able to comprehend God, that indeed would not be God. Therefore the true man is he who is never free from striving, who revolves restlessly and ceaselessly about the light of the Majesty of God. And God is He who consumes man and makes him naught, being comprehended of no reason.[6]

According to the Sufi teachers, the knowledge of the self, ultimately and in essence, leads to the understanding that "manhood" *(rujūliyya)* is also "slavehood" *('ubūdiyya)*, since the reference-point of a genuine self-knowledge is God, who alone possesses "Lordship" *(rubūbiyya)* and majesty *(jalāl)*. Full manhood, therefore, cannot be attained before man becomes aware of his inherent state of subservience and want. Contemporary seekers, whose spiritual search is often bound up with an introspection based on modern, ego-focused psychological systems, may find this double aspect of Sufi manhood challenging.[7]

In order to "know" these polar aspects of the human condition as they truly are, man, say the Sufi teachers, has to acquire special organs of perception, to develop inner, subtle senses. In science and technology, powerful extensions to our minds and senses have been developed. But in order to observe man's true nature, such extensions are not sufficient; a different kind of senses has to evolve. These, Sufis say, are the sense-organs of the subtle heart, of that "divine and spiritual subtlety which... is this in man which perceives and learns and knows."

The search for wholeness is therefore a process in which the *inner* man is cultivated, a process in which the functions of the coarse, physical senses are gradually transmuted into subtle counterparts. "Our path is the path of alchemy," writes Najm ad-Dīn Kubrā, who flourished in the first part of the turbulent 13th century. "The subtle organ of light *(al-laṭīfa an-nūrāniyya)* has to be extracted from those [material] mountains."[8] "The five senses are replaced by other senses," he goes on to explain,

> Other senses open into the unseen *(al-ghayb)*: eyes, ears, [the sense of] smell, mouth, hands, feet, a [different level] of being. [A man] sees and hears and partakes of food from the unseen... and talks and walks and kicks and reaches distant countries.... What ordinary man realizes in sleep... the wayfarer *(as-sayyār)* realizes between sleep and wakefulness.[9]

How does this transmutation happen? An elaborate answer is offered by Rūmī, to whose theory of evolution this chapter is devoted. But at heart his answer is simple, and can be summed up as follows: In order to attain the sought-for inner transformation, the sincere seeker has to live in a state of *conscious neediness*, while being irresistibly *attracted* to an evolved soul.

This chapter has its starting point in a book about Rūmī's theory of man's spiritual evolution, a book which inspired Mrs. Tweedie years ago. She came across this book after returning from India to London, when she was preparing herself for the task for which she had been trained by her teacher.

"What shall I do when I go back to the West?" she had asked him.

"Lecture," Bhai Sahib answered.

"But on what shall I lecture?" she insisted.

"On Sufism."

"How will I be able to do this? You have taught me nothing on Sufism; I don't know much about it," Mrs. Tweedie tried to argue.

"You'll find out."

Mrs. Tweedie started lecturing for the Theosophical Society. In her lectures she would often get carried away by memories of her beloved teacher and the anguished experiences she had had with him during her stay in India. Her lectures were based on her own experiences, since she had taken a vow never to talk on anything except that which she had experienced herself. Yet when she associated her own experiences with the Sufi teaching described in the few books and articles available to her in London (in the late sixties), she realized how accurately they reflected her own experiences. Her lectures thus became the records of a *living tradition* which was stamped with fire upon her very being, her very soul.

One day, in the round reading room of the British Library, she came across a published dissertation, *The Metaphysics of Rūmī*, written by Khalifa Abdul Hakim, a Pakistani scholar, on Rūmī's theory of evolution and spiritual transformation.[10] Reading it, she later said, was like a revelation. She felt how everything which she had experienced at Bhai Sahib's fell into place. The book confirmed to her the validity of her own experiences and destiny from the vantage point of the larger Sufi tradition. It was a confirmation that her training with Bhai Sahib represented a branch of an ancient yet living mystical tree. She was part of a chain *(silsila)* which had proceeded from time immemorial, the chain of love through which the mystical teaching is transmitted from teacher to disciple. "Two things," she would say, "will always be the same: the flow of rivers and the ways of love." Through statements and quotations brought together by Abdul Hakimin his book, she could formulate for herself the nature of the transformation which she had gone through under the guidance of her teacher: *When the need for Truth is as great as the need for air, then this function of need creates the organ by which Truth can be sought out and attained.*

Mrs. Tweedie copied the whole book twice: first by hand and then, at home, on her typewriter. The typed script, as well as an implicit indication by Mrs. Tweedie, initiated the writing of this chapter. It does not purport, however, to be a summary or a paraphrase of Khalifa's dissertation—this will not do justice to the wide spectrum of erudition covered by Khalifa's book. Nevertheless, the central idea which it conveys can be summed up in the author's own words:

> Life is a journeying back to God; it proceeds according [to] a process of evolution. The minerals develop into plants and plants into animals and animals into man and man into superhuman being, ultimately to reach the starting point—a glorious inter-

> pretation of the Koranic verses, 'God is the beginning and God is the end,' and 'to Him do we return'.[11]

"[Rūmī] teaches," Abdul Hakimgoes on to say,

> that there is only one way of rising from the lower to the higher stage and that is by assimilation of the lower into the higher.... [Rūmī] believed that necessity is not only the mother of invention, it is the mother of creation as well. Even God would not have created the heaven and the earth if He had not been urged by an irresistible inner necessity.... For Rumi ... life is nothing but a product of the will to live, and ever dissatisfied with the present equipment, life creates new desires, to fulfill which new organs come into existence.[12]

In Sufi literature one of the most often quoted extra-Qur'ānic traditions revealed by Allāh, a *ḥadīth qudsī*, states the purpose of creation in a boldness rarely encountered in religious traditions. God says: *"I was a hidden treasure, and I desired to be known; therefore I created creation."*[13] Why did God, who is utter fullness, create the world? Because of a desire, a need to be known. In the hidden unknownness of God, there was one thing missing: there was no one to know Him. Thus, the *raison d'être* of creation is God's need to be known. Need is, then, the foundation upon which creation exists. Quoting Rūmī, Abdul Hakimreiterates this idea:

> If there were no necessity the seven heavens would not have stepped out of non-existence; the sun, the moon and the stars could not have come into existence, and *according to his necessity man is endowed with organs. Therefore, oh needy one, in-*

> *crease your need* so that God's Beneficence may be moved (to bestow new instruments of life on you).[14]

It was this passage which inspired Mrs. Tweedie in particular. In the empty space of one line in her typed script she added by hand the following comment: *"It is the function which creates the organ."* What, then, is this organ, and what is the function which creates it?

In his childhood Rūmī was uprooted from his native home in Balkh, one of the main cities of Khurāsān, the capital of the northeastern province of the Muslim Empire. At the turn of the 13th century Rūmī's family emigrated to Anatolya—a land then known to the Muslim world as Rūm, and known to us today as Turkey. Just over a century before Anatolya had been conquered by the Seljuks, a Muslim dynasty originally from the steppes of Central Asia and Mongolia, who took it from the old Byzantine Empire and claimed it for Islam. Konya became the capital of this fairly new Muslim territory. Jalāl ad-Dīn Rūmī and his family settled there, and soon became respectable citizens. In the East which they had left behind, a catastrophe was impending: fearsome hordes of Mongols were about to sweep through the cultivated lands of Central Asia, were about to mercilessly massacre whole communities, to enslave and rape women and children, to destroy the sophisticated cultural centers of Persia and Iraq, to smash the ancient irrigation systems in these lands, and eventually, in the year 1258—barely forty years after

Rūmī's family had left for the West—they were to eliminate forever the Islamic Caliphate from its old capital Baghdad.

It was as though Rūmī's father, a reputable master, had foreseen these coming events in taking his family to the relative safety of Rūm. Here, the young Jalāl ad-Dīn grew up in a culture which was a hybrid of many ancient traditions—Greek, Byzantine, Persian, Turkish, Arab—in a land that for millennia had been the center of cults and mysteries—Hellenic, Gnostic, Christian. In this alchemical laboratory Jalāl ad-Dīn's psyche was forged, distilling through his own unique experiences of love and longing his inimitable gift with words, with music, with poetry. His poetry carries with it the flavor of freedom in the vast steppes of Central Asia, the courage to leave everything behind and look for new territories where the heart can thrive. It is stamped with the commitment to follow to the very end, earnestly and with passion, the heart's tribulation on the path to God, allowing the heart to constantly change, to become freer from judgment, more fluid, "colorless and featureless" through the oscillation between the opposites. At the same time his poetry and didactic prose demand qualities and ethics which emanate from the vision of the Highest.

This, perhaps, is why his poetry has been for centuries a source of inspiration and consolation for many, Muslims and non-Muslims. A devout Muslim himself, he includes all who possess a sincere heart in the Religion of Love *(kīsh-i mehr)*: Pagans, Christians, Jews, Hindus, heretics—if the ultimate state is to become featureless and colorless, what difference do denominations make? His poetry derives from the thirst to transcend the form and to touch the realm of the essence, and therefore it touches the hearts just there, where it meets their own thirst for truth.

Rūmī's teaching of man's evolution, up to a point, coincides with contemporary medieval beliefs and theories on the origin of the universe and on the destiny of man. These theories, sometimes identified as Neoplatonic, were for centuries widespread among Muslims, Christians, Jews, and Pagans. Creation is seen in them as a hierarchical scheme of being, a hierarchy of different planes of existence. The cosmos was envisaged as a series of concentric spheres, one within the other, all *emanating* in a descending order from the One, the Source, the Eternal. The One, in His overflowing dark and hidden luminosity, produced a "sphere," an "other." This sphere was identified by medieval philosophers with the Throne of Glory *(al-'arsh)*, with the cosmological "all-encompassing sphere" *(al-muḥīṭ)*, or with the Universal Intellect *(al-'aql al-kullī)*. This sphere, in its turn, out of its own effulgence produced another sphere, lower than itself, less luminous. Other spheres of existence *emanated* in the same way. These are the spheres of planets and fixed stars. The spheres became denser and dimmer as their distance from the Source increased. The lowest sphere was identified with the moon. Beneath the moon, in what became known as "the sublunar world," lay our universe—the plane of Nature, which became populated by man and other living creatures. This was considered the densest, darkest plane of being. Here, in a material and temporal world, life is governed by the law of "generation and corruption," birth and death. Everything on this plane is composed of the four elements, which, unlike the celestial entities above the moon, are confined by the limitations of time and space.

Seen from the lowermost, this plane, too, reflects a hierarchical scheme. Inanimate entities—minerals, stones, metals—are the densest of all phenomena, since they are the most remote from the Source of Being. As Rūmī intuitively knew, the mineral world only *appears* to be inanimate. In fact, it vibrates with the movement of atoms. Nevertheless, the pace of transformation on this level of being is so slow that it appears to be lifeless.

Above minerals rises the slightly less compact realm of plants and trees. Plants are confined to their place; they are rooted to the earth, but they have freedom of sorts: they move with the wind, they branch out, they produce leaves, flowers, fruit.

Above the vegetative realm lies the realm of animals. Animals are freer than plants or minerals; their makeup is finer, their developmental rhythm faster. But they are still remote from the Source. They are governed mainly by instincts, the most prominent of which is the instinct to survive. Their range of choices is small.

Man, it was believed, soars above these three planes. He is on the highest rung of the sub-lunar ladder. His freedom is greater: the freedom to move and the freedom to make choices. Yet his plane too, compared with the celestial spheres, is remote from the Source, dim, dense, slow. Moreover, man too is part of Nature, made of the four elements, and governed by the laws of "coming-into-being" and "passing-away," fruition and decay.

It was believed that each level of being contains within it the lower one(s). Human beings thus carry within them, in an ascending order, mineral, plant, and animal. For man the process of evolution starts from the moment of conception. He starts as a drop, the product of the meeting between a sperm and an egg. In this state he belongs to the mineral realm. From the drop a fetus develops, a creature which resembles a minute human being, but is closely related to the vegetative realm, since it's rooted to the walls of the uterus and is fed through the mother. When the fetus is born it is ruled mainly by instincts, which associate it with the animal realm: for its survival it needs food, warmth, security, some basic movement, and a lot of sleep. Slowly the human infant grows, and as it grows it learns how to adapt to its environment and circumstances; it becomes wiser, it learns through mistakes and imitation. Its mind develops; it learns how to walk, talk, use its hands and feet, remember things, reason with things, think, express itself, respond, create. For most medieval people the mind, the intellect *(al-'aql)*, became therefore the highest stage of development on the hierarchical ladder on the sublunar levels of creation. A human being, by definition, was conceived of as a creature endowed with mind, and his "rational soul" *(an-nafs an-nāṭiqa)*, which enabled him to speak, think, and make choices, made him the crown of creation and the vice-regent of God on earth.

But within the human being there resides another component, which is not a product of the organic line of evolution—a *subtle* entity *(laṭīfa)* which is not a genuine native of the sub-lunar world. This is a luminous, spiritual energy which is sometimes referred to as "soul." This celestial entity comes from the Source of all being, from the Divine Hiddenness. Its origin is the Spirit of God *(rūḥ)*. "The spirit is of the bidding of my Lord *(ar-rūḥ min amri rabbī)*," says the Qur'ān,[15] and it was therefore understood to be an impenetrable mystery, knowable to no one but God.[16] Within the Spirit of God, the souls of all human beings were contained in a potential, pre-created state. "In the realm of the Spirit," says Rūmī, "we all were one extended substance without beginning and without end: one substance like the sun, clear and without knots, like water."[17]

How did the soul come to reside in man's body of clay? On the mythical Day of Creation God pronounced the sacred "word" *(Logos)* "Be!" *(kun)*, and the created being was.[18] All created beings, it was believed—especially in Sufi circles—angels as well as minerals, were created through the Divine Logos—all except for human beings. The clay of *their* creation was kneaded and shaped by God's own hands.[19] God created man not by a word, which comes from Divine Wisdom *(ḥikma)*, which itself comes from Divine Power *(qudra)*, but by hand-shaping, which comes from Divine Love *(maḥabba)*. Into the clay shaped by His hands God breathed His spirit, and the new-created being, Adam (in Hebrew: [earth-made] man), came into life. Through the breath of God something was planted deep within the clay: man's soul and the seeds of his future awakening. Upon this hidden entity within, an imprint was impressed, a memory of that experience at the beginning of time, an experience of the closest intimacy between man and God, a memory of sheer fulfillment.

From the loftiest of all planes, from a state of bliss and nearness to God, the soul came down to reside within man's body as a stranger in a strange land. It descended through all the celestial spheres, each sphere denser and darker than the one above, and more remote from Home. It came down into this sub-lunar world of birth and death. Here, in the confinement of the earthly body, it became the hidden counterpart of God's spirit: "God possesses nothing in the lofty heavens and in the earth more hidden than man's spirit."[20] The soul is thus part of the Spirit of God: "God is the origin of the human soul, the *asl* [!] (origin, foundation) of it."[21]

The soul's descent has become one of the prevailing themes of medieval religious and philosophical literature. Foreign in this world of matter and darkness, illusion and instability, the soul was placed in an unbearable, tragic situation. Rūmī, like many mystics before and after him, laments the woeful state of exile in which the soul exists in this world. The human condition in this world is described in terms of boundless pains of separation, exile, longing, and foreignness. In the opening lines of the *Mathnawī* Rūmī has given one of the most poignant expressions of these feelings, using the reed, severed from the reed-bed, as symbol of the soul cut off from her source. His proem, the opening poem, includes some of the best-known lines in Sufi poetry, and the heartfelt complaint expressed in them reverberates in the haunting music of the *ney*, the simple reed flute, to this very day:

> Listen to the reed how it tells a tale, complaining of separations—

> Saying, "Ever since I was parted from the reed-bed, my lament hath caused men and women to moan....
>
> Every one who is left far from his source wishes back the time when he was united with it....
>
> The reed is the comrade of every one who has been parted from a friend: its strains pierced our hearts."[22]

But the soul's descent from its lofty place of origin to reside within the human body is for a purpose. Its lamentable state of confinement in the dense and dark prison of the sub-lunar world is in accordance with God's design: to enable man to elevate himself from the limitation and temporality of his corporeal existence in the sub-lunar plane, and to return to the everlasting vastness of his celestial Source: "Life is a journeying back to God; it proceeds according [to] a process of evolution: 'To Him do we return.'"[23]

Thus, according to this ancient belief, the process of man's evolution does not end within the boundaries of the sub-lunar world. It ascends on through all the celestial spheres, towards the realm of the Divine Hiddenness. The soul was planted within man in order to awaken in him the memory and longing for his real home, and in order to help him prepare the organ, the vehicle of transportation, by which he will be able to make the journey back. This is the soul's *function*, and *need* is the organ which it creates. He who becomes fully awakened to his soul's need and to his primordial nearness to God, he who becomes *conscious* of his true desolate position in the hierarchy of being, only he will commit himself to the efforts and dangers of the journey back home.

> Awake awake, the sleepy season is over.
> The swallow flies, its wings radiate
> in the blazing sun.[24]

Rūmī grew up on these beliefs, which for centuries were shared by Muslims, Christians, Jews, and Pagans. Many of the philosophers of his time believed that in order to reach God one had to cultivate and purify the mind, the intellect. The intellect was highly revered as an instrument of spiritual contemplation, illumination, and spiritual communion with the Divine; it was believed to be a luminous spark of the Universal Intellect.

But Rūmī knew otherwise. He was trained in the tradition of lovers. This tradition gives due respect to the mind, but it knows from experience that the mind is useless when it comes to penetrating the mysteries of the affinity and love of soul and God. Mystics and lovers know that, in order to resurrect the soul's primordial proximity to God while on the earthly plane—and without this the soul will not be able to make its way back home—a faculty other than the mind is required, another, subtler body of perception and knowledge. This subtle body is the heart. In Rūmī's words:

> Here the intellect must remain silent, or else lead us astray. For the heart is with Him—indeed, the heart is He.[25]

The religion of love, more ancient than Islam but historically connected with Sufism, has always seen the human *heart,* not the mind, as the core of man's being and as the seat of that special faculty of perception *(baṣīra)* which perceives everything from the vantage point of the soul:

> Oh, (there is) many a one whose eye is awake and whose heart is asleep: what, in truth, should be seen by the eyes of creatures of water and clay?
>
> (But) he that keeps his heart awake—though the eye of his head may sleep, it (his heart) will open a hundred eyes.
>
> ... Be awake..., be a seeker of the (illumined) heart....
>
> But if your heart hath been awakened, sleep sound: thy (spiritual) eye is not absent from the seven (heavens) and the six (directions).[26]

The heart, which Divine Wisdom has designed for the function of communicating with the unseen, contains the subtle organs of perception as tiny seeds, as imperceptible potentialities. For the true function of the soul to come to fruition, these organs have to be awakened and cultivated. This is man's greatest task on earth. Not only does it take a lifetime of pain and effort, but it requires also the ability and resolution to face, with open eyes, fear, loneliness, and death.

Before a new organ of perception can be developed, the human being has to become *"dissatisfied with the present equipment of life."* He must be aware of a need which cannot be fulfilled by the old sense organs, a need which does not belong to the field of worldly desires, a hunger which cannot be met by satisfying the cravings of the appetite. This need has to grow in him to immense proportions, to acquire a devastating magnitude. Otherwise no substantial change from the state of dissatisfaction and disillusionment will take place, only shilly-shallying with fantasies about change. Addicts "know" this quality of need, but how to describe it to non-addicts?

Mrs. Tweedie tells the story of the fish who were separated from each other. When the primordial sea, which had covered the whole of the planet, became fragmented, and when pieces of dry land separated sea and sea, then some fish longed to reunite with their mates in other seas, and their longing was as great as their despair, because they did not have an organ by which to make the journey to that other bit of sea. They were stuck in an agonizing state, and were slowly dying of longing. Many centuries passed, perhaps millennia, but the painful longing did not subside. The fish were dying of it in their multitudes, day by day, year by year, eon by eon. Then one day, a miracle: a little tail, small feet, tiny claws to clutch the earth with. Some fish, with tremendous will power, managed to pull themselves up and out of the sea and onto the earth. Gradually they learned how to breathe, how to crawl, how to hop, how to walk, how to run, how to climb up mountains, how to climb down deep canyons. They could move from their little bit of sea to the vast ocean of their primordial being. But first they had to die of despair and longing. New organs were miraculously created because there was such a great need for them in the fish.

This fable does not reflect a biological observation, and it has little to do with Darwin's theory of evolution or with later theories of mutation. Most modern theories of evolution are based on a concept of mechanistic, accidental, blind sequences of events, while this theory of spiritual evolution is based on a revelatory, purposeful, *and painful* process, in which man collaborates *consciously* with the Divine Will. This process stems from the inner awakening to the fundamental need to return to the source, to the beginning. The awakening is kept in motion by the longing to *merge* into a higher plane of being.

"Every Being has its fixed place [in the Hierarchy of Creation]," writes Khalifa,

> and only in its fixed place it receives its share of Life and Perfection, which is communicated to it by a Being next higher to it, and which it has in turn to communicate to the one immediately lower than itself.[27]

> With Rūmī there is no development by chance variation. For him development consists in the creation of an ever-increasing need for expansion and by assimilation into a higher organism.[28]

In the essence of all created beings lies the need to become fuller, more complete, to develop into a higher, subtler species. This need becomes experienced as passionate love, as desire *('ishq)*, for that which is seen as more complete, more perfect, more luminous:

> All the processes of assimilation, growth and reproduction are manifestations of Love. Without Love there would have been no movement in the Universe.... The indeterminate matter is made to assume, by the inner force of love, various forms and rise higher and higher in the scale of beauty which is identical with perfection.[29]

In the following lines Rūmī sings the praises of the alchemical, transformative power of love (and note the punch-line):

> Through Love all that is bitter will be
> sweet.
> Through Love all that is copper will be
> gold.
> Through Love all dregs will turn to purest
> wine.
> Through Love all pain will turn to
> medicine.
> Through Love the dead will all become
> alive.
> Through Love the king will turn into a
> slave![30]

But what is love? In essence it is a state of *need*. The lover is in need of the beloved, since the beloved reflects something which the lover senses as *missing* in himself. The experience of love exposes a veiled, unconscious desire to unite with an idealized partner who will supply the bits missing in oneself. But Rūmī stresses that when this need awakens, rather than fulfilled it has to be *sustained*. Need, he argues, creates the primary vehicle of change, evolution, and growth. Without need there is no desire; without desire there is no movement. Therefore, to *perpetuate* the state of need is more conducive to change than to satisfy it.

> They say in the end, love is the want and need for something. Hence need is the root, and the needed thing is the branch. I say: After all, when you speak, you speak out of need. Your need brings your words

into existence.... So need is prior, and the words came into being from it.... The branch is always the goal—the tree's roots exist for the sake of its branches.[31]

So the noose of all existences is need: Man's instrument is the extent of his need.

So, oh needful man, quickly increase your need! Then the Sea of Bounty will gush forth in generosity.[32]

Where there are questions, answers will be given; where there are ships, water will flow.

Spend less time seeking water and acquire thirst! Then water will gush from above and below.[33]

In order for an evolutionary change to occur, the need has to be immense and conscious. Sometimes there is a need, but it's not strong enough; the longing for fullness has not yet reached sufficient intensity. The seeker can somehow survive, can learn to hide behind psychological defenses, so that the sense of emptiness is less painful. He suffers, but not enough; he is thirsty, but not yet dying of thirst. He is afraid of losing the relative comfort of a lukewarm, chronic state of frustration. But in *this* process, the Sufi teaching reiterates, only when the seeker reaches a state of despair beyond comfort or consolation will he be able to let go of his painful—yet familiar—patterns of survival. It is not easy to relinquish the familiar for a change whose consequences are unknown, unforeseeable. Therefore the need for change has to become as great as the need for air of a drowning man: "If you want Truth as badly as a drowning man wants air, you will realize it in a split-second."[34]

In the pursuit of this creative need, Rūmī's philosophy turns the logic of conventional pragmatism upside down. We need comfort, therefore we create comfortable things; we need warmth, so we create shelters, clothes, fire, heaters, air-conditioning; we become self-sufficient in order to alleviate the pain of want. Rūmī says: No, don't create anything to fill your emptiness; don't run away from the innate need of your soul.

> Remember what the soul wants,
> because in that, eternity
> is *wanting* our souls!
>
> Which is the meaning of the text,
> *They love That, and That loves them.*[35]

Don't rush to find a solution to your neediness, says Rūmī; stay with it, acknowledge it, live with it, *live it,* become more and more needy, more and more thirsty, colder, poorer, more helpless: "I shall cry and cry until the milk of compassion will boil up on Your lips." This wisdom, says Rūmī, is known to every infant:

> I wonder at this tiny infant who cries, and its mother gives it milk. If it should think, "What profit is there in crying? What is it that causes milk to come?"—then it would not receive any milk. But we see that it receives milk because of its crying.[36]

Growth comes out of need. When neediness becomes intolerable, then a new organ is created out of the needy one's own potentiality. This is the as-yet-unlived potentiality which the soul has planted in the heart. The inner organs of perception, the eyes and the ears of the heart, are given a new intelligence, a new outlook, a new direction, new possibilities. This is how Rūmī advocates it in his direct, passionate, provocative language:

> The cry was heard, "Oh seeker, come! Like a beggar, bounty is in need of beggars!"[37]

> God has given hunger to His elect so that they may become mighty lions.[38]

> Pain is an alchemy that renovates—where is indifference when pain intervenes?
> Beware, do not sigh coldly in your indifference! Seek pain! Seek pain, pain, pain![39]

> Where there is pain, the cure will come; where the land is low, water will run.
> If you want the water of mercy, go, become low! Then drink mercy's wine and become drunk![40]

> God's Mercy is water—it moves only towards low ground. I will become dust and Mercy's object in order to reach the All-Merciful.[41]

Besides the fear of pain there is another fear which has to be faced on the path of evolution: the fear of death. Every new form is born out of a dying old one:

> This process of dying to live is represented by organic life. Inorganic matter becomes organic by dying to itself and living a higher life in the plant and so can the plant be exalted into still higher life by dying unto itself and living in the animal. The whole course of evolution is an illustration of the principle of dying to live.[42]

Can the seeker easily give up the old organs in order to acquire new ones? Can he learn to surrender to the demand "Die before you die?"[43] "Die inside your life, and go on living," advocates Rūmī, paradoxically. His view of death as a prerequisite for birth encompasses the whole range of possibilities open to him who desires to live as a true human being. The soul of such a one knows no limits. In verses often quoted, he exclaims:

> I died as a mineral and became a plant
> I died as plant and rose to animal,
> I died as animal and I was man.
> Why should I fear? When was I less by dying?
> Yet once more I shall die as man, to soar
> With angels blest: but even from angelhood
> I must pass on: all except God doth perish.
> When I have sacrificed my angel soul,
> I shall become what no mind e'er conceived.
> Oh, let me not exist! for Non-existence
> Proclaims in organ tones, "To Him we shall return".[44]

The soul ascends the ladder of evolution with the power of love. On every step it is reminded of the vast, free spaces of *home* where the Beloved abides. The remembrance of the old, forgotten taste of the homeland, the real homeland, gives the soul the courage to die to the known and to leap into the unknown. The lament of separation then turns into a song of jubilation:

How should the soul not take wings
  when from the Glory of God
It hears a sweet, kindly call:
  "Why are you here, soul? Arise!"
How should a fish not leap fast
  into the sea from dry land
When from the ocean so cool
  the sound of the waves reached its ear?
How should the falcon not fly
  back to his king from the hunt
When from the falconer's drum
  it hears the call: "Oh, come back!"?
Why should not every Sufi
  begin to dance atom-like
Around the Sun of duration
  that saves from impermanence?
What graciousness and what beauty!
  What life-bestowing! What grace!...
Oh fly, oh fly, O my soul-bird,
  fly to your primordial home![45]

The willingness to sustain the need, or poverty, of the heart has to be made conscious; there has to be a conscious readiness to endure pain, a willingness to pay the price of evolution. The suffering the seeker is bound to encounter on the soul's journey has to be intentional and conscious. But one cannot overcome the fear of suffering and dying by oneself alone. For the soul's need to surface into full consciousness, the seeker has to be under the influence of a higher being. Alone, he may glimpse *what it is that the soul wants*, but it is almost impossible for these glimpses to ignite fully the sacred fire within. For such an ignition to take place one needs a sun, a *shams,* someone who is nearer the Truth, with whom one shall fall in love, and who will expose that which is fundamentally wanted.

Rūmī, we saw, talks about the desire to develop into a higher species out of love for that species: the moon falls in love with the sun *(shams)*; Rūmī falls in love with his own Shams. When Rūmī met Shams ad-Din of Tabriz, he immediately knew, in a flash, all that he had unconsciously longed to know all along.[46] Shams, the Complete Man, *al-insān al-kāmil,* compared with whom all things fade as a mirage, was for him a whiff of Reality, a scent of that Divine Truth, as real and substantial as it is elusive and mercurial. There is another scheme of things which belongs to that type of man who has attained the state of total poverty and freedom. In this state there are no compromises; he is pure, empty, translucent, one-pointed. Rūmī had these qualities within him, but in an embryonic, potential form. He *needed* this encounter with Shams; it hit him so brutally that he immediately awoke to his own power, his own truth. From that moment on, the old Rūmī died. He had to die. In the face of Reality reflected in Shams, nothing else mattered; everything else was eclipsed, banal, empty. The choice, if there was any, was either this or nothing. His disciples were jealous; they were inwardly dying, and were plotting murder out of jealousy. There can be no fiercer jealousy than what they experienced. Mevlānā, their own light, had left them. They had nothing to do with that wandering, ragged Dervish who completely took over their master. They could do nothing but witness how he had taken away *their* light.

When the desire for the loved one is total, everything devoid of him becomes boring, empty, dead. Apathy takes over. Anyone who has ever experienced falling in love knows this simple and profound truth. When the loved one is around, there is a sense of fullness; everything, even trivialities, becomes full of meaning: every gesture, every turning of the head, every sound, every footstep. But then the beloved is taken away, and everything becomes dull and boring. Everyone who has gone through the early intimations of falling in love knows these feelings. And this is not yet passion, not just yet, only a sense of the fullness of meaning, of an imminent potency which makes existence meaningful, worthwhile, full of sense and sensuality. One lives for this experience; everything else exists only in order to fill the emptiness which the absence of this experience creates.

Now this is so, says Rūmī, on every level of being. Not just human beings live in order to experience the *aliveness*, the fullness of being which comes through love; all things live for love. Atoms, flint stones, pieces of straw, leaves, dogs and butterflies, clouds, little children, angels, galaxies—all are in a constant state of agitation because of the pull of love:

> God's wisdom made us lovers of one another.
> In fact, all the particles of the world
> are in love and looking for lovers.
>
> Pieces of straw tremble
> in the presence of amber.
> We tremble like iron filings
> welcoming the magnet....

The desire of each lover is
that the work of the other be perfected.
By this man-and-woman cooperation,
the world gets preserved.
Generation occurs....
Every part of the cosmos draws toward its mate.[47]

The goal of the attraction for the higher and more perfect, says Rūmī, is procreation. Not the instinctual, chronological line of procreation, but that which marks a stage on the upward journey home. Every new generation that comes into being creates another rung on the evolutionary ladder. Every step on the ladder of conscious evolution emerges from an *awakening* to the beauty of the loved one. Loving, we long to unite with the beloved; desiring, we desire to *become* the beloved. This is the pinnacle of the inner journey, and Rūmī's eloquence proclaims this attainment triumphantly:

> For a time you were the four elements, for a time an animal. Now you have been a spirit, so become the Beloved! Become the Beloved![48]

> When a mineral turns its face toward the plant kingdom, life grows up from the tree of its good fortune.
>
> Every plant that turns toward the spirit drinks from the fountain of life, like Khidr.
>
> Then when the spirit turns toward the Beloved, it spreads its bedroll in everlasting life.[49]

Every fine therapist, every sensitive schoolteacher, knows how powerful love is for healing and growth. In therapy the patient falls in love with the therapist, whatever shape this love takes. In school, pupils are attracted to the teacher more than to the subject taught. Sometimes such an early attraction shapes our life for years to come, and is very fruitful. We learn and make progress through *inspiration,* through *attraction.* Through inspiration and attraction we become ready to exert ourselves, willingly, in the effort of the therapeutic process, or the effort of mastering a subject, or training for a profession, or committing ourselves to the hardships of the mystical path.

But who inspires? He who is inspired. Who creates a desirous passion in us? He who is himself a passionate lover. All of creation is an ascending ladder made of lovers and loved ones. Ultimately, in the whole of creation there are only lover and Beloved.[50]

> Indeed, no lover seeks union without his beloved seeking him....
>
> When the lightning of love for the loved one flashes in *this* heart, know that there is also love in *that* heart.
>
> When love for God has doubled in your heart, without doubt God has love for you....
>
> This thirst in our souls is the attraction of the Water—we belong to It and It belongs to us.[51]

Rūmī teaches that behind the pains of separation, the loneliness of the dark night of the soul, the unrequited loves, the missed opportunities, behind all those ever changing stations of the battered heart, and through the repeated disappointments of earthly relationships, one gains access to the only love-experience which is unconditionally given, the love affair with the sacred within.

It is not easy to distinguish between the attraction which comes from sensual impulses and psychological neediness and the attraction which arises from the need of the soul. This is part of the muddle-up of being a human being. A human being is by definition a muddled-up, compound entity. Therefore it is very rare to have an experience of love purely from the soul's level. But the mystical teaching of evolution upholds that man is evolving towards that which he had been before. Here, in the clay body, man is not whole, he cannot be complete; yet in his depth he carries an image of wholeness and the seeds of completeness.

One of the impacts of a meeting with a *shams*, with one on a higher rung on the ladder of conscious evolution, is the awakening of remorse, repentance, *tawba.* A meeting with such a magnetic center can have, if one is ripe for the experience, a dramatic effect on one's psyche. Questions grab hold of one that won't let go: What have I done with my life? How have I messed it up so carelessly? How have I given up that which is most sacred in me? How did I neglect the noble function which is my true birthright?

It's hard to describe the intensity of this kind of remorse. It does not arise out of fear of confronting an authority figure, or a repentance in the wake of transgressing a religious commandment. Rather, it's a powerful, painful response to the sudden awakening of that substance, that faculty, that talent which one has ignored and slighted. Consider, for example, a person who used to be a competent horse-rider but then neglected his talent out of laziness or disregard. When he meets a rider who is free, noble, in tune with his horse, exhilarated, fulfilled, then remorse, more painful than envy, will rise in him. He realizes that he has neglected the perfection of a function which has been given to him as grace. He has not listened with his heart's ears to his inner need to cultivate and complete this function. When the seeker's soul comes in contact with a soul which has perfected itself, he repents his heedlessness, compromises, excuses. Some are terrified of such a meeting. It is a fear of being exposed, of being found out, like the fear of Adam and Eve in the Garden of Eden, who hid from God out of guilt, fear, and shame. One of the functions of a meeting with such a man or woman is to force these inhibiting but semi-conscious feelings into the open. Without the conscious effort of facing them, the alchemical process in which the dross is burnt away can't take place. This is part of the preparation for death *(al-isti'dad lil-mawt)*, the death of the old self. When the old self dies, like an old potato, the subtle organs can bud. The impact and consequence of such a meeting is one of the implications of the statement *"It is the function which creates the organ."*

Many years ago, in Gurdjieff's *Meetings with Remarkable Men*, I came across an account of an awakening which occurred as a result of a meeting with an evolved human being. This account made a deep impression on me. In many ways it has remained for me a signpost ever since. Here are a few passages from this account:

Far to the south arose the majestic snow-capped peak of the Elbruz, with the great chain of the Caucasian mountains.... Silence reigned all around. No one was on the mountain.... We sat down on a rock and began to eat.... Suddenly my glance rested on the face of Professor Skridlov and I saw that tears were streaming from his eyes.

'What's the matter, old fellow?' I asked him.

'Nothing', he answered, drying his eyes, and then added:

'...What has just happened, has happened to me many times during this period. It is very difficult to explain what takes place in me when I see or hear anything majestic which allows no doubt that it proceeds from the actualization of Our Maker Creator. Each time, my tears flow of themselves. I weep, that is to say, it weeps in me, not from grief, no, but as if from tenderness. I became so, gradually, after meeting Father Giovanni, whom you remember we met together in Kafiristan, to my worldly misfortune.

'After that meeting my whole inner and outer world became for me quite different.... There took place, as it were by itself, a revaluation of all values.

'Before that meeting, I was a man wholly engrossed in my own personal interests and pleasures, and also in the interests of my children. I was always occupied with thoughts of how best to satisfy my needs and the needs of my children.... All my manifestations and experiencings flowed from my vanity. The meeting with Father Giovanni killed all this, and from then on there gradually arose in me that "something" which has brought the whole of me to the unshakeable conviction that, apart from the vanities of life, there exists a "something else" which must be the aim and ideal of every more or less thinking man, and that it is only this something else which may make a man really happy and give him real values, instead of the illusory "goods" with which in ordinary life he is always and in everything full.[52]

When the soul awakens, all values change. All is seen now from the soul's vantage point. Every art form, anything we create, if it lacks that dimension of attraction to a superior sun, becomes temporal, boring, and self-indulging. Sufis say, "For the Sufi only the best is good enough: best clothes, best food, best experiences, the best Friend." Behind this statement lies a commitment that sooner or later every sincere seeker must make: to strive for the flowering and maturation of the very best in him, in her, to dedicate his inner as well as his outer life to the best functioning of the soul which, if God so wills, will create the organ with which to live wholly as a complete human being.

Notes

Bibliography

Index

Notes

Chapter 1, THE NICHE OF LIGHT, pages 1-22

1. Rūmī, *Mathnawī,* II, 1157, quoted in Eva de Vitray-Meyerovitch, *Rûmî and Sufism,* p. 88.

2. Ismail Hakki Bursevi's translation of Ibn al-'Arabī, *Kernel of Kernel,* p. 45.

3. Al-Qushayrī, *Ar-Risāla,* p. 35 (trans. SS, slightly abridged).

4. Al-Ḥakīm at-Tirmidhī, *Nawādir al-uṣūl,* p. 258.

5. Al-Ḥakīm at-Tirmidhī, *Ghawr al-umūr,* fols. 42b-43a.

6. Al-Ḥakīm at-Tirmidhī, *Nawādir al-uṣūl,* p. 338; see also *Masā'il ahl Sarakhs,* p. 165 (Arabic text).

7. Al-Ḥakīm at-Tirmidhī, *Manāzil al-'ibād,* fol. 228b.

8. Al-Ḥakīm at-Tirmidhī, *Kitāb ar-riyāḍa,* p. 71. (Passages from at-Tirmidhī's works trans. and paraphrased SS.)

9. *Bayān al-farq bayna aṣ-ṣadr wal-qalb wal-fu'ād wal-lubb,* pp. 35 ff.

10. *Ḥabb,* seed, is etymologically and semantically linked with *ḥubb* and *maḥabba*—Arabic for love. Al-Qushayrī writes: "It is said that 'love' *(maḥabba)* derives from 'seed' *(ḥabb),* for the seed of the heart is that which gives it vigor.... Love is named *ḥubb* because it is the marrow *(lubāb)* of life"; see *Ar-Risāla,* p. 190. On the different "stations of the hearts" according to Abū al-Ḥusayn an-Nūrī, a 9th- and 10th-century mystic from Baghdād, see Schimmel, *Mystical Dimensions of Islam,* pp. 60f.

11. 'Aṭṭār, *The Conference of the Birds,* pp. 55-6 (ll. 1152ff.).

12. See *Kitāb ar-riyāḍa wa-adab an-nafs,* pp. 116ff. For the *ḥadīth* "God holds the heart between two of His fingers," see Schimmel, *Mystical Dimensions of Islam,* p. 197.

13. For this term and the paradox of freedom in slavehood, see below, ch. 2 (Effort), p. 31.

14. As-Sulamī, *Faṣl fī ghalaṭāt aṣ-ṣūfiyya* (Chapter on the errors of the Sufis), p. 332 (trans. SS).

15. Ibn al-'Arabī, *Al-Futūḥāt al-makiyya,* II, 113.33, quoted in Chittick, *The Sufi Path of Knowledge,* p. 109 (emphasis SS).

16. On the ultimate *annihilation* in a state of *colorlessness* and *featurelessness,* see below, ch. 7 (Color), pp. 155-63.
17. 'Abd al-Qādir al-Jīlānī is the eponym of one of the early Sufi paths *(ṭuruq),* the Qādiriyya; on him and on the *ṭarīqa* which bears his name, see J. S. Trimingham, *The Sufi Orders in Islam,* pp. 40ff.
18. *The Secret of Secrets,* trans. Shaykh Tosun Bayrak al-Jerrahi al-Halveti, p. 87.
19. *The Koran Interpreted,* pp. 356-7.
20. 'Abd al-Qādir al-Jīlānī, *The Secret of Secrets,* p. xlvii.
21. 'Abd al-Qādir al-Jīlānī, *The Secret of Secrets,* pp. xlvii-xlviii.
22. Quoted in Corbin, *The Man of Light in Iranian Sufism,* pp. 72, 73.
23. Quoted in Corbin, *The Man of Light in Iranian Sufism,* p. 73 (emphasis SS).
24. Al-Qushayrī, *Ar-Risāla,* p. 31.
25. *Kitāb ilā Muḥammad ibn al-Faḍl al-Balkhī,* Ms. Leipzig 212, fol. 15b.
26. I. Tweedie, *Daughter of Fire,* pp. 266-7.
27. On *ḥāl* as synonymous also with *lawn,* color, see below, ch. 7 (Color), pp. 149ff.
28. The Arabic text reads: *wa-amma wajd aṣ-ṣūfiyya fa-muṣādafat al-ghayb bil-ghayb;* see *Ādāb al-mulūk,* ed. Bernd Radtke, p.68, l. 19 (trans. SS).
29. Rūmī, *Dīvān-i Kebīr,* verse 274, p. 57.
30. 'Aṭṭār, *The Conference of the Birds,* p. 54.
31. A fine study dedicated to Sufi *shaṭaḥāt* is Carl Ernst's *Words of Ecstasy in Sufism;* see especially Part I, ch. B/1: "Selfhood," pp. 25-8.
32. Quoted in Carl Ernst, *Words of Ecstasy,* p. 27. On Abū Yazīd's ecstatic exclamations, see also Schimmel, *Mystical Dimensions of Islam,* p. 49. Compare with Rūmī's powerful version "Bestami" in *Delicious Laughter,* versions Coleman Barks, pp. 30-31 *(Mathnawī,* IV, 2102-2148).
33. See Carl Ernst, *Words of Ecstasy,* p. 20. See also Schimmel, *Mystical Dimensions of Islam,* pp. 62-9 (and also index). See also Louis Massignon, *The Passion of al-Ḥallāj,* vol. I, pp. 126ff.; and Massignon, *Hallāj, Mystic and Martyr,* pp. 64ff. Compare with 'Aṭṭār's poetic account in *The Conference of the Birds,* pp. 220-22.

34. Michaela Özelsel, *Forty Days, The Diary of a Traditional Solitary Sufi Retreat,* pp. 93-4.
35. For this *ḥadīth qudsī* (an extra-Qur'ānic saying attributed to Allāh), see Schimmel, *Mystical Dimensions of Islam,* p. 190.
36. 'Abd al-Qādir al-Jīlānī, *The Secret of Secrets,* p. 85.

Chapter 2, EFFORT AND THE EFFORTLESS PATH, pages 23-45

1. Quoted in Chittick, *The Sufi Path of Knowledge,* p. 120.
2. Quoted in Özelsel, *Forty Days,* p. 92.
3. Psychological terminology can be confusing when the same term is used with different connotations. *Nafs* can sometimes stand for "soul," especially in philosophical texts, in which instance it is viewed as a subtle, lofty entity which resides within the human heart or mind. In Sufi texts, however, more often than not, *nafs* has a pejorative connotation. "Self" as a rendering of *nafs* should *not* be confused with the way Self is understood in Analytical Psychology: "An archetypal image of man's fullest potential.... A unifying principle within the human psyche [which] occupies the central position of authority in relation to psychological life, and therefore, the destiny of the individual"; see Andrew Samuels, *A Critical Dictionary of Jungian Analysis,* p. 135.
4. In a famous *ḥadīth* the Prophet Muḥammad says: "The worst enemy you have is the *nafs* between your sides"; see Schimmel, *Mystical Dimensions of Islam,* p. 112.
5. I wish to extend my gratitude to N. for his poems.
6. This well-known phrase was coined by Plotinus, a mystical philosopher from Late Antiquity, whose so-called Neoplatonic philosophy inspired mystics as well as philosophers in Late Antiquity and in the Middle Ages.
7. See, e.g., Schimmel, *Mystical Dimensions of Islam,* p. 189; see also below, ch. 9 (Function), p. 188. For a wide perspective on ancient and medieval sources for this and similar formulations of the dictum *Know thyself!,* see Alexander Altmann, "The Delphic Maxim in Medieval Islam and Judaism," pp. 1-40.
8. See Hujwīrī, *Kashf al-Maḥjūb,* p. 32.

9. Al-Qushayrī, *Ar-Risāla,* p. 47 (trans. SS).
10. Al-Hujwīrī, *Kashf al-Maḥjūb,* p. 181 (emphasis SS).
11. For the intricate psychology of *riyā'* in more detail, see Sara Sviri, "Ḥakīm Tirmidhī and the *Malāmatī* Movement in Early Sufism" in *Classical Persian Sufism: from its Origins to Rūmī,* pp. 583-613; see also Sviri, "The *Mysterium Coniunctionis* and the 'Yo-Yo Syndrome': From Polarity to Oneness in Sufi Psychology" in *Jung and the Monotheisms,* p. 202.
12. Michaela Özelsel, *Forty Days,* pp. 56-7.
13. Translation SS, based on Radtke (ed.), *Sīrat al-awliyā',* pp. 14-17, paras. 26-32 (Arabic text).
14. See also Qur'ān 3:54, 13:42.
15. Tweedie, *Daughter of Fire,* p. 221. For Mrs. Tweedie's diary as a Sufi document describing the teacher-disciple relationship, see Sviri, "*Daughter of Fire* by Irina Tweedie: Documentation and Experiences of a Modern Naqshbandi Sufi" in Puttick and Clarke (eds.), *Women As Teachers and Disciples in Traditional and New Religions,* pp. 77-89.
16. The above quotations have been culled and paraphrased from Massignon, *The Passion of al-Ḥallāj,* vol. 3, pp. 113-16.
17. Rūmī, *Dīwān-i Shams-i Tabrīzī,* no. 1723, quoted in Chittick, *The Sufi Path of Love,* p. 345.
18. Bhai Sahib in Tweedie, *Daughter of Fire,* p. 187.
19. Dhū 'l-Faqār is the name of the sword of 'Alī, the Prophet's son-in-law and the fourth Caliph; it symbolizes death and martyrdom.
20. Rūmī, *Mystical Poems 1-200,* trans. A. J. Arberry, pp. 116-17 (no. 139/1095).
21. I wish to extend my gratitude to Margaret Sampson for this insight.
22. For more on al-Ḥallāj's three phases, see Massignon, *The Passion of al-Hallāj* (trans. H. Mason), vol. 3, pp. 40-41.
23. On these Qur'ānic attributes of *nafs* in Sufi psychology, see Schimmel, *Mystical Dimensions of Islam,* p. 112.
24. For a statement made by al-Junayd in which he quotes this verse to describe a state of sobriety in ecstasy, see below, ch. 6 *(Dhikr),* pp. 127-8.
25. In a well-known *ḥadīth* Moses asks God: "Oh, God, who are your Friends *(awliyā')*?" God answers: "Those who are remembered when I am remembered, and when they are

remembered, I am remembered." See, e.g., al-Ḥakīm at-Tirmidhī, *Sīrat al-awliyā'*, p. 57, para. 80 (Arabic text; trans. SS).

26. For this *ḥadīth,* known as *ḥadīth an-nawāfil (nawāfil:* supererogatory acts of worship), see Schimmel, *Mystical Dimensions of Islam,* pp. 43, 133, 144, 277.

27. For the mystical state of *'ayn al-jam',* see also above, ch. 1 (Niche), p. 11.

28. Quoted in Massignon, *The Passion of al-Hallāj,* pp. 41-3.

Chapter 3, DREAMS AND DESTINY, pages 46-76

1. Samuel Taylor Coleridge, *Biographica Literaria or Biographical Sketches of My Literary Life and Opinions,* ed. G. Watson, p. 176 (with thanks to Jeni Couzyn for this quotation).

2. Thomas Merton, *The Mystic Life,* a series of talks on Sufism given at Gethsemani Monastery, unpublished; quoted in Terry Graham, "Sufism: the 'Strange Subject'. Thomas Merton's Views on Sufism" in *SUFI,* issue no. 30, Summer 1996, p. 39.

3. *Al-Futūḥāt al-makkīyya,* II, 684.4, quoted in William Chittick, *The Sufi Path of Knowledge,* p. 154 (emphasis SS).

4. Carl G. Jung, *The Archetypes and the Collective Unconscious, Collected Works* vol. 9i, p. 283, para. 506.

5. Jung, *The Structure and Dynamics of the Psyche, Collected Works* vol. 8, p. 348, para. 673.

6. Jung, *The Structure and Dynamics of the Psyche,* p. 349, para. 673.

7. Jung, *The Structure and Dynamics of the Psyche,* p. 190, para. 388.

8. Jung, *The Structure and Dynamics of the Psyche,* p. 190, para. 388.

9. Gerhard Adler, *Dynamics of the Self,* pp. 34ff.

10. Rūmī, *Mathnawī,* I, 3157-3168, in Coleman Barks (versions), *Delicious Laughter,* pp. 94-5. Note Joseph's words to his brothers, according to the Qur'ān, when they reunite in Egypt: "This is the interpretation of my old dream. God has fulfilled it" (12:101).

11. Henri Corbin, who studied imagination in Islamic mystical philosophy, writes: "This imagination does not

construct something unreal, but *unveils* the hidden reality"; see his *Spiritual Body and Celestial Earth,* p. 12 (emphasis HC). See also Corbin, *Creative Imagination in the Ṣūfism of Ibn 'Arabī,* "Introduction," pp. 6ff. On imagination and its boundaries, see below, ch. 7 (Color), pp. 150ff.

12. This Qur'ānic verse reads: "He let forth the two seas that meet together, between them a barrier they do not overpass"; see *The Koran Interpreted,* p. 557.

13. Quoted in Chittick, *The Sufi Path of Knowledge,* p. 117.

14. Quoted in Chittick, *The Sufi Path of Knowledge,* p. 115. On the world of the imaginal as *barzakh,* see Corbin, *Avicenna and the Visionary Recital,* e.g., p. 161: "...changing the appearances of things, walking on water, climbing Mount Qāf... are psychic events whose scene and action are set in neither the sensible nor the intelligible worlds, but in the intermediate world of the Imaginable, the *'ālam al-mithāl...* the *place* of all visionary recitals. Now, this world is also called *barzakh* as interval extending between the intelligible and the sensible. *It is the world in which spirits are corporealized and bodies spiritualized*" (emphasis SS).

15. Quoted in Chittick, *The Sufi Path of Knowledge,* p. 118.

16. Ibn al-'Arabī relates this expression to a dictum attributed to the 9th-century mystic Abū Sa'īd al-Kharrāz who, when asked, "Through what have you known God?" answered: "Through the fact that He brings opposites together"; see Chittick, *The Sufi Path of Knowledge,* p. 115. See also Corbin, *Creative Imagination in the Ṣufism of Ibn 'Arabī,* pp. 188, 209.

17. On the *coincidence of opposites* in Sufism, see Sara Sviri, "Between Fear and Hope: On the Coincidence of Opposites in Islamic Mysticism," pp. 316-49.

18. Quoted in Chittick, *The Sufi Path of Knowledge,* p. 116.

19. Quoted in Chittick, *The Sufi Path of Knowledge,* p. 119.

20. Quoted in Chittick, *The Sufi Path of Knowledge,* p. 119 (emphasis SS).

21. Quoted in Chittick, *The Sufi Path of Knowledge,* p. 119.

22. The following paragraphs have been culled from Ibn al-'Arabī, *Fuṣūṣ al-ḥikam,* pp. 99ff. (trans. SS).

23. On this *ḥadīth,* see Schimmel, *Mystical Dimensions of Islam,* pp. 382-3. See also below, ch. 4 (Khiḍr), p. 90.

24. For canonical sources for this *ḥadīth,* see Chittick, *The*

Sufi Path of Knowledge, p. 396, n. 6.

25. On the form of Diḥyā al-Kalbī, a handsome Arab youth, which the angel Gabriel assumed in the Prophet's vision, see Corbin, *Creative Imagination,* pp. 217, 223-4.

26. Ibn al-'Arabī, *Fuṣūṣ al-ḥikam,* pp. 99ff. (trans. SS).

27. See al-Ḥakīm at-Tirmidhī, *Buduww sha'n,* pp. 315-43. See also Radtke, "*Tirmiḏiāna Minora,*" pp. 242-98.

28. See al-Hujwīrī, *Kashf al-Maḥjūb,* pp. 210ff. See also Chodkiewicz, *Seal of the Saints,* pp. 27-32.

29. See Radtke (ed.), *Sīrat al-awliyā',* pp. 66-7 (Arabic text; trans. SS).

30. For a dream of Ibn al-'Arabī's wife, Maryam, recorded by her husband, see Ralph Austin, *Sufis of Andalusia,* pp. 22-3.

31. English translation of all passages from at-Tirmidhī's autobiography by Sara Sviri, based on *Buduww sha'n,* ed. Muhammad Khalid Masud, *Islamic Studies* 4 (1965), pp. 315-43.

32. The fact that at-Tirmidhī wakes up sitting in the same position as in the dream may suggest that the dreaming took place in a mosque. If this be so, it may reflect a kind of *istikhāra,* an Islamic practice which echoes the ancient ritual of dream incubation.

33. For the *ḥadīth* "He who sees me in a dream sees [really] me, for Satan cannot embody me" *(man ra'ānī fī 'l-manām fa-qad ra'ānī fa-inna 'sh-shayṭān lā yastaṭī'u an yatamaththala bī),* see al-Ḥakīm at-Tirmidhī, *Nawādir al-uṣūl,* p. 116.

34. The text reads *'afā 'annī* , which may also be rendered "He has released me, He has set me free."

35. See Radtke, "The Concept of *Wilāya* in Early Sufism," p. 490.

36. On at-Tirmidhī's link with Khiḍr in later accounts of his life, see 'Aṭṭār, *Muslim Saints and Mystics,* pp. 244-6. See also below, ch. 4 (Khiḍr), pp. 100f.

37. Qur'ān 21:47.

38. "The Inhabited House," *al-bayt al-ma'mūr,* reference to Qur'ān 52:4.

39. See Hujwīrī, *Kashf al-Maḥjūb,* p. 214. See also Radtke, *Al-Ḥakīm at-Tirmiḏī,* pp. 91ff.

Chapter 4, WHERE THE TWO SEAS MEET, pages 77-101

1. Hafeẓ, "The Song of Spring," adapted from *Dance of Life,* pp. 12, 14, 67.
2. On *waqt, ḥāl,* and the Sufi concept of the mystical "now," see also above, ch. 1 (Niche), pp. 18ff.
3. Some of the information contained in the following passages has been culled from the article "al-KHAḌIR" in *The Shorter Encyclopaedia of Islam,* pp. 232ff., as well as from Stephanie Dalley (trans.), *Myths from Mesopotamia.*
4. *The Koran Interpreted,* Sūra 18:60-82, pp. 295-8.
5. *The Koran Interpreted,* Sūra 18:64, p. 296.
6. *The Koran Interpreted,* Sūra 18:60-64, pp. 295-6 (emphasis SS).
7. Needless to say that this attempt at identifying *Khiḍr* with Andreas is only one of many. For other renditions, see *The Shorter Encyclopaedia of Islam,* pp. 232ff.
8. How this attribute might link Khiḍr and Dhū an-Nūn, the famous 9th-century mystic from Egypt, is not clear, but the similarity is worth noting. It is also interesting to note that the name of Moses' page is Joshua bin Nūn.
9. *Mushkil gushā* is a Persian idiom which means "the remover of obstacles." It has become one of the attributes of the Pole *(quṭb),* whose energy, which emanates from Divine mercy, removes all the obstacles which the sincere seeker encounters on the path. Each generation is believed to have its own *mushkil gushā.* On the term *muḍṭarr,* see above, ch. 2 (Effort), pp. 24ff.
10. *Kalīm Allāh,* he who spoke with God, is the title of Moses in Muslim prophetology. This is based on Qur'ān 4:162, which echoes the Bible, Numbers 12:8.
11. Rūmī, *Mathnawī,* III, 1962ff., trans. R. A. Nicholson, pp. 109-10.
12. On this term, see above, ch. 3 (Dreams), p. 56 and n. 16.
13. *The Koran Interpreted,* Sūra 55:26, p. 558.
14. In Arabic the notion of poverty, need, or lack is designated by the word *faqr,* from which derives *faqīr,* a poor man. It is an attribute of the Sufi who lives in total need of the Beloved. On need and poverty, see also below, ch. 9 (Function).

15. Traditionally, *tawba* is the first "station" *(maqām)* on the Sufi path. Sufi manuals offer various definitions for *tawba,* which, in the normative sense of the term, means "to repent of sins." Thus, for example, Abū al-Ḥusayn an-Nūrī says: "*Tawba* means to withdraw from all things other than God" *(at-tawba: an tatūba min kulli shay'in siwā allāh).* Quoted in as-Sarrāj, *Kitāb al-luma',* p. 68 (trans. SS).

16. Verses SS.

17. One of the many words for "rain" in Arabic is *ghawth,* which literally means help, rescue, the one who rescues. From here derives *ghawth* as an attribute of the spiritual teacher and the Pole.

18. Tweedie, *Daughter of Fire,* p. x. "Die before you die" is an old Sufi tradition which goes back to the Prophet Muḥammad and can be traced back to even older Jewish sources. For this *ḥadīth* in the Sufi tradition, see Schimmel, *Mystical Dimensions of Islam,* pp. 70, 135.

19. On the "Cosmic North," see Henri Corbin, *The Man of Light in Iranian Sufism,* ch. III, pp. 39-60 (and see also index).

20. See *The Koran Interpreted,* Sūra 18:65-78, pp. 296-7.

21. See *The Koran Interpreted,* Sūra 18:79-82, pp. 297-8.

22. See also below, ch. 6 (Dhikr), pp. 137f.

23. On the *ḥadīth* "The breath of the Merciful comes to me from Yemen," see Schimmel, *Mystical Dimensions of Islam,* pp. 28-9. For more information on Uways al-Qaranī and the *uwaysiyyūn,* see al-Hujwīrī, *Kashf al-Maḥjūb*, pp. 83-4. See also Schimmel, *Mystical Dimensions,* p. 125. See also Corbin, *Creative Imagination in the Ṣūfism of Ibn 'Arabī,* pp. 32-3.

24. Based on Moḥammad Ebn-e Monavvar, *The Secrets of God's Mystical Oneness,* pp. 93-4.

25. 'Aṭṭār, *Muslim Saints and Mystics, Episodes from the Tadhkirat al-Auliyā' ('Memorial of the Saints'),* p. 244.

26. On at-Tirmidhī's link with Khiḍr through the dreams of his wife, see above, ch. 3 (Dreams), pp. 61-5.

27. 'Aṭṭār, *Muslim Saints and Mystics,* pp. 244-6.

Chapter 5, EROS AND THE MYSTICAL QUEST, pages 102-123

1. Quoted in Inayat Khan, *The Hand of Poetry,* trans. Coleman Barks, p. 39.
2. Rūmī, *Discourses,* quoted in Chittick, *The Sufi Path of Love,* p. 204.
3. Jeni Couzyn, *In the Skin House,* p. 53.
4. Tweedie, *Daughter of Fire,* p. 222.
5. Tweedie, *Daughter of Fire,* pp. 180-81.
6. *Khalq* means both "creation" in general and "human beings," "mankind," in particular.
7. See Plato, *Symposium,* trans. W. H. D. Rouse, pp. 85-9 (Aristophanes' speech).
8. *Al-Futūḥāt al-makiyya* II: 399.28, quoted in Chittick, *The Sufi Path of Knowledge,* p. 131.
9. *Al-Futūḥāt al-makiyya* III: 429.4, quoted in Chittick, *The Sufi Path of Knowledge,* p. 132.
10. *Al-Futūḥāt al-makiyya* I: 459.1, quoted in Chittick, *The Sufi Path of Knowledge,* p. 131.
11. *Al-Futūḥāt al-makiyya* II: 487.34, quoted in Chittick, *The Sufi Path of Knowledge,* p. 130.
12. *Al-Futūḥāt al-makiyya* II: 437.20, quoted in Chittick, *The Sufi Path of Knowledge,* p. 131.
13. *Al-Futūḥāt al-makiyya* II: 459.1, quoted in Chittick, *The Sufi Path of Knowledge,* p. 131.
14. *Al-Futūḥāt al-makiyya* II: 399.28, quoted in Chittick, *The Sufi Path of Knowledge,* p. 131 (emphasis SS).
15. *Al-Futūḥāt al-makiyya* II: 437.20, quoted in Chittick, *The Sufi Path of Knowledge,* p. 131.
16. The term *umm al-kitāb* is based on Qur'ān 43:4, which reads: "...and behold it is in the Essence of the Book, with Us; sublime indeed, wise"; see *The Koran Interpreted,* p. 505. See also *The Shorter Encyclopaedia of Islam,* p. 601.
17. The esoteric meaning and power of letters are an unmistakable aspect of Jewish mysticism. See, for instance, A. Kaplan, trans., *Sefer Yezira. The Book of Creation.* See also M. Idel, *Kabbalah New Perspectives,* pp. 97ff. For letter mysticism in Sufism, see Schimmel, *Mystical Dimensions of Islam,* Appendix 1, pp. 411-25.
18. Al-Ḥakīm at-Tirmidhī, *Nawādir al-uṣūl,* p. 212.

19. Tweedie, *Daughter of Fire,* p. 149.
20. *Al-Futūḥāt al-makiyya* II: 459.1, quoted in Chittick, *The Sufi Path of Knowledge,* p. 131.
21. Rūmī, *Discourses,* trans. A. J. Arberry, p. 87. The Divine Logos articulated in the creative Be! *(kun)* is based on several Qur'ānic verses, e.g. 2:117, 3:59, 6:73, 40:68.
22. Rūmī, *Discourses,* trans. A. J. Arberry, p. 87.
23. Rūmī, *Discourses,* trans. A. J. Arberry, p. 33.
24. Ibn al-'Arabī, *Bezels of Wisdom,* trans. R. W. J. Austin, p. 274, quoted in Austin, "The Sophianic Feminine in the Work of Ibn 'Arabī and Rumi," p. 239.
25. Quoted in Austin, "The Sophianic Feminine in the Work of Ibn 'Arabī and Rumi," p. 243.
26. Mahmud Shabistari, *The Secret Rose Garden,* trans. Florence Lederer, pp. 34-5.
27. Jeni Couzyn, *In the Skin House,* p. 44.
28. Rūmī, Quatrain 558, quoted in *Open Secret,* trans. John Moyne and Coleman Barks, p. 11.
29. Rūmī, Quatrain 1300, quoted in *Open Secret,* trans. John Moyne and Coleman Barks, p. 19.
30. Rūmī, Quatrain 1794, quoted in *Open Secret,* trans. John Moyne and Coleman Barks, p. 22.
31. 'Aṭṭār, *The Conference of the Birds,* p. 60 (ll. 1235-1258).
32. 'Aṭṭār, *The Conference of the Birds,* pp. 73-4 (ll. 1534-1576).
33. 'Aṭṭār, *The Conference of the Birds,* p. 75 (ll. 1577-1595).
34. Hafeẓ, *Love's Perfect Gift,* p. 63.
35. On this *ḥadīth (inna Allāha jamīl yuḥibbu 'l-jamāl),* see Schimmel, *Mystical Dimensions of Islam,* p. 291.
36. Ancient Jewish traditions *(midrash)* tell that when the women of Egypt, who were chopping vegetables, saw Joseph walking on the wall of the city, they became so stupefied by his beauty that they cut their fingers and were oblivious of pain. This is referred to also in the Qur'ān, 12:30-31, in a somewhat different version. For a Sufi interpretation of the women's oblivion, see al-Hujwīrī, *Kashf al-Maḥjūb,* p. 32.
37. Abdulrahman Jāmī, *The Book of Joseph and Zuleikha,* trans. Alexander Rogers, pp. 35-6.
38. Al-Qushayrī, *Ar-Risāla,* (Exhortation to Novices), p. 184 (trans. SS).

39. Culled, paraphrased, and collated from the following works by al-Ḥakīm at-Tirmidhī: *Aṣ-Ṣalāt wa-maqāṣiduhā* (On the Purpose of Prayer), pp. 20, 94-5, and *Kitāb ar-riyāḍa wa-adab an nafs* (The Training of the *Nafs)*, pp. 34ff., 92ff.

Chapter 6, DHIKR, pages 124-144

1. On the inner layers of the heart, see above, ch. 1 (Niche), pp. 5-8.
2. Rūmī, *Mathnawī,* I, 3154, quoted in Chittick, *The Sufi Path of Love,* p. 160.
3. Sahl ibn 'Abdallāh at-Tustarī was a 9th-century Sufi teacher close to the Baghdadi circle. On him, see Schimmel, *Mystical Dimensions of Islam,* pp. 55f. See also Gerhard Böwering, *The Mystical Vision of Existence in Classical Islam.*
4. Quoted in Schimmel, *Mystical Dimensions of Islam,* p. 169. For another version, told by 'Aṭṭār, see his *Ilāhī-nāma, Book of God,* trans. J. A. Boyle, Discourse VI, 8, pp. 105-6.
5. Quoted in A. H. Abdel-Kader, *The Life, Personality and Writing of al-Junayd,* p. 76.
6. Quoted in as-Sarrāj, *Kitab al-luma',* p. 49 (trans. SS).
7. Al-Kalābādhī, *The Doctrine of the Sufis,* trans. A. J. Arberry, pp. 166-7.
8. Michaela Özelsel, *Forty Days,* trans. A. Gaus, p. 19.
9. Rumi, *Mathnawī,* III, 2072-2076, quoted in Abdul Hakim, *Metaphysics of Rūmī,* p. 16.
10. On the cosmological concepts of "planes" and "spheres," see below, ch. 9 (Function), pp. 196-200.
11. Abū Naṣr as-Sarrāj, *Kitāb al-luma', Bāb 'ākhar fī tafsīr ḥikāya dhukirat 'an Abū Yazīd* (another chapter on the interpretation of an anecdote attributed to Abū Yazīd), p. 464 (trans. SS).
12. As-Sarrāj, *Kitāb al luma',* (another chapter on the interpretation of an anecdote attributed to Abū Yazīd), p. 466: *inna -l iltifāt wal-ishtighāl bil-mulāḥaẓa ilā -l-kawn wal-mamlaka khud'a ' inda wujūd ḥaqā'iq at-tafrīd wa-tajrīd at-tawḥīd* (trans. SS).
13. As-Sarraj, *Kitāb al-luma',* (another chapter on the interpretation of an anecdote attributed to Abū Yazīd), p. 467: *...'inda ahl an-nihāya ... al-iltifāt ilā ayyi shay'in siwā -llah*

khud'a (trans SS).

14. As-Sarrāj, *Kitāb al-luma', Bāb fī waṣf samā' al-murīdīn wal-mubtadī'in* (chapter describing the listening of novices), p. 358 (trans. SS).

15. Rūmī, *Dīwān,* 1647, quoted in Chittick, *The Sufi Path of Love,* p. 327.

16. On this aspect of the *nafs,* see above, ch. 2 (Effort), p. 29.

17. On other rules laid down by the Naqshbandi masters, see below, ch. 8 (Etiquette), pp. 169-73.

18. As-Sulamī, *Risālat al-malāmatiyya,* p. 104.

19. See Hasan Shushud, *Masters of Wisdom of Central Asia,* p. 26.

20. On this aspect of Khiḍr's work, see above, ch. 4 (Khiḍr), pp. 98-101. For more information on the Naqshbandi *dhikr,* see J. G. J. ter Haar, "The Naqshbandī Tradition in the Eyes of Aḥmad Sirhindī," in Gaborieaux, Popovic, and Zarcone (eds.), *Naqshbandis,* pp. 83-92.

21. *"Ud'ū rabbakum taḍarru'an wa-khufyatan."*

22. This anecdote is told with more detail in *Al-Anwār al-qudsiyya fī manāqib as-sāda an-Naqshbandīyya (The Sacred Lights in Praise of the Naqshbandi Masters),* pp. 111-12.

23. Tweedie, *Daughter of Fire,* p. 821.

24. Quoted in Hasan Shushud, *Masters of Wisdom of Central Asia,* p. 38.

25. On *tawajjuh,* see Schimmel, *Mystical Dimensions of Islam,* pp. 237, 366. See also M. Chodkiewicz, "Quelques aspects des techniques spirituelles dans la *ṭarīqa* Naqshbandiyya," in *Naqshbandis,* pp. 70ff.; and J. G. J. ter Haar, "The Naqshbandi Tradition," in *Naqshbandis,* pp. 86ff.

26. Ar-Rakhāwī, ed., *al-Anwār al-qudsiyya fī manāqib as-sāda an-Naqshbandīyya (The Sacred Lights in Praise of the Naqshbandi Masters),* p. 6.

27. *Al-Anwār al-qudsiyya fī manāqib as-sāda an-Naqshbandīyya,* p. 114.

28. *Al-Anwār al-qudsiyya fī manāqib as-sāda an-Naqshbandīyya,* p. 131.

29. For this *ḥadīth qudsī,* see Schimmel, *Mystical Dimensions of Islam,* p. 168.

Chapter 7, THE COLOR OF WATER, pages 145-163

1. Quoted in Inayat Khan, *The Hand of Poetry,* trans. Coleman Barks, p. 20.

2. 'Aṭṭār, *The Conference of the Birds,* p. 191.

3. On Abū Yazīd and his ecstatic *shaṭaḥāt,* see above, ch. 1 (Niche), p. 20.

4. As-Sarrāj, *Kitāb al-luma',* p. 57 (trans. SS). In al-Qushayrī, *Ar-Risāla,* p. 142, this statement is attributed to al-Junayd; see *Principles of Sufism,* trans. B. R. von Schlegell, p. 322.

5. An extraordinary phenomenon of a total loss of the ability to see colors is described by the neurologist Oliver Sacks; see "The Case of the Colorblind Painter" in *An Anthropologist on Mars,* pp. 3-41.

6. Jacques Lusseyran, *And There Was Light,* pp. 10-13.

7. See also above, ch. 1 (Niche), p. 18.

8. On the importance and function of imagination as the bridge *(barzakh)* between the two worlds in which the mystic lives, see above, ch. 3 (Dreams), pp. 55-7.

9. See Corbin, *The Man of Light in Iranian Sufism,* p. 78. Corbin, the French scholar and philosopher, developed his influential theory of the "imaginal," the *mundus imaginalis.* This, as has been discussed above (ch. 3), is the realm from which dream-images and visions emanate, a realm in which these images and visions have a concrete reality and are not merely the so-called figments of fantasy. Corbin's theory is based on his in-depth study of the teachings on imagination of Kubrā, Ibn al-'Arabī, and other medieval mystics and philosophers. On the *mundus imaginalis,* see also Corbin, "*Mundus Imaginalis* or the Imaginary and the Imaginal," in *Spring* (1972), pp. 1-19.

10. Quoted in Corbin, *The Man of Light in Iranian Sufism,* pp. 77-8 (emphasis HC).

11. Quoted in Corbin, *The Man of Light in Iranian Sufism,* p. 78.

12. Quoted in Corbin, *The Man of Light in Iranian Sufism,* pp. 79-80.

13. Ibn 'Aṭā' Allāh, *The Book of Wisdom,* trans. V. Danner, p. 85.

14. Ibn 'Aṭā' Allāh, *The Book of Wisdom,* p. 68.

15. Tweedie, *Daughter of Fire,* p. 187.

16. Quoted in Chittick, *The Sufi Path of Knowledge,* p. 376.
17. Al-Kalābādhī, *The Doctrine of the Sufis,* trans. A. J. Arberry, pp. 126-7.
18. *The Conference of the Birds,* p. 166.
19. *The Conference of the Birds,* p. 205.
20. *The Conference of the Birds,* p. 212.
21. *The Conference of the Birds,* p. 213.
22. *The Conference of the Birds,* p. 220.
23. Tweedie, *Daughter of Fire,* p. 729.
24. Tweedie, *Daughter of Fire,* p. 631. On the state of *jam',* see above, ch. 1 (Niche), and note in particular the quote from al-Qushayrī on p. 2 (n. 3).
25. On Moses' meeting with Khiḍr, see above, ch. 4 (Khiḍr), pp. 95-7.
26. Quoted in Corbin, *The Man of Light in Iranian Sufism,* p. 112.
27. This conventional interpolation means that, while the author offers his commentary, he humbly makes the reservation that only God knows the truth.
28. As-Sarrāj, *Kitāb al-luma',* p. 57 (trans. SS).
29. *Al-Anwār al-qudsiyya fī manāqib as-sāda an-Naqshbandiyya,* p.131. See also Hasan Shushud, *Masters of Wisdom of Central Asia,* p. 44. See also above, ch. 6 (Dhikr), p. 142.

Chapter 8, SUFI ETHICS AND ETIQUETTE,
pages 164-186

1. Colin Thubron, *The Lost Heart of Asia,* p. 105.
2. As-Sulamī, *The Way of Sufi Chivalry,* p. 37.
3. Books on *ādāb* available in English for further reference are: al-Ghazzālī, *On the Duties of Brotherhood,* trans. M. Holland; al-Hujwīrī, *Kashf al-Maḥjūb,* trans. R. A. Nicholson, ch. XXIII, pp. 334-66; al-Qushayrī, *Principles of Sufism,* trans. B. R. von Schlegell, ch. 40, pp. 308-15; as-Suhrawardī, Abū Najīb, *A Sufi Rule for Novices,* trans. M. Milson; as-Suhrawardī, 'Umar ibn Muḥammad, *The 'Awārif al-ma'ārif,* trans. W. Clarke, esp. pp. 30-48; as-Sulamī, *The Way of Sufi Chivalry,* trans. Tosun Bayrak al-Jerrahi.
4. This saying is attributed by al-Qushayrī to al-Kattānī; see *Ar-Risāla,* (Chapter on Sufism), p. 127. Note also the

following saying recorded by al-Qushayrī: "Sufism consists of noble characteristics shown at a noble time by a noble man among noble people," quoted in *Principles of Sufism,* p. 303.

5. Al-Hujwīrī, *Kashf al-Maḥjūb,* p. 39.

6. Al-Hujwīrī, *Kashf al-Maḥjūb,* p. 39.

7. In the Arabic text the word for "man," *'abd,* literally means "slave."

8. Quoted in as-Sarrāj, *Kitāb al-luma',* p. 80 (trans. SS).

9. Rūmī, *Dīwān,* 1331, quoted in Chittick, *The Sufi Path of Love,* pp. 218-19.

10. As-Sulamī, *The Way of Sufi Chivalry,* pp. 40-41.

11. Al-Qushayrī, *Ar-Risāla,* (Chapter on Sufism), p. 127.

12. As-Sulamī, *The Way of Sufi Chivalry,* p. 42.

13. Quoted in Nicholson, *Studies in Islamic Mysticism,* p. 46.

14. Al-Kalābādhī, *The Doctrine of the Sufis,* p. 11.

15. As-Sulamī, *Risālat al-malāmatiyya,* p. 90 (trans. SS).

16. Quoted in al-Qushayrī, *Ar-Risāla,* (Chapter on Sufism), p. 128.

17. As-Sulamī, *The Way of Sufi Chivalry,* p. 42.

18. For the *ḥadīth* "Qualify yourself with the qualities of God," see Schimmel, *Mystical Dimensions of Islam,* p. 142.

19. Sunni *sharī'a* is the religious law and practice of Orthodox (Sunni) Islam. It was formulated in four main legal schools during the 8th century.

20. Tweedie, *Daughter of Fire,* p. 9.

21. Tweedie, *Daughter of Fire,* p. 20.

22. Quoted in al-Qushayrī, *Ar-Risāla,* (Chapter on Sufism), p. 127.

23. Rūmī, *Discourses,* trans. A. J. Arberry, p. 18.

24. As-Suhrawardī, Abū Najīb, trans. M. Milson, *A Sufi Rule for Novices,* pp. 35-6.

25. Tweedie, *Daughter of Fire,* p. 220.

26. "The 'people of the portico,' a group of pious companions of the Prophet, were considered by the Sufis as the ideal prototype of Islamic piety." (This is the original footnote in M. Milson (trans.), *A Sufi Rule for Novices,* p. 36, n. 24.)

27. As-Suhrawardī, *A Sufi Rule for Novices,* pp. 35-6.

28. On the "existential" aspect of the Sufi tradition, see also above, ch. 1 (Niche), pp. 16-18.

29. Al-Ghazzālī, *The Alchemy of Happiness,* trans. C. Field and E. L. Daniel, pp. 5-6.

30. Al-Hujwīrī, *Kashf al-Maḥjūb,* p. 39.
31. J .G. Bennett, *The Masters of Wisdom,* p. 102. Fuller summations of the Naqshbandi rules can be found in the following studies: J. G. Bennett, *The Masters of Wisdom,* pp. 102-4; A. Schimmel, *Mystical Dimensions of Islam,* pp. 364f.; J. S. Trimingham, *The Sufi Orders in Islam,* pp. 202-4.
32. Saint Augustine, *Confessions,* p. 195.
33. Saint Augustine, *Confessions,* pp. 200-1.
34. On *hūsh dar dam,* see also above, ch. 6 (Dhikr), pp. 135, 137, 142.
35. As-Sulamī, *Nasīm al-arwāḥ (The Breath of Souls),* p. 163 (trans. SS).
36. Hospitality has always been of the utmost importance in the East: "Invite guests, offer feasts, and be hospitable," writes as-Sulamī. See his *The Way of Sufi Chivalry,* p. 40.
37. See as-Sulamī, *Risālat al-malāmatiyya,* pp. 91-2 (trans. SS).
38. Tweedie, *Daughter of Fire,* p. 261.

Chapter 9, "IT IS THE FUNCTION WHICH CREATES THE ORGAN," pages 187-219

1. Quoted in al-Qushayrī, *Ar-Risāla,* (chapter on Poverty), p. 123.
2. As-Suhrawardī, Shihāb ad-Dīn, *Risālat al-abrāj (The Epistle of the Towers),* quoted in Henri Corbin, *Avicenna and The Visionary Recital,* p. 19.
3. Al-Ghazzālī, *Iḥyā' 'ulūm ad-Dīn,* vol. III, book I, p. 4 (trans. SS).
4. This is based on a prophetic *ḥadīth,* "God created Adam in His image," which in itself is based on Genesis 1:26-27. On this *ḥadīth,* see Schimmel, *Mystical Dimensions of Islam,* p. 188.
5. On the central *ḥadīth* "He who knows himself knows his Lord" *(man 'arafa nafsahu faqad 'arafa rabbahu),* see above, ch. 2 (Effort), p. 26.
6. Rūmī, *Discourses,* trans. A. J. Arberry, p. 48.
7. In this context, note the interesting observations made by Michaela Özelsel in her *Forty Days,* pp. 110-12.
8. Kubrā, Najm ad-Dīn, *Fawā'iḥ al-jamāl,* p. 5 (Arabic text, para. 12; trans. SS). The "mountains" are the four

elements of which everything in the material world, including the human body, is composed.

9. Kubrā, *Fawā'iḥ al-jamāl,* p. 18 (Arabic text, para. 41; trans. SS).

10. *Metaphysics of Rūmī* by Khalifa Abdul Hakim was originally submitted as a doctoral thesis at Heidelberg University; it was then published in Lahore in 1933 by The Ripon Printing Press.

11. Abdul Hakim, *Metaphysics of Rūmī,* p. 25. The Qur'ānic verses quoted are 57:3 and 2:156 respectively.

12. Abdul Hakim, *Metaphysics of Rūmī,* pp. 31-2.

13. On this *ḥadīth qudsī,* see also above, ch. 5 (Eros), p. 108.

14. Abdul Hakim, *Metaphysics of Rūmī,* p. 32, n. 1. See also Nicholson's translation of *Mathnawī,* II, 3274-3280: " ... without need ... God does not give anything to any one.... Need, then, is the noose for (all) things that exist: Man has instruments in proportion to his need. Therefore quickly augment thy need, O needy one, in order that the Sea of Bounty may surge up in lovingkindness."

15. Sūra 17:85.

16. On the mystery of the spirit within the heart, see also above, ch. 6 (Dhikr), pp. 135f.

17. Abdul Hakim, *Metaphysics of Rūmī,* p. 12.

18. See Qur'ān 2:117, 3:59, 6:73, 16:40, 19:35, 40:68.

19. See Qur'ān 38:75. On the creation of man "by God's Hands," see Schimmel, *Mystical Dimensions of Islam,* p. 188

20. *Mathnawī,* VI, 2877, quoted in Chittick, *The Sufi Path of Love,* p. 27.

21. Abdul Hakim, *Metaphysics of Rūmī,* p. 25.

22. *Mathnawī,* I, 1-11, trans. R. A. Nicholson, p. 5.

23. Abdul Hakim, *Metaphysics of Rūmī,* p. 25.

24. Verses SS.

25. Rūmī, *Mathnawī,* I, 3489, quoted in Chittick, *The Sufi Path of Love,* p. 38.

26. Rūmī, *Mathnawī,* III, 1222-1225, trans. R. A. Nicholson, p. 69.

27. Abdul Hakim, *Metaphysics of Rūmī,* p. 28.

28. Abdul Hakim, *Metaphysics of Rūmī,* p. 34.

29. Abdul Hakim, *Metaphysics of Rūmī,* p. 35.

30. Quoted in *Look! This is Love,* trans. A. Schimmel, p. 17.

31. Rūmī, *Discourses,* quoted in Chittick, *The Sufi Path of*

Love, p. 207.

32. Rūmī, *Mathnawī,* II, 3279-3280, quoted in Chittick, *The Sufi Path of Love,* p. 207.

33. Rūmī, *Mathnawī,* III, 3211-3212, quoted in Chittick, *The Sufi Path of Love,* p. 207.

34. A saying from one of the *Upanishads,* quoted in Tweedie, *Daughter of Fire,* p. x.

35. Rūmī, *Mathnawī,* III, 4440, quoted in Coleman Barks (versions), *Feeling the Shoulder of the Lion,* p. 61.

36. Rūmī, *Discourses,* quoted in Chittick, *The Sufi Path of Love,* p. 211.

37. Rūmī, *Mathnawī,* I, 2744, quoted in Chittick, *The Sufi Path of Love,* p. 208.

38. Rūmī, *Mathnawī,* V, 2838, quoted in Chittick, *The Sufi Path of Love,* p. 208.

39. Rūmī, *Mathnawī,* VI, 4303-4304, quoted in Chittick, *The Sufi Path of Love,* p. 208.

40. Rūmī, *Mathnawī,* II, 1939-1940, quoted in Chittick, *The Sufi Path of Love,* p. 208.

41. Rūmī, *Dīwān,* 1400, quoted in Chittick, *The Sufi Path of Love,* p. 209.

42. Abdul Hakim, *The Metaphysics of Rūmī,* p. 40.

43. On this *ḥadīth,* see above, ch. 4 (Khiḍr), p. 88.

44. Quoted in Nicholson, *The Mystics of Islam,* p. 168.

45. Quoted in *Look! This is Love,* trans. A. Schimmel, pp. 76-7.

46. On Rūmī's meeting with Shams, which is told and retold in many versions, see, e.g., Schimmel, *The Triumphal Sun,* pp. xvi-xvii; see also Schimmel, *I am Wind You are Fire.*

47. Rumi, *Mathnawī,* III, 4400-4420, quoted in Coleman Barks, *Feeling the Shoulder of the Lion,* pp. 58-60.

48. Rūmī, *Dīwān,* 22561, quoted in Chittick, *The Sufi Path of Love,* p. 78.

49. Rūmī, *Mathnawī,* VI, 126-128, quoted in Chittick, *The Sufi Path of Love,* p. 78.

50. See also above, ch. 5 (Eros), pp. 104ff.

51. Rūmī, *Mathnawī,* III, 4393-4399, quoted in Chittick, *The Sufi Path of Love,* p. 209.

52. G. I. Gurdjieff, *Meetings With Remarkable Men,* pp. 245-6.

Bibliography

'Abd al-Qādir al-Jīlānī. *The Secret of Secrets*. Trans. Shaykh Tosun Bayrak al-Jerrahi al-Halveti. Cambridge: The Islamic Texts Society, 1992.

Abdel-Kader, A. H. *The Life, Personality and Writing of al-Junayd: a study of a 3rd/9th-century Mystic*. London: Luzac & Co., 1976.

Abdul Hakim, Khalifa. *The Metaphysics of Rumi*. Lahore: The Ripon Printing Press, 1933.

Adler, Gerhard. *Dynamics of the Self*. London: Coventure, 1979.

Altmann, Alexander. "The Delphic Maxim in Medieval Islam and Judaism." In *Studies in Religious Philosophy and Mysticism*, Alexander Altmann, pp. 1-40. London: Routledge & Kegan Paul, 1969.

Arberry, A. J. *Sufism: An Account of the Mystics of Islam*. London: Allan & Unwin, 1950.

'Aṭṭār, Farīd ad-Dīn. *The Conference of the Birds*. Trans. Dick Davis and Afkham Darbandi. London: Penguin Classics, 1984.

——. *The Ilāhī-Nāma or Book of God*. Trans. John A. Boyle. Manchester: Manchester University Press, 1976.

——. *Muslim Saints and Mystics: Episodes from the Tadhkirat al-Auliyā' ('Memorial of the Saints')*. Trans. and ed. A. J. Arberry. London: Routledge and Kegan Paul, 1966 (1979).

Augustine, Saint. *Confessions*. Trans. H. Chadwick. Oxford and New York: Oxford University Press, 1992.

Austin, Ralph W. J. "The Sophianic Feminine in the Work of Ibn 'Arabī and Rumi." In *The Legacy of Mediaeval Persian Sufism*, ed. Leonard Lewisohn, pp. 233-245. London and New York: KNP, 1992.

——, trans. and ed. *Sufis of Andalusia*. Sherborne, Gloucestershire: Beshara Publications, 1988.

Barks, Coleman. See Rūmī, Jalāl ad-Dīn.

——. *The Hand of Poetry*. See Khan, Inayat.

Bennett, J. G. *The Masters of Wisdom*. Santa Fe, New Mexico: Bennett Books, 1995.

Böwering, Gerhard. *The Mystical Vision of Existence in Classical Islam: The Qur-ānic Hermeneutics of the Sūfi Sahl at-Tustarī (d. 283/896).* Berlin and New York: de Gruyter, 1980.

Bursevi, Ismail Hakki. *Translation of Kernel of Kernel by Muhyiddin Ibn 'Arabī.* Sherborne, Gloucestershire: Beshara Publications, no date.

Chittick, William C. *The Sufi Path of Knowledge, Ibn al-'Arabī's Metaphysics of Imagination.* Albany: State University of New York Press, 1989.

——. *The Sufi Path of Love, The Spiritual Teachings of Rumi.* Albany: State University of New York Press, 1983.

Chodkiewicz, Michel. "Quelques aspects des techniques spirituelles dans la *ṭarīqa* Naqshbandiyya." In *Naqshbandis,* eds. M. Gaborieau, A. Popovic, and T. Zarcone, pp. 69-82. Istanbul-Paris: Éditions Isis, 1990.

——. *Seal of the Saints: Prophethood and Sainthood in the Doctrine of Ibn 'Arabī.* Trans. L. Sherrard. Cambridge: The Islamic Texts Society, 1993.

Coleridge, Samuel Taylor. *Biographia Literaria or Biographical Sketches of My Literary Life and Opinions.* Ed. G. Watson. London and New York: J. M. Dent & Sons and E. P. Dutton & Co., 1960.

Corbin, Henri. *Avicenna and the Visionary Recital.* Trans. W. R. Trask. Dallas: Spring Publications, 1988.

——. *Creative Imagination in the Ṣūfism of Ibn 'Arabī.* Trans. R. Manheim. Princeton, N. J.: Princeton University Press, 1969.

——. *The Man of Light in Iranian Sufism.* Trans. N. Pearson. New Lebanon, NY: Omega Publications, 1994.

——. "*Mundus Imaginalis* or the Imaginary and the Imaginal." *Spring* (1972), pp. 1-19.

——. *Spiritual Body and Celestial Earth: From Mazdean Iran to Shi'ite Iran.* Trans. N. Pearson. Princeton, N.J.: Princeton University Press, 1977.

Couzyn, Jeni. *In the Skin House.* Newcastle upon Tyne: Bloodaxe Books, 1994.

Dalley, Stephanie, trans. (with introduction and notes). *Myths from Mesopotamia: Creation, The Flood,*

Gilgamesh and Others. Oxford: Oxford University Press, 1989.

Ebn-e Monavvar, Moḥammad. *The Secrets of God's Mystical Oneness*. Trans. and annotated J. O'Kane. Costa Mesa and New York: Mazda Publishers, 1992.

Ernst, Carl. *Words of Ecstasy in Sufism*. Albany: State University of New York Press, 1985.

Friedman, Yohanan. *Shaikh Ahmad Sirhindi: An Outline of His Thought and a Study of His Image in the Eyes of Posterity*. Montreal: McGill University Press, Institute of Islamic Studies, 1971.

Gaborieau, M.; Popovic, A.; and Zarcone, T.; eds. *Naqshbandis. Historical Developments and Present Situation of a Muslim Mystical Order*. Proceedings of the Sèvres Round Table, 2-4 May 1985. Istanbul-Paris: Éditions Isis, 1990.

Ghazzālī (al-), Abū Ḥāmid Muḥammad. *The Alchemy of Happiness*. Trans. C. Field and E. L. Daniel. New York and London: M. E. Sharpe, 1992.

——. *Mishkāt al-anwār* ("The Niche for Lights"). Trans. W. H. T. Gairdner. Lahore: Sh. Muhammad Ashraf, 1952.

——. *On the Duties of Brotherhood*. Trans. M. Holland. London: Latimer New Dimension, 1975.

Gurdjieff, G. I. *Meetings With Remarkable Men*. London: Routledge & Kegan Paul, 1979.

Haar, Johan G. J. ter. "The Naqshbandī Tradition in the Eyes of Aḥmad Sirhindī." In *Naqshbandis*, eds. M. Gaborieau, A. Popovic, and T. Zarcone, pp. 83-93. Istanbul-Paris: Éditions Isis, 1990.

Ḥāfeẓ. *Dance of Life*. Washington, D.C.: Mage Publishers, 1987.

——. *Love's Perfect Gift, Rubaiyat of Hafiz*. Versions Paul Smith. Melbourne, Australia: New Humanity Books, 1988.

Hujwīrī, 'Alī ibn 'Uthmān al-Jullabī. *Kashf al-Maḥjūb*. Trans. R. A. Nicholson. London: Luzac & Co., 1911 (1976).

Ibn al-'Arabī, Muḥammad ibn 'Alī. *The Bezels of Wisdom*. Trans. with introduction R. W. J. Austin. New York: Paulist Press, 1980.

——. *Al-Futūḥāt al-Makiyya (The Meccan Revelations).* See Chittick, William C., *The Sufi Path of Knowledge.*
——. *The Kernel of Kernel.* See Bursevi, Ismail Hakki.
——. *Sufis of Andalusia.* See Austin, Ralph W. J.
Ibn 'Aṭā' Allāh. *The Book of Wisdom.* Trans. Victor Danner. New York: Paulist Press, 1979.
Idel, Moshe. *Kabbalah New Perspectives.* New Haven and London: Yale University Press, 1988.
Jāmī, Abdulrahman. *The Book of Joseph and Zuleikha.* Trans. Alexander Rogers. London: David Nutt, 1892.
Jung, Carl G. *Collected Works 8, The Structure and Dynamics of the Psyche.* Trans. R. F. Hull. London and Henley: Routledge and Kegan Paul, 1969.
——. *Collected Works 9i, The Archetypes and the Collective Unconscious.* Trans. R. F. Hull. London: Routledge and Kegan Paul, 1968.
Kalābādhī (al-), Abū Bakr. *The Doctrine of the Sūfīs.* Trans. A. J. Arberry. Cambridge: Cambridge University Press, 1935 (1979).
Khan, Inayat. *The Hand of Poetry: Five Mystic Poets of Persia.* Trans. Coleman Barks. New Lebanon: Omega Publications, 1993.
The Koran Interpreted. Trans. A. J. Arberry. Oxford: Oxford University Press, 1964.
Lewisohn, Leonard, ed. *Classical Persian Sufism: from its Origins to Rūmī.* London and New York: KNP, 1993.
——, ed. *The Legacy of Mediaeval Persian Sufism.* London and New York: KNP, 1992.
Lusseyran, Jacques. *And There Was Light.* Trans. E. Cameron. London: Floris Classic, 1964.
Massignon, Louis. *Hallāj, Mystic and Martyr.* Ed., abridged, and trans. H. Mason. Princeton, N.J.: Princeton University Press, 1995.
——. *The Passion of al-Ḥallāj: Mystic and Martyr of Islam.* Trans. H. Mason. 4 vols. Princeton, N.J.: Princeton University Press, 1982.
Naqshbandis. See Garborieau, M.; Popovic, A.; and Zarcone, T.; eds.
Nicholson, R. A. *The Mystics of Islam.* London: G. Bell and Sons, 1914 (reprint 1975). (The 1975 edition was published in London by Routledge and Kegan Paul.)

——. *Studies in Islamic Mysticism.* Cambridge: Cambridge University Press, 1921.
Özelsel, Michaela. *Forty Days, The Diary of a Traditional Solitary Sufi Retreat.* Trans. A. Gaus. Brattleboro, Vermont: Threshold Books, 1996.
Plato. *Symposium (The Banquet).* In *Great Dialogues of Plato,* trans. W. H. D. Rouse, eds. E. H. Warmington and P. G. Rouse, pp. 69-117. New York: Penguin Books, 1984.
Qushayrī (al-), ʻAbd al-Karīm Abū al-Qāsim. *Principles of Sufism.* Trans. B. R. von Schlegell. Berkeley: Mizan Press, 1990.
Radtke, Bernd. "The Concept of *Wilāya* in Early Sufism." In *Classical Persian Sufism: from its Origins to Rumi,* ed. Leonard Lewisohn, pp. 483-496. London and New York: KNP, 1993.
——, ed. *Drei Schriften des Theosophen von Tirmiḏ.* Beirut and Stuttgart: Franz Steiner Verlag, 1992.
—— *Al-Ḥakīm at-Tirmiḏī: Ein islamischer Theosoph des 3./9. Jahrhunderts.* Freiburg: K. Schwarz Verlag, 1980.
——. "Tirmiḏiāna Minora: Die Autobiographie des Theosophen von Tirmiḏ." *Oriens* 34 (1994), pp. 242-298.
Rūmī, Jalāl ad-Dīn. *Delicious Laughter: Rambunctious Teaching Stories from the Mathnawī.* Versions Coleman Barks. Athens, GA: Maypop Books, 1990.
——. *Discourses (Fīhi mā fīhi).* Trans. A. J. Arberry. London: John Murray, 1961.
——. *Dîvân-i Kebîr.* Trans. Nevit O. Ergin. Walla Walla, WA: Turkish Republic Ministry of Culture & Current, 1995.
——. *The Essential Rumi.* Trans. Coleman Barks and John Moyne. San Francisco, CA: Harper, 1995.
——. *Feeling the Shoulder of the Lion.* Versions Coleman Barks. Putney, Vermont: Threshold Books, 1991.
——. *Look! This is Love.* Trans. Annemarie Schimmel. Boston and London: Shambhala, 1990.
——. *The Mathnawī of Jalaluddin Rumi.* Ed. and trans. R. A. Nicholson. London: E. J. W. Gibb Memorial Trust, 1930 (1982).
——. *Mystical Poems of Rumi 1-200.* Trans. A. J. Arberry.

Chicago: The University of Chicago Press, 1968.
——. *Mystical Poems of Rumi, 201-400.* Trans. A. J. Arberry. Boulder, Colorado: Westview Press, 1979.
——. *Open Secret.* Trans. John Moyne and Coleman Barks. Putney, Vermont: Threshold Books, 1984.
——. *Selected Poems from the Dīwān-i Shams-i Tabrīz.* Ed. and trans. R. A. Nicholson. Cambridge: Cambridge University Press, 1898 (1952).
——. See Chittick, William C., trans. and ed. *The Sufi Path of Love.*
Ruspoli, Stephanie. "Reflexions sur la vie spirituelle des Naqshbandi." In *Naqshbandis*, pp. 95-107. Istanbul-Paris: Éditions Isis, 1990.
Sacks, Oliver. *An Anthropologist on Mars.* New York: Vintage Books, 1996.
Samuels, Andrew; Shorter, Bani; and Plaut, Fred. *A Critical Dictionary of Jungian Analysis.* London and New York: Routledge & Kegan Paul, 1987.
Schimmel, Annemarie. *I am Wind You are Fire, The Life and Work of Rumi.* Boston and London: Shambhala, 1992.
——. *Mystical Dimensions of Islam.* Chapel Hill: The University of North Carolina Press, 1975.
——. *Pain and Grace, A Study of Two Mystical Writers of Eighteenth-Century Muslim India.* Leiden: E.J. Brill, 1976.
——. *The Triumphal Sun: A Study of the Life and Works of Mawlana Jalaloddin Rumi.* London & The Hague: East-West Publications, 1978, 1980.
Schlegell, B. R. von, trans. *Principles of Sufism.* Berkeley: Mizan Press, 1990.
Shabistarī, Maḥmūd. *The Secret Rose Garden of Sa'd ud Din Mahmūd Shabistarī.* Trans. Florence Lederer. Lahore: Sh. Muhammad Ashraf, no date.
Shorter Encyclopaedia of Islam. Leiden: E. J. Brill, 1974.
Shushud, Ḥasan Lutfi. *Masters of Wisdom of Central Asia.* Trans. M. Holland. Moorcote, North Yorkshire: Coombe Spring Press, 1983.
Suhrawardī (as-), Abū Najīb. *A Sufi Rule for Novices.* Trans. M. Milson. Cambridge, Mass.: Harvard University Press, 1975.

Suhrawardī (as-), 'Umar ibn Muḥammad. *The 'Awārif al-ma'ārif.* Trans. W. Clarke. New Delhi: Taj Company, 1891 (revised edition 1984).

Sulamī (as-), Abū 'Abd ar-Raḥmān. *The Way of Sufi Chivalry.* Trans. Tosun Bayrak al-Jerrahi. Rochester, Vermont: Inner Traditions International, 1983 (1991).

Sviri, Sara. "Between Fear and Hope: On the Coincidence of Opposites in Islamic Mysticism." *Jerusalem Studies in Arabic and Islam,* vol. 9 (1987), pp. 316-349.

——. "The *Coincidencia Oppositorum* and the 'Yo-Yo Syndrome': From Polarity to Oneness in Sufi Psychology." In *Jung and the Monotheisms: Judaism, Christianity, Islam,* ed. J. Ryce-Menuhin, pp. 192-213. London and New York: Routledge, 1994.

——. "*Daughter of Fire* by Irina Tweedie: Documentation and Experiences of a Modern Naqshbandi Sufi." In *Women As Teachers and Disciples in Traditional and New Religions,* eds. E. Puttick and P. B. Clarke, pp. 77-89. Lampeter and New York: The Edwin Mellen Press, 1993.

——. "Ḥakīm Tirmidhī and the Early *Malāmatī* Movement." In *Classical Persian Sufism: from its Origins to Rumī,* ed. Leonard Lewisohn, pp. 583-613. London and New York: KNP, 1993.

Teilhard de Chardin, J. *The Phenomenon of Man.* London: Collins Fountain Books, 1977.

Thubron, Colin. *The Lost Heart of Asia.* London: Penguin Books, 1995.

Trimingham, J. S. *The Sufi Orders in Islam.* Oxford: Oxford University Press, 1971.

Tweedie, Irina. *Daughter of Fire.* Inverness, CA: The Golden Sufi Center, 1986.

Vitray-Meyerovitch, Eva de. *Rûmî and Sufism.* Trans. S. Fattal. Sausalito, CA: The Post-Apollo Press, 1987.

BOOKS IN ARABIC

Ādāb al-mulūk. See Radtke, Bernd (ed.).
Al-Fāwī, Maḥmūd 'Abd al-Fattāḥ. *At-Taṣawwuf al-wajh wal-wajh al-ākhar.* Cairo: Maktabat az-zahrā', 1995.
Ghazzālī (al-), Abū Ḥāmid. *Iḥyā' 'ulūm ad-dīn.* Beirut: Dār al-qalam, no date.
Al-Ḥakīm at-Tirmidhī (Pseudo- ?). *Bayān al-farq bayna aṣ-ṣadr wal-qalb wal-fu'ād wal-lubb.* Ed. Nicholas Heer. Cairo: Dār iḥyā' al-kutub al-'arabiyya, 1958.
Al-Ḥakīm at-Tirmidhī. *Buduww sha'n.* Ed. Muhammad Khalid Masud. *Islamic Studies* 4 (1965), pp. 315-343.
——. *Ghawr al-umūr.* Ms. Esat (Istanbul) 1312, fols. 33a-87b.
——. *Kitāb ar-riyāḍa wa-adab an-nafs.* Eds. A. J. Arberry and A. H. 'Abd al-Qādir. Cairo: Maktabat al-ādāb aṣ-ṣūfiyya, 1947.
——. *Kitāb ilā Muḥammad ibn al-Faḍl al-Balkhī.* Ms. Leipzig 212, fols. 15b-17b.
——. *Manāzil al-'ibād min al-'ibada.* Ms. Ismail Saib (Ankara) 1571, ff. 220a-237b.
——. *Masā'il ahl Sarakhs.* In *Drei Schriften des Theosophen von Tirmiḏ,* ed. Bernd Radtke, pp. 138-168 (Arabic texts). Beirut and Stuttgart: Franz Steiner Verlag, 1992.
——. *Nawādir al-uṣūl.* Beirut: Dār ṣādir, 1970 (?) (reprint of Istanbul: 1293h.).
——. *Aṣ-Ṣalāt wa-maqāṣiduhā.* Ed. Husni Nasr Zaydan. Cairo: Dār al-kitāb al-'arabī, 1965.
——. *Sīrat al-awliyā'.* In *Drei Schriften des Theosophen von Tirmiḏ,* ed. Bernd Radtke, pp. 1-134. Beirut and Stuttgart: Franz Steiner Verlag, 1992.
Ibn al-'Arabī, Muḥammad ibn 'Alī. *Fuṣūṣ al-ḥikam.* Ed. Abū-l-'Alā' 'Afīfī. Beirut: Dār al-kitāb al-'arabī, 1946.
——. *Al-Futūḥāt al-makiyya.* Eds. Yahyā Othmān and Ibrāhīm Madkūr. 13 vols. Cairo: Al-hay'a al-miṣriyya al-'āmma lil-kitāb, 1972-1990.
Kubrā, Najm ad-Dīn. *Fawā'iḥ al-jamāl wa-fawātiḥ al-jalāl.* Ed. Fritz Meier. Wiesbaden: Franz Steiner Verlag, 1957.
Qushayrī (al-), 'Abd al-Karīm Abū al-Qāsim. *Ar-Risāla fī*

'ilm at-taṣawwuf. Beirut: Dār al-kitāb al-'arabī, no date. See also Schlegell, B. R. von.
Radtke, Bernd, ed. *Ādāb al-mulūk.* Beirut and Stuttgart: Franz Steiner Verlag, 1991.
Rakhāwī (ar-), Muḥammad, ed. *Al-Anwār al-qudsiyya fī manāqib as-sāda an-Naqshbandiyya.* Cairo: Maṭba'at as-sa'āda, 1344h./(1925).
Sarrāj(as-), Abū Naṣr. *Kitāb al-luma' fī at-taṣawwuf.* Eds. 'Abd al-Ḥalīm Maḥmūd and 'Abd al-Bāqī Surūr. Baghdad and Cairo: Dār al-kutub al-ḥadītha wa-maktabat al-muthannā, 1960.
Sulamī (as-), Abū 'Abd ar-Raḥmān, *Faṣl fī ghalaṭāt aṣ-ṣūfiyya.* In *At-Taṣawwuf al-wajh wal-wajh al-ākhar,* ed. Maḥmūd 'Abd al-Fattāḥ al-Fāwī. Cairo: Maktabat az-zahrā', 1995.
——. *Risālat al-malāmatiyya.* In *Al-Malāmatiyya waṣ-ṣūfiyya wa-ahl al-futuwwa,* ed. Abū -l-'Alā' 'Afīfī. Cairo: 'Īsā al-Bābī al-Ḥalabī, 1945.
——. *Nasīm al-arwāḥ.* In *Majmū'a t āthār Abī 'Abd ar-Raḥmān as-Sulamī,* ed. Nasr Allah Pur Javadi. Tehran: Markaz-i bakhsh-i dānishgāhī, 1990.

The Index

E

F

N

O

P

S

Y

Z

INDEX OF QUR'ĀNIC VERSES

Acknowledgments

The Golden Sufi Center:

Information and Publications

Autobiographical Notes

Acknowledgments

For permission to use copyrighted material, the author gratefully wishes to acknowledge: Aris & Phillips Ltd., for permission to quote from *Mathnawi,* translated by R.A. Nicholson (© 1982); Bennett Books, for permission to quote from *The Masters of Wisdom* by J. G. Bennett (© 1980); Bloodaxe Books Ltd., for permission to quote from *In the Skin House* by Jeni Couzyn (© Bloodaxe Books, 1994); University of Chicago Press, for permission to quote from *Mystical Poems of Rumi,* translated by A. J. Arberry, edited by Dr. Ehsan Yarshater (© 1968); Islamic Text Society and Drakes International Services, for permission to quote from *The Secret of Secrets* by Abd al-Qudir al-Jalani (© 1992); Maypop Books, for permission to quote from *Delicious Laughter,* translated by Coleman Barks; Omega Press, for permission to quote from *The Man of Light in Iranian Sufism* by Henri Corbin (© 1978); Paulist Press, for permission to quote from *The Book of Wisdom* by Ibn 'Ata Allah, translated by Victor Danner (© 1979); Penguin Books Ltd., for permission to quote from *The Conference of Birds* by Farīd ad-Dīn 'Aṭṭār, translated by Afhham Dardandi and Dick Davis (© Penguin Classics, 1984); Princeton University Press, for permission to quote from *The Passion of al-Hallāj* by Louis Massignon, translated by Herbert Mason (© 1988 by PUP); Shambhala Publications Inc., for permission to quote from *Look! This is Love: Poems of Rumi,* translated by Annemarie Schimmel (© 1991), reprinted by arrangement with Shambhala Publications Inc., 300 Massachusetts Avenue, Boston, MA 02115; Threshold Books, 139 Main St., Brattleboro, VT 05301, for permission to quote from *Feeling the Shoulder of the Lion,* translated by Coleman Barks (© 1991), *Open Secret,* translated by John Moyne and Coleman Barks (© 1984), and *Forty Days* by Michaela Özelsel (© 1996); and State University of New York Press for permission to quote from *The Sufi Path of Knowledge: Ibn al-Arabi's Metaphysics of Imagination* (© 1989) and *The Sufi Path of Love, The Spiritual Teachings of Rumi* (© 1983) by William C. Chittick.

THE GOLDEN SUFI CENTER is a California Religious Non-Profit Corporation dedicated to making the teachings of the Naqshbandi Sufi Path available to all seekers. For further information about the activities of the Center and Llewellyn Vaughan-Lee's lectures, write to:

The Golden Sufi Center
P.O. Box 428
Inverness, California 94937

Tel: (415) 663-8773
Fax: (415) 663-9128
e-mail: GoldenSufi@aol.com
website: http://users.aol.com/GoldenSufi/gsc.html

OTHER TITLES PUBLISHED BY THE GOLDEN SUFI CENTER

BY IRINA TWEEDIE

DAUGHTER OF FIRE:
A DIARY OF A SPIRITUAL TRAINING WITH A SUFI MASTER

BY LLEWELLYN VAUGHAN-LEE

THE BOND WITH THE BELOVED:
THE MYSTICAL RELATIONSHIP OF THE LOVER AND THE BELOVED

~

IN THE COMPANY OF FRIENDS:
DREAMWORK WITHIN A SUFI GROUP

~

TRAVELLING THE PATH OF LOVE,
SAYINGS OF SUFI MASTERS

~

SUFISM, THE TRANSFORMATION OF THE HEART

~

THE PARADOXES OF LOVE

ABOUT THE AUTHOR

SARA SVIRI, Ph.D., studied Arabic and Islamic Studies at the Hebrew University of Jerusalem, where she later taught in the Department of Arabic. She currently holds the Catherine Lewis Lectureship in medieval studies at University College, London. She has written numerous articles on Sufism and other topics from a Sufi perspective, including depth psychology and dreams. For the last few years she has lectured extensively in Europe and the U.S. on Sufism.